LOVE YOU MADLY, HOLLY WOODLAWN: A WALK ON THE WILD SIDE WITH ANDY WARHOL'S MOST FABULOUS SUPERSTAR

fh

Feral House
1240 W. Sims Way
Suite 124
Port Townsend, WA 98368
www.feralhouse.com
info@feralhouse.com

Design by Ron Kretsch

Cover photo by and used courtesy of Peter Palladino

LOVE YOU MADLY, HOLLY WOODLAWN

BY JEFF COPELAND

For Robert, whose curiosity and intrigue jump-started this journey in the first place.

And for my parents, who believed I could do it, even when I didn't know how.

FOREWORD

J EFF COPELAND AND I ARE NOT ACQUAINTED. Nonetheless, I have a strong feeling that we are, dare I say it, soul sisters. We are members of a specific tribe, the glamour-hungry gays of yore who fled the disapproving oppression of small-town life, our Dorothy bags bursting with Hollywood dreams. To quote Jeff, we were "the strange bruised fruit of society, the outcasts who were damned to hell from the get-go."

But our Hollywood, mine and Jeff's, was not a *Hooray for Hollywood* Hollywood. Our Hollywood was a place of low expectations, faded glamour, crummy apartments and dragging mufflers. Our Hollywood was cheap, tacky and tawdry. There was no finesse or chrome or gloss in our L.A. Instead, there were gas shortages, sunbaked stucco and smog alerts. Coyotes were sneaking into fancy neighborhoods, eating pets and abducting babies. The Manson murders were recent history.

The headlines which greeted me when I arrived in Tinseltown throbbed with reports of new terrors: the Hillside Strangler, and later the Wonderland Murders. Instead of a glittering utopia, I found a place of small-time cults, sad stripper stores on Hollywood Boulevard filled with dead-stock merchandise, lousy health-food restaurants which weren't even remotely healthy, hookers in bikinis on Sunset, male gang-members wearing bright yellow hair-rollers and blue hairnets, and, in the more affluent neighborhoods, middle-aged geezers with hairy chests and medallions, sporting thick Sy Sperling toupées and driving rag-top Cadillacs. Are you starting to get the picture?

There were no historic statues in our L.A. unless you count Bullwinkle and Randy's Donuts and the Tail o' the Pup, which we did. And there was no future looming. This *was* the future and it was cheap and dusty and not futuristic at all.

The momentum of the early '70s—Coppola, Polanski, Bogdanovich, Scorsese—had fizzled and been replaced by *Three's Company*, *Laverne and Shirley*, and "tentpole" blockbuster movies—*Jaws*, *Alien*, *Close Encounters*, *Star Wars*—movies which filled the Hollywood Toystore with rivers of licensed merch. In addition to this commercial fodder, there were so-bad-they-are-good movies like *Moment by Moment* staring Lily Tomlin and John Travolta. Lily played the female romantic lead and Travolta played "a drifter named Strip," and it wasn't a comedy.

The movie void referred to above was filled with new genres of edgy and fabulous filth which were right up our respective boulevards. There were art-house punky movies like *Desperate Living*, *Thundercrack* and *Eraserhead*, directed by John Waters, Curt McDowell and David Lynch, respectively. The whole red-carpet, who-are-you-wearing, who does your Botox, TMZ, ET, *Vanity Fair*, Harvey Weinstein, Fashion Police, Oscars, Globes, Brangelina, Kim and Kanye explosive reinvention of Hollywood was eons away, as was the marriage of celebrity and fashion. In our L.A., celebs dressed themselves.

You are doubtless wondering why, if it was all so gnarly and so naff, did Jeff and I, the glamour-obsessed bruised fruits, not throw our rotting selves onto the nearest compost heap. Let me be crystal (Carrington) clear: The void, the valley of low expectations, this Los Angeles of the late '70s and early '80s was *the most deliriously fabulous place in the world*.

Our City of Angels was an incredible Petri dish where anything might grow. The stakes, like the rents, were so low that the only way was up. Our L.A. was, most importantly, an improvisational place of improbable encounters. At any moment you might, for example, meet a former Warhol superstar and forge a freaky bond. Jeff met his, and I met mine.

Upon arrival in Hollywood I checked into the long-gone Tropicana Motel in West Hollywood. My room was situated directly above Duke's Coffee Shop, a storied eatery. Every day I woke up to the sound of the breakfast racket, directly below me. An aroma of coffee and hot lard rose up through the walls and floor, into my lungs and into the fibers of my clothing. My fragrance during this period was a subtle blend of Folgers and Pam. Fortunately it was the punk rock era and everyone was a tad smelly.

Duke's attracted a swinging mix of confident misfits. Sitting at the counter was the best way to meet unconventional superfreaks. I am thinking in particular of Pat Ast, former Warhol superstar and plus-size bad girl. Pat was a Duke's regular.

Red-headed Pat had appeared, albeit fleetingly, in *Midnight Cowboy*, one of the greatest movies of the twentieth century. Halston repeatedly put jolie-laide Pat on his fashion runway alongside sleek giantesses such as Anjelica Huston and Pat Cleveland. Tossing a chunky reprobate such as Pat into the mix was a revolutionary move. Pat then became a Warhol protegée/superstar, starring in *Women in Revolt*, alongside our heroine Holly Woodlawn, and then *Heat*. In this latter movie Miss Ast played Lydia, a volatile and grumpy motel owner. Rumor has it that *Heat* was partially shot at the Tropicana, which might explain Pat's enduring allegiance to the motel coffee shop. Like Holly Woodlawn or Candy Darling, or Jackie Curtis or Divine, Pat was an underground legend and an unhinged supernova of fabulosity. And like Holly she was excitable, though Holly was undeniably the more excitable of the two.

Andy Warhol responded to excitability. He cast Holly Woodlawn in two unforgettably deranged movies: *Trash* and, as mentioned above, *Women in Revolt*. Explaining his decision, Andy noted that his cis-gendered female superstars "couldn't seem to get excited about anything," whereas the Factory drag queens "could get excited about *anything*."

Fast-forward a decade: The crummy L.A. of the late '70s and early '80s was the perfect crash-pad for fading Warhol superstars. Reading Jeff Copeland's account of his years with Holly Woodlawn, I repeatedly (and narcissistically) returned to my fizzy time with Pat, the laughs, the mood swings, the outings to the Fake Club, the histrionics, followed by more laughs.

Like Holly, Pat had come to Los Angeles to reignite her superstardom. Both ladies were endowed with a lethal mixture of insecurity and full-throttle confidence. When Andy Warhol said, "If you can convince yourself that you look fabulous, you can save yourself the trouble of primping," he was surely thinking of his stomping superstars Holly and Pat. With their ferocious chutzpah, these girls demanded attention and adoration.

After laughing and crying through Jeff's account of his dogged efforts to harness Holly's manic charisma—highlights include flying dentures and a chilly encounter with Vampira—and catapult her back to relevance, I began to wonder about my breakfasts with anarchic fun-loving Pat. Had I dodged a bullet . . . or missed an opportunity? Should I, could I, have become Pat's *éminence grise*, her *aide-de-camp*, her factotum, her . . . biographer?

Like Holly, Pat was a circus act of impulsive exhibitionism. I was fascinated, but ultimately too wary of getting my emotional nylons snagged to get too close. Brave Jeff, on the other hand, cleaved to his muse in a roller-coaster symbiosis which ultimately produced two books.

When *A Low Life in High Heels* hit the bookstores I devoured it, as did many others. Not only had Mr. Copeland given the world an empathetic snapshot of an excitable Warhol mainstay, he had also, patiently and successfully, used his writing skills to give Holly a second shot at fame. Bravo, Jeff. And moi?

By the late '80s I had moved to New York. Barneys, my employer, was hosting a fashion show at a branch store in Costa Mesa, south of Los Angeles. The budget did not allow for supermodels. As a result, we decided to go with "interesting creative personalities." When it came to casting, all eyes were on me. "You lived in L.A. You know the score. Rustle up some of your kooky pals," hectored my colleagues. Feeling a bit like a mode-ish version of Corky St. Clair, I dived into my Rolodex.

Still at the same number, Pat picked up after the second ring. When I offered her the gig she played hard to get. Clearly she did not want me to think she was idly stroking on Fabulash while waiting for DeMille to call. "Yes, I know it's in a suburban shopping mall," I gushed, "but Peggy Moffitt, Djimon Hounsou and Lypsinka have already said yes!" After a few groveling callbacks, La Ast finally relented, but with some provisos: a fee, a limo and a bottle of vodka.

The day of the show arrived. Many of my "models" carpooled from Hollywood. Some drove themselves. The star arrived in her limo, swigging from her swag. In no time Pat's excitable persona infected her fellow mannequins with a spirit of reckless Mardi Gras. As I watched my chorines smoking, primping and swigging, I could feel any remaining vestiges of professionalism slithering out of the room.

Showtime!

Watched by open-mouthed attendees, my "creative interesting personalities" vamped and vogue'd down the escalator with reckless abandon. I won't go into details; suffice it to say that the subsequent headline on the *Orange County Register* read "NEARLY NUDE MODELS IN SHOPPING MALL SHOCKER."

And then came the grand finale. Pat, arms akimbo, grinning from ear to ear, her signature henna'd frizz rippling in the updraft, waved from the descending escalator like a visiting dignitary. Mouths opened wider. To Costa Mesa suburban eyes, unfamiliar with the Ast backstory, she had every appearance of a crazy lady who had bum-rushed the occasion.

Anxious to underscore Pat's celebrity—and make sure she did not fall and break her neck—I ran to the bottom of the escalator and grabbed her waving hand. We locked eyes. I bowed. Gazing at me with teary gratitude, she uttered a few words which I will never forget.

"It's just so great to be back on the runway."

Despite having traded in Halston's lacquered catwalk in the Olympic Tower for a suburban shopping mall escalator, Pat was radiant. Her poignant bottomless desire for recognition and the belief in the comeback trumped everything. *Thank you Mr. DeMille. Thank you for this escalator and this shopping Mall. Thank you for putting me back where I belong.*

Post script: Books about the writing of biographies of uncooperative or illusive subjects are a rare and special genre. Thanks to Mr. Copeland, I now have two. As I write, my new copy of *Love You Madly, Holly Woodlawn* sits on my bookshelf right next to Robert Plunket's *My Search for Warren Harding*. I feel sure there are others in existence. I fully intend to find them.

—SIMON DOONAN.

Simon Doonan is the author of many books, including DRAG: *The Complete Story* and *The CAMP 100: Glorious Flamboyance, from Louis XIV to Lil Nas X.*

CHAPTER 1

I T WOULD HAVE TAKEN A YEAR TO SAVE THE MONEY I needed to get to Hollywood, and that was too long to wait because I had the nerve to go now. Bold, audacious, unrelenting nerve.

"It's like betting on a racehorse," my mother said.

We were standing at a bank teller's window and she'd exchanged twelve hundred dollars for traveler's checks. An unlit cigarette hung out of her mouth as she fumbled through her purse for a lighter. She was agitated. Twelve hundred dollars was a lot of money in 1985. I certainly couldn't have saved it on my own when I was going to college. Even though I'd worked my way through school, I could barely afford my books and food. And when I graduated the previous week with a B.A. in media studies from Webster University, a small liberal arts school in St. Louis, Missouri, I was knee-deep in student loan debt.

That's why I borrowed twelve hundred dollars from my parents, so I could lasso the dream while it was alive and kicking, harrowing and thrilling, charged with excitement and a sense of urgency. I was afraid that if I didn't go for it now, I'd never go at all, and my dream of working in Hollywood would just fade away and disappear into nothing.

My parents were earnest, hard-working blue-collar folks. My father was a small-town barber and my mother worked in a flower shop. Their money was hard-earned and even harder to save. It was a big deal for them to lend

Four years old…when my only friend was imaginary, and my life dream could be summed up in four words: Ding! Dong! Avon calling! 1967.

me twelve hundred dollars so I could pursue a career that had no guarantees of panning out. I didn't have a job to go to, but I was determined to find one. I was a starry-eyed dreamer with big hopes, big dreams, and not a lick of sense … yet somehow, I thought I knew everything.

"It's like betting on a racehorse, kid," Mom said again, nervous, as she handed me a white envelope stuffed with traveler's checks.

"Always remember you're a blue blood," she said, even though I technically wasn't. In my mother's mind that didn't make a difference. People are what they believe themselves to be, she reasoned, and that's all that mattered. All of Dottie Copeland's kids were blue bloods, which really meant we had more class than the white trash down the street. Even though we lived in the ugliest house on the block, Mom made sure we knew we were better.

We were in the car now, driving through the small town I couldn't wait to escape. I never really belonged here, but this was where I'd gotten stuck, in a provincial suburb forty miles west of St. Louis, where people were ordinary, complacent, and fearful of the city.

"You kids come from good, hard-working American stock," Mom said. Our family lineage traced all the way back to an Irish horse thief who earned his freedom by fighting in the Revolutionary War.

High-water bell bottoms and clown shoes. The only thing that could have made this outfit worse was a Junior Miss Rhinestone Setter. 1974.

"Your father and I are very proud of you. We want you to do well, to make something of yourself. And you can't do that here," she reasoned. "So when you get to California, for God's sake, don't do porno!"

"Mom!" I said, embarrassed. "I'm not driving all the way to Hollywood to work in porn!"

According to my mother, working in porn was the ultimate disgrace, worse than losing all my teeth and living in a trailer. I didn't understand why she'd even be concerned, because the thought of working on anything that wasn't Academy Award-winning or at least airing on a major television network never even crossed my mind. My intent was to make my parents proud, not embarrass them. After all, I had humiliated them enough when I was a little boy.

My father had big dreams for me from the time I was born. He looked forward to teaching me how to play ball and shoot hoops, and he hoped to forge the kind of relationship he hadn't experienced with his own father. But as we both learned, sometimes a dream is nothing more than misguided hope that sours over time.

I wasn't like the other little boys in town. While they played ball, wrestled and fought, I stayed inside and watched old black-and-white movies on television. I was riveted by every melodramatic gasp, slap, and gunshot, punctuated by a chilling orchestral score, that caused my eyes to widen and hairs to stand on end. Old movies called to me in a way that was profound and inspiring. Sports, on the other hand, made me anxious. Yet my father was determined to transform me into an all-American basketball star. When I resisted, he offered money.

"If you make ten baskets in a row, I'll give you a dollar," he said.

"Jeffrey, if you're a good basketball player, you can get a scholarship to college," Mom said. "There are professional basketball players who make millions of dollars."

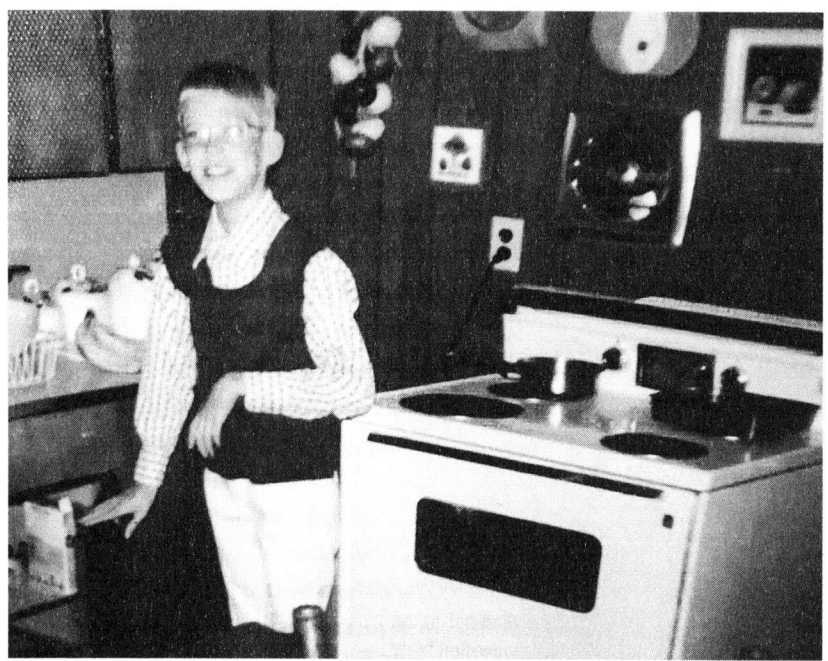

My limp wrist phase. This pose was inspired by a beautiful woman I'd seen in my mother's *Cosmopolitan* magazine. 1975.

But not even a million bucks could make me like basketball or any other sport. I had other interests, which I confided to my mother.

"For crying out loud, you're only seven years old!" she scoffed. "You're not having a Tupperware party!"

I also wanted to be an Avon lady but kept that to myself. I knew I was different. It seemed the older I got, the more unusual I became.

When I was eight, I developed compulsive nervous tics. I shook my head every few seconds, banged my elbows on tables whenever I had the chance, and occasionally made odd faces. I also wet the bed.

"Dottie," my father warned. "There's something wrong with that boy."

Even my paternal grandmother was aghast at my behavior.

"Well, my lands!" she howled when I had a tic fit at her house on Easter Sunday. "Jeff, you've got to stop doing that because people are going to think you're not right."

I knew that when I wrote Santa and asked for a Suzy Homemaker toy oven and got a Tonka truck instead. I was all wrong. Even though it was never said, it was implied. Eventually, my mother took me to see a pediatrician. The doctor never said that I was an embarrassment or a disappointment, but by the age of eight, that's how I felt. I knew I wasn't the type of son my father would have chosen if he'd had a choice. Who would want a little boy who couldn't play sports, shook his head all the time, and compulsively banged his elbows on tables?

The son my father dreamt of having actually belonged to his best friend, and I always heard about his athletic accolades.

"Why can't you be like him?"

That question was never asked, but I still heard it loud and clear. While my dad's best friend hit the jackpot with his little boy, my father got saddled with the booby prize. Throughout my childhood, I always knew I was his greatest disappointment.

Over time, as my father grew more frustrated with my interests, he withdrew further into his own. He cared about me, and he said he loved me, but as a young boy, I knew he didn't understand me, and sometimes that irritated him. So I did my best to stay out of his way.

When I was thirteen, my nervous tics and bedwetting miraculously stopped. But then I was thrown into a far bigger crisis: puberty. My boyish face changed into a festering horror of acne. My hair got so curly it was impossible to comb, so I brushed it straight, which made it look worse.

"That's embarrassing!" Dad shouted with disgust.

It was ironic that the son of a barber would have such awful hair.

"It looks like you've got a thatched roof on your head," he said.

"I'm an ugly piece of shit!" I cried one night at the dinner table. "No one likes me."

"For crying out loud!" Mom barked.

"Look at him," Dad blurted. "Bawling his head off. Goddamn! What's wrong with him, Dottie?"

"Denny," she said, glaring at him. "Just shut up."

My father couldn't relate. When he was my age, he was handsome, athletic, and well-liked. My mother, on the other hand, knew exactly what I was going through.

"You're just a late bloomer," she told me later. "The good news is you have a lot to look forward to."

My mother told me many stories of how she was bullied and mistreated by cute, mean-spirited cheerleaders who all grew up to be old, miserable, wrinkled, and drunk . . . by the time they were twenty-eight. I thought snotty, stuck-up cheerleaders who turned into shit-faced trolls was the best revenge ever, and I couldn't wait to see that comeuppance.

In the eighth grade, "Hey, fag!" was my new nickname and I heard it daily. Up until that time, I didn't know anything about homosexuality, but I did know that I couldn't take my eyes off the beautiful muscular boys. At first, I thought these attractions were a passing phase and reasoned that I liked those athletic boys because I wanted to be like them. But over time, as those strange feelings persisted, I came to a horrible realization.

At night, when I said my prayers, I pleaded with God to make me normal. And every night, those prayers were ignored. After a year of begging, I finally came to terms with the truth. I was gay. As I lay in bed

The fabulous Rona Barrett: my hero and guiding light. 1979.
Courtesy of Rona Barrett.

and talked to God about my sexuality, I heard the theme from *The Tonight Show Starring Johnny Carson* that carried from the opposite end of the house. It was an exciting, high-energy overture that I heard regularly at night when I was in bed, and it comforted me like a favorite childhood lullaby.

"From Hollywood, *The Tonight Show* starring Johnny Carson..." said Ed McMahon, the show's announcer and Johnny's on-set sidekick.

Watching Johnny Carson was my mother's nightly ritual. It was a time when she could finally settle down for some peace and quiet after a long day at the flower shop, where she worked six days a week.

On this night, as she sat curled on the couch, smoking a Benson & Hedges menthol cigarette, she listened to Carson's opening monologue. And at that moment, something unusual happened and she was struck with a vision.

"It was the strangest thing," she told me the next evening as she prepared a dinner salad in our kitchen. "I was watching Johnny Carson last night and all of a sudden..." She paused.

"What happened?" I asked as I filled drinking glasses with water and placed them around the table.

"You were on *The Tonight Show*," she said.

"What?" I shouted in disbelief.

"You were talking with Johnny Carson. I saw it plain as day. You were grown up, on *The Tonight Show*, and you were with Johnny Carson."

"Why?"

"I don't know. It only lasted a moment. But you were in Hollywood."

In my mind, there was no greater place than Hollywood, California, because that's where all the movie stars lived. And my mom was convinced that God, Jesus Christ, and Johnny Carson had given her a divine sign.

At the time, Rona Barrett was the reigning queen of Hollywood gossip, and I watched her daily on television. After reading her autobiography, *Miss Rona*, I was convinced Hollywood was my only hope for a better life. It's where I could make right all that was wrong and, most importantly, make both of my parents proud.

When I was seventeen, I told my mother I wanted to pursue a career in entertainment journalism.

"I want to interview movie stars when I grow up, Mom."

"Why wait?" she said. "Do it now. Carol Channing is coming to the Muny Opera in St. Louis. Interview her."

I sat at the kitchen table and looked at my mother like she was crazy. Carol Channing was a major star.

"I can't get an interview with Carol Channing."

"You're a kid, you can do anything," Mom reasoned. "People will help you because you're not a threat."

"But I'm just a kid," I said. "No one is going to take me seriously."

"Bullshit," she said.

"But how am I going to meet Carol Channing?"

My mother thought about that for a moment.

"I have a great idea," she said. "Flowers in a soda bottle."

"What?" I was confused.

"Carol Channing is going to love it!" Mom said, her eyes flashing with excitement. "You're going to send her flowers in a soda bottle because you can't afford to send her anything else. Trust me. Of all the beautiful arrangements she receives, flowers in a soda bottle is what she'll remember. And she'll be so touched, she'll give you an interview."

Mom was an award-winning floral designer, and she made daisies in a soda bottle look fantastic. So I wrote Carol Channing a card requesting an interview for my school newspaper and attached it to the soda bottle, and

If you can't hang with the popular kids in school, then go hang with the Hollywood stars. They're more interesting. With actress Dody Goodman in her dressing room at the Westport Playhouse. She was a doll. 1981.

Photo by Terry Smith.

then Mom and I drove to St. Louis and delivered the flowers to the Chase Park Plaza Hotel, where Carol Channing was staying.

A day later, I got a call from Carol Channing's assistant. Carol Channing loved the flowers and wanted to meet with me. But unfortunately, the day before we met, her friend Gower Champion died and she flew back to New York for his funeral. My interview was canceled, but my intent was set. A month later, I landed an interview with Pearl Bailey. Cloris Leachman, Brett Somers, Phyllis Diller, and Toni Tennille followed.

My father was impressed, especially when I showed up on the evening news with a comic legend named Bob Hope. I spent my senior year in high school freelancing as an entertainment reporter for a large St. Louis newspaper chain. I had my own press credentials before I had my high school diploma!

When Josh Logan came to St. Louis to direct *Mr. Roberts*, I took him to lunch and interviewed him about his amazing career on Broadway and in Hollywood. I was bowled over when he said his favorite actress to direct was Marilyn Monroe. It was during our conversation that I realized I didn't want to just interview famous people. I wanted to work with them, like Josh Logan worked with Marilyn Monroe.

Phyllis Diller refused my request for an interview, so I ambushed her at a local book signing. She admired my persistence and gave me an interview on the spot, which drew a huge crowd. When I mistakenly prefaced a question with the phrase "at your age," she had a hissy fit and caused such a stink, you would have thought I called her an old fart. 1981.
Photo by Terry Smith.

"I want to write TV shows and stage plays," I said one night at the dinner table.

"Well, that sounds like fun," Mom said.

"Yep," Dad agreed. "It does sound like fun."

I would never be the basketball star my father dreamt of having for a son, but he encouraged and supported me so that I could be a star in other ways.

"You kids can be whatever you want," Mom said. "This is America. Just go for it."

And I did, like an Irish horse thief hell-bent on freedom. One week after college graduation, I was moving to Los Angeles to pursue a career in television and film.

My father bought new tires for my 1976 Plymouth Volaré, then sat at the kitchen table with a road map and plotted my course. My mother hit a sale at K-Mart, where her nesting instinct went into overdrive and she loaded up on washcloths, towels, pots and pans, silverware, dishes, sheet sets, pillows, curtains, soap, canned tuna, a toaster, and an awful green vinyl kitchen trash can. My most precious treasure was a black 1950 Royal typewriter that I carefully placed onto the floorboard behind the driver's seat.

The next morning, we were up at the crack of dawn. Grandma, who had come to see me off, fried up a mess of eggs and made a pot of weak coffee. My two sisters chattered with excitement about my new adventure. Mom, momentarily overwhelmed by the chaos, smoked a cigarette on the porch.

"You should be there in three days," my father said as he gave me the road map he'd been working on that clearly outlined my journey in red ink. "Don't forget to check your oil."

"I won't forget. And I'll call you tonight to let you know where I am."

My mother came into the kitchen, dressed in her long housecoat. She looked distressed.

"He's going to California!" Grandma wailed as if I were heading to the state pen.

"Well, I've about had enough of this," Mom blurted. "Get your ass out of here. Goodbye!"

I knew she was kidding. Her caustic outburst was just for show.

"I'm going!" I said.

I hugged and kissed them all, and soon was backing my car out of the driveway and into the street. The necessities of life clanked and rattled in the back seat and the green vinyl trash can wobbled from side to side. My family stood on the front porch, waving and crying.

"Bye, Jeffrey!" my two sisters hollered and waved.

"Hollywood or bust!" I yelled and stepped on the gas. The engine roared, the tires screeched, and I sped away.

Madonna's "Into the Groove" blasted on the radio, and my body tingled with excitement as the old Plymouth barreled over the hills that led out of that small Missouri town. Those hills would eventually be cleared and bulldozed for an expansive, picture-perfect community of model homes and franchise restaurants that would be a dream come true for thousands of upwardly mobile, middle-class families. But I was on my way to seek another kind of fortune, one that would ultimately spin into a disaster and change me forever.

MAE WEST in
"Go West Young Man"
Warren WILLIAM · Randolph SCOTT
ALICE BRADY · ELIZABETH PATTERSON · LYLE TALBOT
GROUCHO · CHICO · HARPO
RIP-ROARING WITH LAUGHS, GIRLS, SONGS!
MARX BROS.
GO WEST
ASTOR PICTURES Presents
BING Crosby in "The Road to Hollywood"
Luis Alberni
Ann Christy
Dick Stewart
Katherine Ward
with
Matty Kemp
Eddie Phillips
Vernon Dent
Alice Adair
Directed by BUD POLLARD
8 GREAT SONG HITS
Norma SHEARER and Clark GABLE
in CLARENCE BROWN'S production of IDIOT'S DELIGHT

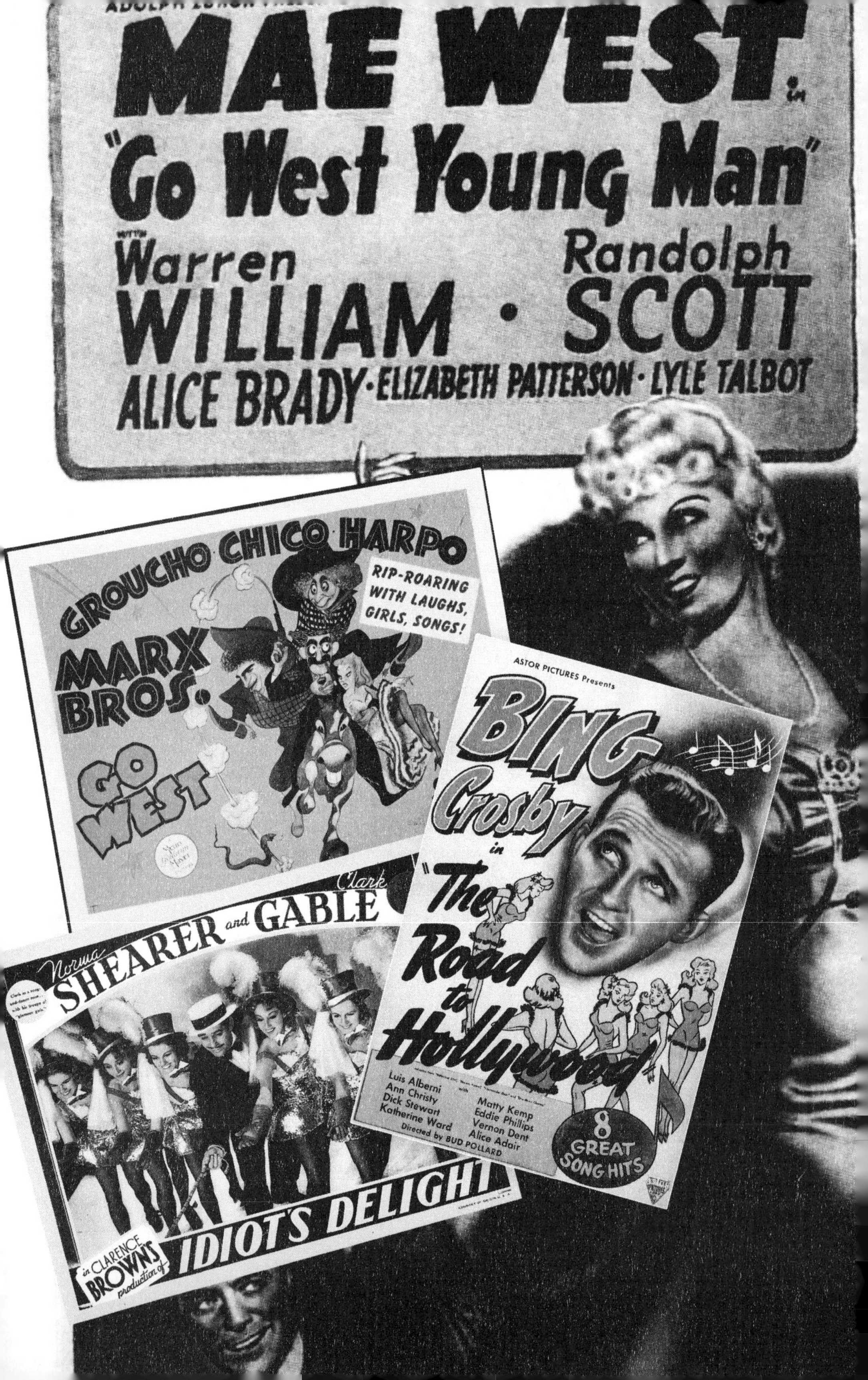

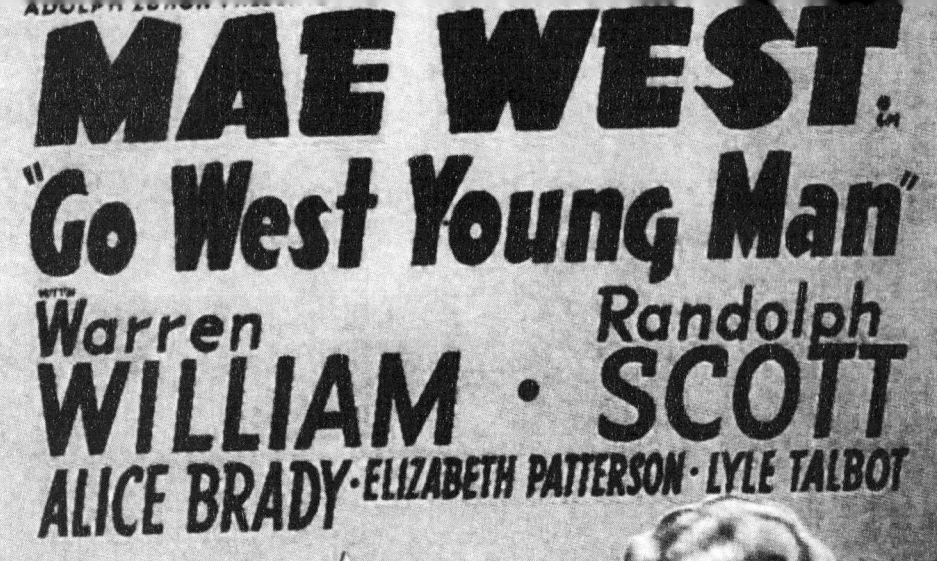

CHAPTER 2

THE SEEMINGLY ENDLESS DRIVE ALONG HIGHWAYS 44 and 40 was nothing more than a blur. Oklahoma, Texas, New Mexico, and Arizona were just states in the way, and I made no time for scenic distractions. I had to get to Los Angeles and only stopped at motels when it became necessary to sleep, or stopped for gas when it looked like I might run out.

By the time I crossed the California state line and drove into a town called Needles, I was tired and bleary-eyed, and my legs and back ached. The Plymouth Volaré wasn't doing much better. Its HOT ENGINE light glared at me from the dashboard, and a jolt of panic shot through my body.

The hot sun was blinding; the Mojave desert looked desolate and God-forsaken.

"Oh, God, please don't let the car break down here," I said aloud as I pulled in to a dusty gas station. I parked in the shade and walked into the shanty, where I found a lean, scruffy-faced attendant. When I told him that my car had overheated, he shrugged.

"Ain't got no mechanic today," he barked, chewing on a toothpick.

It didn't make a difference because I couldn't afford a mechanic anyway.

"Where you headed?" he prodded.

"Los Angeles."

11955 MOJAVE DESERT, NEAR BARSTOW, CALIF.

"Hollywood," he snickered. His mouth stretched into a grin and he giggled to himself. His teeth were yellow and tobacco-stained. "That's what they all say," he continued. "The Wagon Wheel Motor Lodge ain't too far, if you want to spend the night and leave the car here."

I stood motionless, not quite sure what to do. The idea of getting stranded in Needles, California, made me anxious. I watched that toothpick roll between his grinding teeth and felt vulnerable to unscrupulous shysters out to take advantage of my situation. All I could think was I had to get to Los Angeles. It was only 270 miles away. I was so close. So terribly close.

At that moment, I remembered a handsome kid in high school. He had the beauty of a teen idol: dark hair, brown eyes, olive skin, chiseled jaw, and a smile that made me weak. We carpooled together while working a summer job before he left for college. He drove an old junky station wagon, and whenever his car overheated, he turned on the car's heater, and somehow that caused the engine to stay cool. I didn't understand how that worked and pondered it for a moment. Could I actually drive through the Mojave desert with the heater on? Was that even possible?

If I left the car at the gas station and waited for it to be fixed, how much would that cost? Two hundred dollars? Six hundred dollars? And what if it couldn't get fixed right away? What if it took days to get the right parts? What if I blew all the money I had in Needles and never made it to Hollywood? Ever!

Screw the heat. After filling my car with gas and topping off the radiator with coolant, I rolled down my car windows, started the engine, turned the heater on full blast, and drove away. A row of barricades with flashing yellow caution lights caught my attention. They blinked in the distance, signaling a rough road ahead, but I paid them no mind. I was too blinded by my ambition to recognize or even understand the prophecy of my predicament.

To my great relief, the HOT ENGINE light went off and the temperature gauge slowly moved into the normal range. As I drove down that lone stretch of highway, I thought about that beautiful kid I'd known for only a few weeks. He was so handsome, he should have gone to Hollywood. But instead he went to Bible college and became a Christian missionary. He'd never know how much his brief friendship meant to me or the impact it had on my road trip to California. *Funny how people come into our lives for a reason,* I thought.

While the heater kept the Plymouth running, it made the drive through the hot desert almost unbearable. Sweat trickled down my forehead and stung my eyes. My shirt, my pants, even my underwear were drenched in perspiration. It's a wonder I didn't die of heatstroke. But no matter how miserable I felt, I refused to stop driving. I had to keep going. I had to make it to Hollywood. Just push forward, I told myself, because if you stop, you might not ever get there. And so, with a heavy foot and blurred vision, I ripped through the scorched desert and ignored the sweltering hell.

Four hours later, nightfall had draped the outskirts of Los Angeles with a fluorescent purple hue. My contact lenses felt dry and sticky, and the freeway signs were blurred. I was lost in a sea of fast-moving traffic with thousands of glowing red taillights ahead of me. Speeding cars raced by, and reckless, aggressive motorcyclists startled me as they roared between the cars and wove in and out of the freeway lanes.

While my chugging, sluggish Plymouth struggled to keep up, it suddenly dawned on me I didn't know where to go. I was in such a hurry to get to Hollywood, I didn't put any thought as to where I'd land once I'd arrived. I just assumed I'd figure it out. I never considered the possibility of arriving at night with compromised vision.

A friend in college told me that Hollywood was gang-ridden and dangerous, and arriving at night in a car that was packed to the headliner with housewares put me on edge. I didn't feel comfortable parking my car on the street or in an open parking lot. What if gang members shattered my windows and stole every pot, pan, and pillowcase I owned? What if they stole the green plastic trash can that I could never live without? The thought of hooligans breaking into my car made me a nervous wreck.

I exited the 101 Freeway into Hollywood and followed the stream of traffic as it traveled down Highland Avenue. I didn't know where I was going. I was just following red taillights and figured I'd wind up somewhere. In the distance, through my itchy contact lenses that kept sticking to my eyelids, I saw a blurred lighted Holiday Inn sign and felt a huge sense of relief.

"Thank you, Jesus, for a trusted national hotel chain!" I said aloud.

I checked in, took a shower, and called my parents.

"I'm in Hollywood," I said. "I made it. Finally!"

"We are so proud of you," Mom said.

"Jeff, are you doing okay?" Dad chimed in. "Don't forget to check your oil."

"I'm doing great, Dad," I said. "Tomorrow I'm going to get an apartment, and then I'm going to look for a job."

My parents were happy, and I didn't want to spoil the moment by telling them my car overheated in the desert. What was the point? It would only cause them unnecessary stress and worry. Besides, I'd get a job soon and have the car fixed. It was no big deal. I went to bed that night and dreamt about my exciting future and all the wonderful things that were to come my way.

The next morning, my eyelids were so red and itchy I couldn't wear my contacts. I rooted through my suitcase and found the old horn-rimmed eyeglasses that I kept as a backup. The round faux tortoiseshell frames had been broken and glued back together because I was too poor to replace them in college, but they were functional and I was glad to have them.

Shortly afterward, I checked out of the Holiday Inn and set out to find an apartment. I wanted a safe place to live, someplace where I could unpack all my stuff and focus on finding a job. So I bought a *Los Angeles Times* and sat outside a hot dog stand (that was actually shaped like a huge hot dog in a bun) and perused the rental classifieds. I found a single apartment in Pasadena for $300 that sounded good, dropped a dime into the nearby pay phone, and called the number. A woman answered and she sounded nice. She raved over the unit, explained it had new paint and appliances and said she was reviewing applications that week. I didn't know anything about the application process. I thought I'd just pay her the first month's rent and move in.

"No, that's not how it works," she explained. "Where are you from?"

When she learned that I'd just moved to California and was unemployed, she declined to show me the unit.

"But I have money," I said.

"But you don't have a job," she reasoned. "What's your credit rating?"

"What's that?" I asked.

The wonderful Tail o' the Pup hot dog stand was located at 451 N. La Cienega Blvd. in 1985. It's moved a few times since then. Today you can find it at 8512 Santa Monica Blvd. in West Hollywood.
Photo by Josh Lim.

I had no idea what a credit rating was because I didn't have a credit card.

"Oh, dear," she sighed and then kindly explained, "You're screwed, honey. You can't compete with these other applicants who've got good stable jobs and excellent credit. You better go back to Missouri."

I called several other landlords, and they echoed the same sentiment. So, unable to get a place to live, I decided to get a bank account so my money would be safe. I found a Security Pacific Bank on Santa Monica Boulevard in West Hollywood and went inside to open an account and make a deposit.

"I'm sorry," the branch manager said. "You need to have a California ID to get an account "

I went to the Bank of Hollywood and was told the same thing.

"How do I get a California ID?" I asked.

"If you're legal, you go to the DMV. If you're not legal, you go to the black market on Sixth and Alvarado, give fifty bucks to a fat tattooed cholo named Cheeto and pray to God you don't get robbed and shot."

For corn's sake! Now I had to find the Department of Motor Vehicles. In 1985, years before cell phones and Google, Americans used a telephone directory called the Yellow Pages to locate businesses. These books were stationed at pay phones throughout the city. So I found one and located the address of the DMV. But I had no idea how to get to that address because I had no point of reference and had to ask strangers on the street for directions.

"Do you know where the DMV is on Cole Street?" I asked a man at a newsstand.

"It's further west," he said. "Cole runs north and south. Head west on Hollywood, hang a left on Wilcox, and follow it down toward Melrose."

"Is that near Cahoonga Street?" I asked.

"Cahoonga?!" he laughed. "Where are you from?"

"Missouri."

"It's pronounced Ca-WANG-ga," he said. "Cahuenga runs north and south, parallel to Vine. Since you're new in town, you should buy yourself a Thomas Guide."

The Thomas Guide was a book of Los Angeles maps about an inch thick and set me back thirty-five dollars. So I sat in my car, cracked open the Thomas Guide and was immediately overwhelmed. The book was divided numerically and alphabetically, and to me, it was convoluted and mind-boggling. A street would start on page A4 and continue on page G12. I stared at the multicolored squares and tried to decipher the myriad lines. After blowing thirty-five bucks, I was just as lost with the Thomas Guide as I was without it. Finally, I got frustrated and decided to drive down Sunset Boulevard. It was a main thoroughfare, and surely it would get me where I needed to go . . . or at least I hoped.

Sunset Boulevard traversed a variety of cultures and lifestyles. It began or ended at the Pacific Ocean, depending on how you were looking at the map, and wound through the hills of upscale neighborhoods like Brentwood and Beverly Hills, then entered West Hollywood, where traffic came to a crawl as it snaked through the famous "Sunset Strip," and then continued through Hollywood, Silver Lake, and the gang-ridden neighborhoods of Echo Park.

As I drove east on Sunset with the heater on, I could tell this street was about buying, selling, coercing, and manipulating. Tenacious immigrants waved maps to the stars' homes. Rock musicians peddled their gigs. Low-rent hookers prowled for their next trick. Actors pimped their faces in café windows, car washes, and print shops that had walls covered with 8x10 glossies. Whether it was a Hollywood agent brokering a deal at a posh eatery or a weathered Guatemalan hawking roses on the corner, Sunset Boulevard was a street where everyone hustled.

In the '80s, Angelyne's billboards were all over Hollywood.

Even the billboards that dominated Sunset Boulevard were relentless in their exaltation of sex, beauty, and blockbuster films. Back home in Missouri, billboards pushed all-you-can-eat buffets and Jesus. In Hollywood, they glorified movie stars, Calvin Klein underwear, a hot Marlboro man, and a colossal scantily clad sexpot with platinum blonde hair and big boobs. Her name, Angelyne, shouted at me in bold black typeface. I would find out later that Angelyne was a local legend of sorts who was famous simply for being on billboards and driving around town in a hot pink Corvette. Everyone in Hollywood knew who she was, but most people didn't know *what* she was, whether it be a singer, actress, stripper, sugar baby, or a bored housewife. She was just Angelyne, and that was all that mattered.

"Welcome to the land of bullshit and glitter!" Angelyne cooed at me like a Jayne Mansfield knockoff, and then she laughed because I was dumb enough to imagine a billboard could talk in the first place.

The message I gleaned from this barrage of hype was that beauty in all its forms was all that really mattered in this strange new world, and beauty was everywhere: on street corners, in traffic, at the dry cleaners. Even the grocery store checker looked like a male model. As I wandered aimlessly trying to find my way, I didn't need a pair of faux tortoiseshell eyeglasses to clearly see a man's value in this town was based solely on how he looked and the type of car he drove.

When I was a kid, I imagined I'd go to Hollywood and magically feel like I belonged. But compared to everyone I saw around me, I didn't belong at all. This was not the Hollywood of my dreams; this was like going back to junior high. I felt more inadequate than ever and realized I'd been lured to the "film capital of the world" by a fantasy that was nothing more than a ruse. And to think I'd spent three days of relentless driving and most of my parents' money to get here.

"It's like betting on a racehorse."

My mother's words had a chilling tone because the racehorse felt more like a bird with a broken wing, flapping frantically, running in circles, desperate for refuge. I never did find the DMV that day. I made a wrong turn, mistakenly got on a freeway, and drove east when I should have been driving west. Lost and confused, I wound up at the Shangri-La motel in Norwalk, thirty miles outside of Los Angeles. After checking in, I made my way to the coffee shop and collapsed in one of its orange-and-turquoise vinyl booths. A sleepy-eyed waitress shuffled my way and flashed a big smile with crooked teeth.

"How you doing, hon?"

She wiped the wood-grain Formica tabletop with a damp rag, then shoved a menu in my face. "Be right back to take your order," she snapped, and then she was gone.

My gaze drifted out the window to a pathetic little pool that was surrounded by orange-and-white metal umbrellas. And then suddenly, a woman, stark-ass naked, bolted out of a room. She cackled with laughter and jumped into the water.

"Shit!" she cursed as she flung the mop of wet hair out of her face. "I forgot my Bud! Jimmy, bring out that six-pack, will you?"

Just then, a bald, heavyset man in Hawaiian trunks came running after her, six-pack in hand. He jumped into the pool, nearly on top of her.

"You som' bitch!" she snorted, playfully splashing water his way. Jimmy grabbed her and pulled her close, causing her to chortle even more.

The waitress came back to my table with an order pad in hand. Her name tag read "Arlene."

"That dumb hussy-assed skank! She knows she's not supposed to be drinking in that pool," she groused. "That is a code violation!"

"She's naked," I said in disbelief.

"Ain't it awful?" Arlene frowned and grumbled, "You can count the pimples on her flabby, overpriced ass from here!"

Then she leaned forward and her mouth stretched into a mischievous snaggletoothed grin.

"I'll give you a better deal any old day. How'd you like to try the orange snapper special?"

A wink of her eye told me more than I cared to know.

That night, in the dingy motel room, I sat on the bed that rocked and squeaked as I counted what was left of my traveler's checks. I needed to find a permanent place to stay. I needed to find a job. And I needed to get my car fixed because I couldn't drive around forever with the heater on. But I had only eight hundred dollars left, which I kept inside a rolled sock, hidden inside my suitcase.

I pulled out my Thomas Guide and tried to make sense of where I was tonight and where I'd go tomorrow. I'd spent the entire day lost and confused and never got to where I wanted to go. I was anxious, frustrated, overwhelmed, and so ignorant and ill-prepared.

I fell back onto the rickety bed and said a prayer, asking God, Jesus, and the whole universe for help. Tomorrow would be a better day, I told myself. Just relax. But I was too tense. To relieve some stress, I popped a quarter into the Vibro-Matic metal box attached to the bed's headboard, which promised a tingling relaxation massage. I sprawled across the mattress and waited for something to happen. And the more I waited, the more gypped I felt.

CHAPTER 3

THE NEXT MORNING, I HIT THE ROAD AND GOT LOST for three whole years. Maybe even four, now that I think about it. I flopped from one place to the next, renting a room here, renting half a bed there, and once was so desperate I rented space on a floor.

Getting a job in film and television was almost impossible. I had no idea how to find that kind of work. Like a bumpkin, I actually walked up and down Sunset Boulevard in a three-piece suit and dress shoes, knocked on office doors, and personally delivered my résumé. When that was a bust, I stood outside Paramount Pictures and handed my résumé to anyone who'd take it.

"You should get a *Daily Variety*," a passerby told me. "Check the production charts and send your résumé to the companies starting production."

And so I did. I spent a few weeks scouring the production charts, sending out résumés, and making follow-up calls, and I got nothing in return. It's one thing to dream about working in Hollywood, but to actually do it was more difficult than I'd ever imagined. I was such a fool. I thought I'd hit the streets of Hollywood and be welcomed with open arms. I believed I was that special. But in reality, I was just one more hopeful schmo who was getting in the way of other schmoes who were clamoring for a piece of the glitter-encrusted pie. And there were hundreds, if not thousands, hungering for that one coveted piece.

When I stumbled upon the tawdry section of Santa Monica Boulevard known as "Hustler Row," where the gay prostitutes peddled their wares, I wondered about their hopes and dreams. I knew all too well how they wound up selling themselves on the street and shuddered at the thought of being so desperate I'd have to do it myself.

The song "I'll Be Good" by René & Angela loudly pumped over a boom box while the boys prowled the street from La Brea Avenue all the way east to Western. As they worked the boulevard like it was their own sordid runway, I sat in a burger joint and watched them through a window. They strutted and posed, basking in the glow of a defiant sun that colored the sky with blazing magenta hues.

That night, as I sat in my shabby room, low on cash and in desperate need of a production job, wondering how I'd pay the rent, doing the unthinkable came to mind. If I was ever going to get noticed, I had to outfox the competition and charm the gatekeepers.

"If they're not going to hire you," I said aloud, "then they're going to win you."

My brain fired with creative energy. I hoisted that old heavy typewriter onto a makeshift desk that I'd fashioned out of a cardboard box. The typewriter's carriage had gotten bent from the weight of the car seat during the long drive, but thankfully it still worked; I just couldn't return the carriage with a quick swipe of the hand.

I cracked open *Daily Variety* and read the production charts, which listed every TV show and movie in the works as well as the addresses of their respective production offices.

I created this for Jodie Foster after I heard she was looking for an assistant. The kit included a small clay pot, a bag of dirt, a plastic toy shovel, and a packet of forget-me-not seeds. She was not impressed. In referencing the price of postage, she responded, "Well…that was worth twenty-nine cents!"

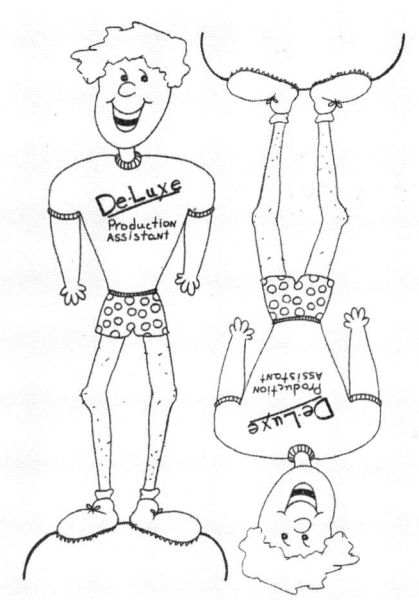

The paper doll gimmick that catapulted me over the gates at Paramount. While some folks were lucky enough to sleep their way into "the biz," I had to take a more ridiculous approach.

"Congratulations, Pee-wee Herman!" I typed, rolled the paper up one notch, manually repositioned the carriage, then typed some more. "This is your lucky day! You've just won your own production assistant from the Jeff Copeland P.A. Clearing House Giveaway."

I was not going down without a fight. I rolled the paper up one notch, carefully returned the carriage and continued to type. "Enclosed you will find a scale model of this wonderful prize to color and set on your desk."

Three humorous paragraphs followed, listing my stellar qualifications, which included typing on a broken typewriter. Then I drew a cartoon caricature of myself, cut it out, and glued it to a cardboard backing.

When I finished creating the paper doll and re-read the letter, I knew this crazy gimmick was certainly one of the most original ways to submit a résumé. It would surely stand out from the rest. And so I sat at my old broken typewriter and banged out another letter, and then another one after that. I typed so many letters and cut out so many paper dolls that my fingers hurt.

Two days later, I landed my first job.

"We can't pay you anything," the producer explained. "But it's a great way to make contacts."

I figured working for free was better than not working at all, so I jumped at the chance. It was a strange little film that starred Lorne Greene of the TV series Bonanza and involved musicians T-Bone Burnett and John Doe, comedian Phil Hartman, John Avila of Oingo Boingo, the band Los Lobos, and a hilarious character actress named Bunny Summers.

I loved being on the set and worked ten hours a day for two weeks. Although I wasn't getting paid, I got three meals a day for free. When the shoot was over, the producers showed their appreciation by giving me a case of Lipton Cup-a-Soup, and I was happy to get it. A few days later, I got a call from the location manager.

"I'm working on another movie and we need production assistants," he said. "Are you available?"

"Yes!" I said, and he gave me a phone number. I called the production office, set up an interview, and hightailed it to Sunset Boulevard, where I found the address on a narrow low-rise Art Moderne structure that was built on a hill.

I entered the building on the side street and found the small, dreary, windowless front office. When I walked inside, it was chaos: phones rang, people hollered. Several tarted-up actresses sat in a row and waited to audition. A production secretary named Cindy manned the front desk and wrestled with the phone lines.

"Cindy!" barked an agitated, over-caffeinated little man with a big belly as he charged through a doorway and dropped some script pages on her desk. "I need five copies of these sides!"

"Cindy!" another voice yelled. "Get me Johnny Depp's agent!"

"Cindy!" another person hollered.

The demands on Cindy seemed endless and unreasonable, and as she answered the incoming calls and juggled the relentless requests, I could see she was frazzled.

"Can I help you?" she asked, putting two calls on hold and shooting me an exasperated look.

"Hi, my name is Jeff Copeland. I'm here to interview for the production assistant job."

"One sec," she said, taking the résumé from my hand and darting into a nearby office.

I sat down next to four bleached-blonde actresses who were all hoping to get the part. To my left was a typing stand where a modern electric typewriter sat. I admired the machine. It was so much better than the one I had.

"Jeff, he'll see you now," Cindy said and motioned for me to go inside the production manager's office. When I entered, I found a burly giant sitting behind a desk, staring at my résumé.

"Hi, my name is Jeff Copeland," I said.

"Hmmmm," he grunted. His eyes glanced up at me, then back down at my résumé. He wasn't impressed.

"I'm a very hard worker," I said.

"We'll call you," he frowned. "Thanks for stopping by."

My heart sank. I didn't have time to wait for a phone call that would never come. I needed work now and this office clearly needed help, but he wasn't even going to give me a chance.

I ducked out of his office and passed by the overpainted blondes, while the phone lines rang and unseen faces screamed "Cindy!" I knew that when I walked out of that office door, I'd never get called back. I needed that job more than anything. It was the only lead I had. After six weeks in Los Angeles, all I had to show for it was an empty case of Lipton Cup-a-Soup. I was out of money, and I was desperate . . . so desperate I was ready to drive back to Missouri, but I didn't have enough money for the gas.

I walked past Cindy as I headed for the door and thanked her for her time. Then, as if right on cue, a handsome young writer who looked more like a male model came running from the back.

"Cindy, I need these pages typed right away," the writer said in a frantic tone.

Multiple phone lines rang and Cindy was struggling to keep up. Clearly overwhelmed, she shrugged with an exasperated look on her face. The beautiful writer looked frustrated, and that's when I stepped forward and snatched the pages out of his hand.

"I'll type those," I said. I sat behind the rickety typing stand and fired up the IBM typewriter. It jolted to life with an electric hum.

Cindy looked at me in disbelief.

"I can type," I said, feeding the machine a blank page. "Sixty-five words a minute. Consider it done."

"Do you work here?" the writer asked.

"No," I said. "But she's crazy busy and I don't have anything else to do."

The production manager came to his doorway and shot me a curious look.

"I'll work the day for free," I said. "Like a free trial. No obligation."

By the end of the day, I'd landed a full-time gig on a cheap B-movie that was helmed by a flamboyant film director who yelled everything he said and stomped around the office in pink satin short-shorts, cowboy boots, and a sweatshirt ripped at the neck. I worked twelve hours a day, six days a week, and made a flat rate of $200. No overtime. No health insurance. Not even Lipton Cup-a-Soup. But I was determined to stick it out because opportunities were slim for an inexperienced rube like me and I figured if I worked hard enough, this opportunity would lead to something better. I also wanted my parents to believe the racehorse they'd bet on was finally getting somewhere.

I hopped from one short-term gig to the next—six weeks on a feature film, two days on a short, one day on a commercial, and six months at the Broadway department store in men's sportswear, where I hustled and networked, always jonesing for a break. One day, a man came in to buy some pants. We chatted as I rang up his sale. I told him I moved to Hollywood to work in the movies and he said he worked at Warner Bros. When I told him I was a writer, he replied, "I need a writer for a movie I'm working on right now."

"Oh, wow," I said. "We should go to lunch."

"People don't go to lunch here," he laughed. "They *do* lunch." And with that, he handed me his business card, which had a big Warner Bros. logo on it. "Give me a call."

A week later, we were at Astro Burger on Santa Monica Boulevard.

"It's a horror movie," he said, squirting a wad of ketchup onto a pile of fries. "It takes place in a fast food restaurant. I'm calling it 'Deep Fried.' Get it?"

No, I didn't get it, but whatever. Then he proceeded to describe the first victim: a snarky high school cheerleader who gets French-fried when her head is dunked in a vat of hot, bubbling grease.

"Wow," I said, thinking, *Well, it beats working on a porno . . . sort of.*

"This is a great opportunity for you," he said, then smiled. "Do you have a big cock?"

"What was that?" I asked, nearly choking on my burger.

"How big is your dick?"

I was gobsmacked. "Dude, what—Why would you even ask me that?"

"You want to be a writer," he said with an arrogant smirk. "You're not a writer yet. Look, I want to work with you but I need you to make it worth my while."

"Worth your while? What about worth *my* while? You told me you were a producer."

"I am a producer."

I pulled out his business card and pointed out the fine print beneath his name.

"It says here you work in payroll. How is that being a producer?"

I thought this lunch would be a good networking opportunity, but learned a valuable lesson instead. There were a lot of charlatans in Hollywood. This guy would never rank with the real movers and shakers of the film industry, but he talked a good game, drove a flashy car, and took advantage of starry-eyed hopefuls, who weren't yet savvy enough to know the difference. But I caught on quick.

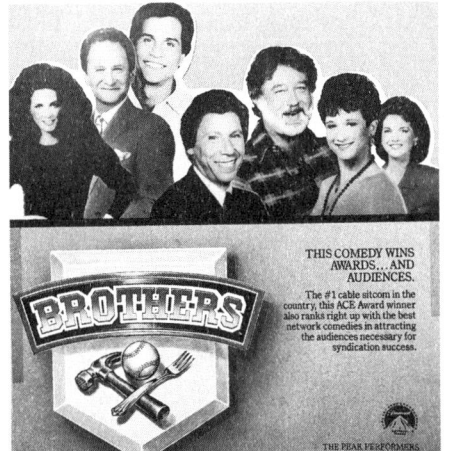

A 1986 promo for Showtime's TV series *Brothers*. In those days, cable TV shows couldn't win Emmy Awards. Instead, cable shows competed for Cable Ace Awards, which always seemed kinda shitty to me. Who the hell wants one of those?

My fortune changed for the better when I landed a production assistant position at Paramount on a TV series called *Brothers*. It was a huge break. Finally, I was on my way to greatness! Or so I thought. I celebrated by financing a car I couldn't afford: a beautiful red Pontiac Fiero.

Working at Paramount was an incredible experience. But after working as a P.A. on *Brothers* for a year, I got bored. While I was grateful to have the job, it offered no opportunities for advancement. I was told I'd never write for the show, so don't even try. And I was surrounded by crew members (grips, gaffers, script supervisors, secretaries) who harbored their own creative ambitions. Some wanted to write and produce, others wanted to direct or do camera work. Even the studio guard slipped me his headshot because he wanted to act. They were all waiting for their turn, and some of these folks had been waiting for twenty years! The stagnation bothered me, and I was afraid I'd get stuck in the P.A. trench and never get out.

I needed to create an opportunity that would catapult my career in the direction I wanted to go, but I didn't know how to do that . . . until one morning a short, dark blonde powerhouse charged into the office wearing a miniskirt, black leggings, and boots.

"Do you guys have sugar? I need to borrow some sugar."

"Sure, it's right here," I said and showed her the way.

"Thanks," she smiled, taking several packets, and then she ran out the back.

"That's Debra Hill," said the production secretary. "She's really nice. She works next door."

Debra Hill was a movie producer whose career skyrocketed when she wrote and produced the blockbuster movie *Halloween* with John Carpenter. Debra produced that movie on a shoestring budget of $325,000 and it grossed over $40 million at the box office. I figured if a horror film could launch Debra Hill's career, it could certainly launch mine. So, in a fit of inspiration, I banged out a screenplay that was the same low-budget schlock the Hollywood bottom feeders had been churning out for years, only my version had a twist of dark humor. A month later, I asked Debra to read it. She took a copy but never responded. Why would she? She was too busy producing major movies. She didn't have time to be bothered by a Hollywood peon who was bucking for attention.

I soon came to understand that aspiring to work as a writer in Hollywood was like climbing a greased slide. I needed a mentor, someone to take interest in my writing, guide me through the obstacles, and catapult me over the hurdles. But no one legitimate in my immediate circle wanted to take me under his or her wing. So one day, I boldly asked our network executive if he would read my screenplay. I figured if I couldn't get support from my bosses, perhaps I'd get it from their boss.

"Don't you know who I am?" he responded curtly, then shot me a long cold stare. I was humiliated and began to apologize when he waved me aside, walked away, and never spoke to me again.

The nerve of that queen! I was so frustrated, discouraged, and pissed off. But then finally, one day, when I least expected it, my telephone rang and everything changed for the better. Well . . . sort of.

PARAMOUNT PRESENTS

JAMES STEWART
KIM NOVAK
IN ALFRED HITCHCOCK'S
MASTERPIECE

1400 POUNDS OF FROZEN FURY that moves like man!

HALF HUMAN

HALF-MAN, HALF-BEAST but ALL MONSTER!

Starring JOHN CARRADINE

THE STORY OF THE LOVE LIFE OF THE SIDESHOW

DO SIAMESE TWINS MAKE LOVE?

CAN A FULL GROWN WOMAN TRULY LOVE A MIDGET?

WHAT SEX IS THE HALF MAN HALF WOMAN?

DWAIN ESPER PRESENTS

FREAKS

MYSTERY!

ISLAND OF LOST MEN

with ANNA MAY WONG
J. CARROL NAISH
ERNEST TRUEX ★ ERIC BLORE

KIRK DOUGLAS

THE BIG CARNIVAL

JAN STERLING

BOB ARTHUR · PORTER HALL · PRODUCED & DIRECTED BY BILLY WILDER

'VERTIGO'

CHAPTER 4

"This script is great," the director said. "I'd like to put a year option on it."

Hearing those words gave me a long-awaited thrill. Finally, I was in the Hollywood game . . . or so I wanted to believe. While the real movers and shakers of Tinseltown negotiated their script deals over lunch at posh eateries like Spago and Le Dome, I was negotiating mine on a Saturday morning at Ernie's Taco House in North Hollywood.

The director wasn't really a director at all. He was just another production assistant at Paramount who was trying to forge his way into filmmaking. The producer, also a Paramount lackey, worked as a glorified file clerk. Together they set out to make a film that would launch their careers, and I was honored that they chose to do it with my script.

"How much?" I asked, knowing full well an option on a screenplay averaged ten thousand dollars.

"Twenty-five bucks," said the producer between bites of his taco.

"Twenty-five bucks?!"

"You'll make it up on the back end," he said, which meant I'd take it up the back end like most aspiring writers in town.

"That's all we got," the director explained.

"But that's not enough to pay for this lunch," I reacted.

"Look, Jeff, we want to work with you. We believe in your story," said the producer.

The fact that they liked my work made me want to pay *them* twenty-five bucks, just so I could hear their compliments again. I was starved for opportunity and validation. I didn't need twenty-five dollars. I needed to know my screenplay was worth producing. The fact that these guys believed in it meant the world to me, so I signed their option and dreamt about my name flying up on the big screen.

"I signed a movie deal!" I told my parents with great excitement. They thought I was on my way to living in Beverly Hills and so did I. But for now, I was holed up in a tiny dump in the St. Katherine Apartments, located in the low-rent section of Hollywood. But there was hope of better things to come. During this time, I finagled my way into a writer's secretary position on the show *Brothers*, which tripled my salary, thanks to overtime. I paid back the money I borrowed from my parents. I decorated my apartment and bought a beautiful 1930s mohair sofa and a 1930s floor model radio. And for a moment, everything was just perfect.

And then my boss got fired—or departed due to creative differences, depending on whom you asked. Whatever the reason, I was let go because I no longer had someone to assist. Then that janky movie deal that I signed for my horror script, the one that I was so proud of, went kaput due to a lack of financing. Suddenly, I was in over my head, swallowed by debt, no bright future in sight, while my landlady banged on the door and hollered that my rent was due.

Thanks to Debra Hill and Paul Reubens, I landed an assistant gig on a Pee-wee Herman circus movie. The money might have been shit, but the fun was out of this world and I loved being on that set. The cast, crew, animals—everything was great. And when it was over, I was back to square one, living on canned corn and mashed potatoes, and wondering when the next paycheck was coming.

It was a precarious life in Hollywood. Up one minute, down the next, always struggling to find my way. Good fortune would come, and then it would vanish or distort, and become something entirely unrecognizable ... like a horrid reflection in a funhouse mirror. But through it all, I clung to the hope that one day my writing would pay off, even though I couldn't get anyone of merit to read my new script. Everyone was just too busy—even my crusty old landlady, Babe Yancey, who told me she could have been a movie star herself, if she had the time.

On the set of *Big Top Pee-wee* at the Disney Ranch in Newhall. 1988.
Photographer unknown.

"I was so good-looking, I'd walk down Hollywood Boulevard and they'd all stop and stare," she said, taking my script, cracking it open, and giving it a quick glance. Her wrinkled, red-painted mouth twisted into a grimace. "I don't got time to read this stilted dialogue. I was married to a writer once. Nothing but trouble."

The gleaming promise I showed as a kid was tarnished now as I trudged from one menial job to the next, answering phones and making coffee. Writing was my only escape. I couldn't afford to go to movies so I stayed home and wrote my own. I pounded my feelings onto the typewriter keys, writing stories about drunks, whores, and retards who couldn't get what they really longed for in life. As a twenty-four-year-old gay man, that's exactly what I'd become . . . a drunk, retarded whore who was fraught with angst, frustration, fear, and the pressure to win. And win big.

"It's like betting on a racehorse."

But a workhorse conditioned to believe it was a thoroughbred didn't stand a chance, or so it seemed. I was a long shot. My parents thought I was doing great. But they were ignorant and didn't know the difference. I'd seen the budgets at Paramount. I understood the real meaning of greatness. It was a job that paid $40,000 a week to write and produce. That's what greatness was; that was the magic cure-all. That was my American dream! But it didn't happen. The raw nerve and relentless drive that had gotten me here was turned against me now, and the hunger to win ate me alive. I came to Hollywood knowing exactly what I wanted, and in three years learned to settle for what I could get: a shit temp job as a data entry clerk in an accounting department at Paramount. It paid the bills . . . barely. But it was more than I could say for the screenplays I wrote at night, that just seemed to languish and die.

A rare, behind-the-scenes photo of actress Bunny Summers and Paul Reubens.
Photo (most likely) by Bruce Talamon.
Courtesy of Author's collection.

One night, as I sat in my little apartment, surrounded by pages I'd written that no one of importance would ever read, everything just fell apart. Sadness swelled. Anger raged. My brain was on fire. I wanted to scream, but my throat was tight. I was so sick of being the chump who clocked in every day to watch someone else's dream come true. I was tired of feeling like a monkey on a stick . . . or a circus elephant that had been tortured into submission and fed peanuts to do tricks. The imagination that always sustained me now hurled voices of self-hate and doubt.

"You were never good enough," it said. "If you were, you'd be somewhere by now."

Now I was really fucked. I needed to see a shrink, but all I could afford was a six-pack of Budweiser. I popped the tab on the first can and guzzled it whole.

"The Hollywood Walk of Fame ain't no cakewalk, sugar puss," that nasty voice taunted. "If you can't handle having your nose rubbed in the gravel and shit, you just get the hell out. What are you sticking around for?"

"Because I don't have anywhere else to go!" I cried out.

That was the horrible truth. Making it in Hollywood was all that I had, it was all that mattered. The basis of my self-worth was that meaningless and that shallow. Where else was I going to go? What else did I have to look forward to? There was nothing else for me except the pressure to write.

WRITE! With a jagged edge that cuts to the bone, you piece of shit.

WRITE! So you can get away from the ravages of AIDS because the romance you long for smells of putrid rot.

WRITE! So you can churn out story after story about the dregs of society that are just reflections of your broken pathetic self.

WRITE! Because it's the only goddamn hope you have for something better.

The "I'll show you" determination that grew out of my inadequacies as a child now raged like a monster. My nerves were chewed raw, the inner torture was unbearable, and that's when I burst into tears and succumbed to my worst nightmare. I was a failure. Trapped in a body I never really liked and cursed with an awful ambition I could never satisfy.

There was only one way out of this horror show: Ethel Merman. Thank God for the original Broadway cast album of *Gypsy*! I cranked up my stereo and blasted myself into a Mama Rose stupor. After crushing the sixth beer can and throwing it against the wall, I fell back onto my Murphy bed, drunk and despondent, and swam in my delirium while Ethel chewed up the scenery with "Rose's Turn."

CHAPTER 5

IN THE SUMMER OF 1988, HOLLYWOOD WAS IN THE throes of a crippling writers' strike that lasted five months. In those days, reality television didn't exist, so when the union writers stopped writing, production came to a halt and an eerie paralysis settled over the town.

Once again, I was laid off. I had to get a job fast and figured my interest in writing would translate well to public relations, so I grabbed the phone book, sat on my Murphy bed, and flipped through the Yellow Pages until I found a long list of entertainment publicity firms. Starting with the letter A, I picked up the phone and dialed.

"Hello, my name is Jeff Copeland and I'm calling to see if you have any assistant positions available."

Three exhausting hours later, when I'd gotten to Rosenbaum/Finnegan/Blithe, my luck changed for the better.

"We are looking for a secretary," the office manager said in an imperious tone. "Can you come in today?"

R/F/B Public Relations was a legendary PR firm that handled major stars, some of the biggest in Hollywood. It was located in a bright turquoise-colored building on a tired stretch of Wilshire Boulevard known as Miracle Mile, right

Fabulous Wilshire Boulevard...back when it actually was fabulous in the 1950s.
Photo: Ellis-Sawyer

across the street from the old Flying Saucer diner, where five bucks would get me a weak cup of coffee and a burger, if I had five bucks to spare.

I took the elevator to the top floor and found the walnut-paneled lobby that was covered with framed magazine covers of all the megastars the firm represented. After introducing myself to the receptionist, I took a seat on the Naugahyde sofa and let my eyes wander over the impressive array of smiling faces on every major publication, including *Vogue, TV Guide, People, Vanity Fair...*

"Those are just a few of the stars in our glittering roster of clients," purred a woman who suddenly appeared in an opened door behind me. She had orange hair and a breathy voice that sounded much younger than her true age, which was at least sixty-five.

"I'm Dorie Clark, we spoke on the phone."

Her handshake was warm and inviting. Her faded beauty strained under the weight of a forced smile.

"Come back to my office," she said with a twinkle in her eye as she opened the beautifully polished door and led me across a corridor into her inner sanctum. She wore a loose-fitting purple dress and had a sensuous and commanding stride, like a tigress on the prowl. Her black slingback open-toed shoes were out of style.

"So tell me about yourself, Jeff," she said as she sat behind her desk and massaged lotion into her brown-spotted hands.

I told her what she wanted to hear while I marveled at her strange allure, attractive but repellent, like a crushed flower that had been pressed between the pages of a book and intentionally forgotten for forty years. I could tell she was quite a siren in her day before gravity took its toll and the gin blossoms started to show. I was particularly fascinated with her smudged lipstick.

"So, why do you want to work in PR?"

As I spoke, she stood and adjusted the blinds on her window. From that angle, I noticed she should have worn a girdle.

"We're all writers here," she concurred, then sat back down and hiked up her leg to smooth out her stocking. "I was a writer. Television mostly. Can you take dictation?"

"Yes," I lied.

"How many words can you type per minute?"

"Sixty-five."

"Hmmmm." She stared at me for a moment, put her index fingers to her misshapen lips. "When were you born? What day?"

"February 25."

"Pisces." She smiled and her eyes lit up. "You're hired. Can you start tomorrow?"

"Yes, absolutely," I said with enthusiasm.

The next morning at nine, Dorie gave me a tour of the "factory," where flacks churned out newsworthy cow pies that were sprinkled with glitter and fed to all the editors, columnists, and stringers around the world. Even the scent of strong floral perfume that danced in Dorie's wake couldn't hide the stench of bullshit. It almost made it worse.

As Dorie sauntered through the galley of offices, I was surprised at how disheveled the place looked. It was so different from the glamorous PR firm that was sold to me in the front lobby.

"You'll be providing support for two very busy publicists," she said as we passed diligent assistants who seemingly cowered in her presence as they focused intently on their typing tasks at hand. Then we rounded the corner, and in the distance I saw a cheap wooden desk that was propped up on a concrete block because it was missing a leg.

"Peter is a young guy," she continued. "A little nervous, but extremely kind. Mack, on the other hand, is old-school. Here's your desk," she said, and I was impressed it had four legs.

Then she took me into Peter's office.

"Peter, this is Jeff Copeland. He's your new assistant."

Peter was a tall, dark, thirty-two-year-old man with a lean build and handsome features.

"Hey, nice to meet you. Welcome," he said with a warm smile and a firm handshake. Afterward, Dorie took me into the adjacent office to meet my other boss, Newt Mackleberry.

"Mack, I want you to meet Jeff Copeland."

"Is that the new secretary?" he said and grimaced.

"That's me."

I extended my hand to a crabby, white-haired curmudgeon who spoke with a Southern drawl. He was clearly unimpressed.

"You take dictation?" he asked without taking my hand.

"Yes, I do."

"Good. Sit down. I've got some missives I need to get out."

"Get busy, boys," Dorie chuckled and slinked away.

"Where's your pad and pen?" Mack barked.

"Oh! I'll be right back."

I ran out to my desk and pulled open a drawer, which dislodged from its track and fell to the floor.

"Oh, Jesus Christ!" I said in a near panic. Inside the broken drawer, I found a steno pad and a mess of loose pens. I grabbed what I needed and hurried back into the old grump's lair, where he dictated a bunch of jibber-jabber that I scribbled down as best I could. Thankfully, Mack spoke slowly, which gave me time to create my own version of shorthand. When he finally finished rattling off all the recipients of the carbon copies, I stood up to go type the letter.

"Where do you think you're going?" he snapped. His tone was demeaning.

"I'm going to type it," I said, wanting to get to that typewriter while the letter was still fresh in my memory.

"I'm not done," he said. "Sit back down."

I dutifully sat down and Mack started to dictate another long-winded letter. I didn't think the wind in that blowhard was ever going to end. Mack dictated eight letters, and by the time I sat down to transcribe what looked like chicken scratch into the word processor, Peter came rushing out to my desk.

"Jeff, I need you to type up this release right away."

He handed me his own mess of scratch. As I tried to make out his writing, Mack's phone started to ring.

"Newt Mackleberry's office," I answered.

"You stupid ass!" screamed a woman on the other end. Before I could speak, she erupted into an explosive rant about the goddamn flowers and the dumbass who fucked them up. I had no idea what she was talking about. When I tried to explain that I was new and I wasn't at fault, she got even more infuriated.

"Who the fuck do you think you're talking to?" she screamed.

"Is that Judy?" bellowed Mack.

"Judy who?" I asked.

"Judy who the fuck do you think, you pipsqueak pussy!" she yelled. "Get Mack on the phone!"

"One moment please," I said kindly then transferred the call, or so I thought. Unfortunately, I disconnected the old pooch! And when she called back, she was so rabid I thought she was going to chew her way through the phone line. Then Peter's phones started ringing and before I could get to them all, Mack's lines lit up again.

"Jeff, I need that release!"

"Where are those missives?"

Never before had I experienced so much stress and pressure. At noon, I was so frazzled, I made a beeline for the nearest 7-11, bought a Budweiser, and chugged it for lunch. I couldn't believe the glamorous and exciting world of entertainment publicity was this horrible.

Later that afternoon, a little old man charged through the R/F/B corridor and hollered, "Ickity! Kookity!"

The old codger rounded the corner and saw me sitting behind my desk. We locked eyes and I felt like a chimp caught in the scope of a poacher's rifle.

"Where's Ickity?" he demanded.

"Um . . . I don't know," I shrugged, then thought, *What the fuck is an Ickity?*

"Kookity!" he screeched. "Where's Kookity?"

Then suddenly, two male assistants came bustling from opposite ends of the suite like Pomeranians running at their master's beck and call.

"Coming, Sol!" one of them howled.

"Get in my office," shouted the old turd. That's when I realized he was Sol Finnegan, the legendary mastermind of the firm, who spearheaded the Los Angeles branch.

To those who were footing the $10,000 monthly retainer, Sol Finnegan came across as a kind, respectable gentleman who manipulated magazines and newspapers to their benefit. But to the working-class schmoes like me, who shoveled that crapola for three hundred bucks a week, Sol was a sawed-off mean-tempered troll who kept his two assistants in a perpetual fluster with his relentless demands. The turnover rate for assistants was so high, Sol called one "Ickity" and the other "Kookity" so he wouldn't have to remember their names.

Sol Finnegan encouraged assistants throughout the office to write "items," which were pithy blurbs about his celebrity clients that could be submitted to national newspaper columnists like Liz Smith and Shirley Eder. It didn't matter whether or not the item was truthful. What mattered most was that it made an impression. I submitted several and always made a bad impression, which became apparent when I was passed over for a junior publicist position. When I asked Dorie Clark for the reason, she sighed, her mouth drooped at the corners, and then she shrugged.

"Sol says you can't write," she said.

I might have been ignorant about a lot of things, but I'd been in Hollywood long enough to know you didn't have to be a good writer to be successful. There were plenty of hacks who made great livings writing stupid sitcoms, nighttime soaps, and bad movies. So whether or not I could write was a moot point. I wanted to write, and I was determined to write whether Sol Finnegan believed in me or not.

One morning, while I sat at my desk and tried to decipher ten pages of illegitimate shorthand, I received a surprising telephone call from the director who had optioned my horror script, the one that couldn't get bankrolled. The movie had finally gotten financed and was going into production in Minnesota. It was a small deal, he said, so he had to make some cuts to accommodate the reduced budget.

"Oh," I said. "What did you cut?"

"About ninety pages," he said.

Well, that was a horror! I'd invested a lot of time, energy, and two-liter bottles of Pepsi into writing that 120-page script. Learning it had been cut down to a thirty-page short was disappointing. When the movie was finished six months later and I finally saw it on the big screen, it was even worse. The movie wasn't bad. It was well made, went on to play film festivals, and even won an award. It just wasn't mine. The actors, the lighting, the mood, and even the music were so different from what I'd initially imagined when I was pounding at the typewriter keys. That's when I knew it wasn't enough to be just a writer. The director was the real storyteller in the film medium. It was the director's vision that trumped all. The only way to experience true creative satisfaction was to be a filmmaker.

The Lovely Carol, a real woman who was sometimes mistaken for a drag queen. She was so funny, so beloved and brought much-needed joy to the gay community during a very dark time. 1995. *Photo by Lisa Harrington, courtesy of The Lovely Carol Archives.*

After the screening party, the producer drove me home because I was too drunk to do it myself. That night I lay sprawled on the thin mattress of my Murphy bed in my little dark apartment with strange shadows cast upon the walls. I was tucked inside my own little world now . . . alone and frustrated, twirling in a state of inebriation. I felt trapped and dreaded the thought of taking dictation the next day. It was all so demeaning. That's when a low-rent hooker stepped out of the shadows and into the tawdry glow of an imagined neon light. She had a jones for narcotics and harbored the volatile charms of a beautiful young killer she hid from the police in her East Hollywood apartment. It was a one-sided romance, and it lingered in my mind like a haunting melody. Even the next day, while I gritted my teeth during sessions of long-winded dictation, that story danced along the periphery of my subconscious like a provocative striptease.

After my missives were typed and stacked neatly on Mack's desk for signature, I took a moment to scratch story notes onto a steno pad when the telephone rang.

"Newt Mackleberry's office," I said.

"Jeff, it's Beverly," announced the lively voice on the other end.

Beverly was a friend of mine who worked as a popular West Hollywood comedian known as "The Lovely Carol." She apologized for the short notice and explained she needed someone to run a video camera that night while she played hostess on the red carpet at a swanky birthday party in Santa Monica. The party was being thrown by a CBS television executive; it sounded like a good networking opportunity.

"All you have to do is work the camera for about an hour," she said. "It doesn't pay, but there's plenty of free food. Are you interested?"

A chance to eat something other than mashed potatoes, boxed macaroni, and canned corn was a golden opportunity in my book. Unfortunately, rush-hour traffic from Mid-Wilshire to Santa Monica was a nightmare. By the time I got there, most of the party guests had already arrived. Then to make matters worse, I couldn't figure out how to turn on the camera. When I finally got it up and running, I couldn't get it to focus.

I believed I could do anything if I put my mind to it, but this experience blew that theory to hell. I felt terrible and apologized. Thankfully, The Lovely Carol just laughed it off.

"Oh, put that camera away and go have a cocktail," she said.

As I made my way to the buffet, the one thing I did focus on was a curious enigma standing by the bar, chatting with friends. *Is that a man?* I wondered. *Or is that a woman?* When it comes to gender in America, the unknown can make one wary, if not downright afraid. In the land of Missouri where I was born and raised, the issue could provoke some folks to reach for their guns.

"Shoot that varmint!" pretty much summed up their level of tolerance for anything that was nonconforming and queer. But I was intrigued with this strange person whose gender I could not discern, and that perplexity haunted me throughout the night.

My friend Tom Bate suddenly appeared at my side, holding a plate filled with crab cakes. As he stuffed two into his mouth, I motioned to the unusual being across the way.

"Who is that?"

"Oh, that?" Tom spoke with his mouth full.

"Is that a man?" I asked.

"That's Holly Woodlawn," he said, shoving another crab cake into his mouth.

"Hollywood who?" I was confused.

"No. Holly is the first name," he explained. "Woodlawn is the last."

"Holly Woodlawn. So, that's a woman?" I uttered but wasn't quite convinced.

"I'm not sure," he laughed. "Whatever it is starred in Andy Warhol movies back in the '70s."

It must be a woman, I thought. And in that very moment, Holly Woodlawn looked my way and I caught her eye. She smiled briefly. I felt rude for staring and turned away. We never spoke that night. But later in my Hollywood apartment, as I tried to fall asleep to the racket of police helicopters and shopping carts being pushed down the sidewalk outside my window, Holly Woodlawn kept coming to mind, and her androgyny was as loud as the urban chaos that kept me awake.

The next day I tried to stay focused on my menial typing tasks for Newt Mackleberry, but Holly Woodlawn kept twirling into my thoughts and tugging at my concentration. That evening, while roaming the streets of West Hollywood, I wandered over to Video West on Larrabee and picked up a popular gossip rag called *The Hollywood Kids*. I was surprised to find Holly Woodlawn on the cover. After reading her interview about the movies she made with Andy Warhol, I was convinced that this Holly person was the "star" I needed for the movie I wanted to make, a dark, gritty drama filmed in black-and-white.

The next morning I dialed the information operator on my old rotary telephone.

"Hello, Operator. I'd like the number for Holly Woodlawn, please," I said, fingers crossed.

"Hollywood who?"

"The last name is Woodlawn. W-O-O-D-L-A-W-N."

"You said the first name is Holly?" she asked.

"Yes."

I was taken aback when the operator actually gave me Holly's phone number. I quickly jotted it down and then dialed the number.

"Hello," a deep voice sang on the other end of the line.

"Hi, my name is Jeff Copeland. I'm trying to reach Holly Woodlawn."

"This is Holly."

"Hi Holly, I'm a filmmaker and I have a wonderful movie I'm working on—it's a drama and I would love for you to star in it. Do you have time to go to dinner and talk about it?"

Now I was just like every other bullshitter in town.

"Well, sure," Holly said. "What time can you pick me up?"

Coincidentally, Holly Woodlawn lived a few blocks away on the corner of Cherokee Avenue and De Longpre Avenue in a two-story building called the Park Cherokee Apartments. It was across the street from a notorious park that was frequented by prostitutes and drug dealers. When I knocked on the door of her ground-floor apartment, I heard a loud "Come in!"

"Hi, Holly," I said as I entered the dingy, sparsely furnished living room and was immediately greeted by a small, mangy Lhasa Apso dog. At that moment, Holly came out of the bathroom without makeup, draped in a white terry cloth bathrobe.

Up until this time, I still had no idea if Holly was a man or a woman—not that it made a difference. I didn't really care. All I wanted was a star for my movie.

"Make yourself at home, hon," Holly said. "I'll just be a minute." And with that, the bathrobe parted, like a curtain unveiling a naughty peep show. Loud cymbals crashed! Horns blew TA-DA! And all doubt and mystery as to whether Holly was a man or a woman flew out the window. There was no mistaking that prized hog for a vagina. That broad put the long in schlong, and it made me a nervous wreck. I tried not to look but had to peek just to make sure I wasn't imagining things.

"Thank God you didn't cut it off!" is exactly what went through my head as I tried to focus on the sniffing dog in front of me. Holly retreated into her bedroom.

"What a gorgeous dong—DOG!" I reached down and pet its head.

"That's my daughter. Her name is Honey," Holly said, then emerged a moment later dressed in a pair of white Bermuda shorts, a print short-sleeved shirt, and espadrilles. Tonight Holly Woodlawn was going out as a man, but his pencil-thin eyebrows, lack of facial hair, and androgynous vocal inflection perplexed me. He was a male . . . physically, for the most part. But like a strange chameleon, he could be a woman, too.

"What a cute car," Holly said as she sank into the passenger side of my Pontiac Fiero. That car might have been the worst investment I'd ever made, but it paid off handsomely when Holly Woodlawn mistook it for a Ferrari.

"I love Italian sports cars!" she said.

"Me, too," I smiled.

If there was one thing I'd learned while working in entertainment publicity, it was to let people believe in the illusion. I shifted the car into gear and we sped off to the French Quarter restaurant in West Hollywood. Over dinner and several glasses of chardonnay, I told Holly about the dramatic screenplay I had written especially for her . . . even though it wasn't quite finished.

"When do we shoot?" she asked as she lit up a cigarette.

"Well, that depends on how quick I can raise the money."

Raise the money? If Holly had any sense, she would have told me to fuck off and hopped a bus home. But she didn't know any better and neither did I. We were a perfect match.

SOME LIKE IT HOT

Carmen **MIRANDA** · Michael **O'SHEA** · Vivian **BLAINE**
(The Sewing Machine...)

SOMETHING
FOR THE
BOYS
Technicolor

Phil **SILVERS** · Sheila **RYAN**
Perry **COMO** · Glenn **LANGAN** 20th
CENTURY-FOX
Directed by **LEW** **SEILER** · Produced by **IRVING** **STARR**

The
LADY OF
SCANDAL
Ruth
CHATTERTON

BASIL **RATHBONE**
RALPH **FORBES**
NANCE **ONEIL**
Directed by
FRANKLIN

METRO-
GOLDWYN-
MAYER

**ALL
TALKING**
PICTURE

WILLIAM **FOX**
PRESENTS
THEDA BARA
IN
THE SHE-DEVIL
THE STORY OF A BEAUTIFUL WOMAN WITHOUT A CONSCIENCE
STORY BY **NEJE HOPKINS** · STAGED BY **J·GORDON EDWARDS**
A **THEDA BARA** SUPER PRODUCTION
FOX FILM CORPORATION

CHAPTER 6

A WEEK LATER, I STOPPED BY HOLLY'S APARTMENT AND delivered my first draft of the script.

"*The Dark Side of Morning*," she said, reading the title page.

"It takes place between midnight and early dawn," I explained.

Holly loved the title. She didn't give two shits about the story. All that mattered was that she was the star. A few days after that, I called her on the phone and invited her over to my apartment for dinner so we could discuss the project.

"What would you like to eat?" I asked her.

"Chardonnay, darling. And plenty of it."

I picked Holly up in front of her building and drove her to the St. Katherine Apartments on Fountain near Wilcox, whereupon she mistook the large two-story Spanish Colonial building for my mansion. When I opened the front door and revealed it was an apartment house, the disappointment on her face was obvious. Her expression only got sadder when we entered my tiny single apartment and she saw I had a Murphy bed that swung out of the closet.

"Oh. How sweet and charming your little apartment is," she said. "Darling..." And then she got serious. Dead serious. "Where's that bottle of wine?"

Holly's fantasy of my being a well-heeled movie producer driving a Ferrari went bust. Instead, I was a struggling nobody driving a Pontiac and could barely afford car insurance, much less chardonnay. So it's no wonder she latched onto that bottle and didn't let go the entire night.

But despite the crushing reality, that evening Holly Woodlawn and I developed a friendship. While I fried chicken and whipped mashed potatoes, Holly and I chatted and genuinely hit it off. I liked her sense of humor and endearing charm, and she liked my hopeful, optimistic spirit. She also liked that I was employed by a major public relations firm that handled big-name superstars. In Hollywood, it's all about connections. And even though my only real connection was to the IBM Selectric typewriter as a secretary, I was eager to help Holly in any way that I could, because I genuinely liked her and I wanted to see her succeed.

An ad for Holly's debut at the Backlot Cabaret in West Hollywood. 1988.

At the time, Holly was preparing to make her Los Angeles cabaret debut at a West Hollywood nightspot called the Backlot, and I volunteered to help promote the show by writing press releases and sending them to all the papers. In an effort to increase her exposure, I also asked my co-worker Teresa Conboy, who managed the R/F/B computerized mailing list, to input Holly's name and address so she'd be invited to the firm's red carpet gala events. Teresa was happy to help, a move that garnered Holly a fortune in free publicity, as those parties were covered by major press photographers. Even the low-class paparazzi who weren't invited inside staked out the front in hopes of getting a shot of a star they could sell to the *Enquirer*.

One memorable event was held in Beverly Hills at Chasen's, one of the swankiest restaurants in town. Holly got all dolled up and looked great wearing a big, beautiful wig, a long green sequined dress, and colorful high heels. But the press wasn't paying her any mind because the big mainstream celebrities were getting all their attention. So I leaned surreptitiously into a photographer's ear.

"See that gal over there in the green?" I whispered. "That's Holly Woodlawn."

"Hollywood who?" he muttered.

"Holly Woodlawn. She's an Andy Warhol superstar. You know, from the Lou Reed song 'Walk on the Wild Side.'"

"Oh." He looked at me, confused, trying to remember.

"You know," I said. "'Holly came from Miami, F-L-A. Hitchhiked her way across the U.S.A.' She's a pop icon legend."

"Oh, yeah," he said. His brain neurons sputtered and fired, and his eyes lit up. "I remember."

"Can you do me a favor and just take her picture?"

"Sure," he replied.

He walked over to Holly.

"Hey Holly, you mind if I take a few?"

"Oh, sure, hon," Holly said, striking a dramatic pose. She was flattered that someone recognized her as a celebrity. When one photographer started to take pictures, the others swarmed in like pigs to a trough. All of a sudden, Holly was caught in a feeding frenzy of rapid-fire cameras. She smiled and posed, devouring each and every flash like a fame-hungry starlet.

At that moment, I was very proud of the media circus I'd created. Dorie Clark wasn't impressed and bristled at the sight of Holly cavorting with the photographers. She sidled up beside me and shook her head in disgust.

"That is not a woman!" she muttered, zeroing in on Holly like a sniper with laser focus, seemingly upset by the glamour gal who suddenly stole everyone's attention. I didn't say anything because I thought it was best to feign ignorance.

Dorie tugged on my shirt sleeve.

"That is not a woman!" she declared.

"Are you sure?" I asked, concerned that Dorie was going to make a scene. Dorie craned her neck for a better look, then frowned and shook her head.

"That is *not* a woman," she huffed for the last time and then stormed off in another direction. I was intrigued by Dorie's reaction. Why was she so upset? Was a man dressed as a woman that awful? Was that a threat to her own femininity? Was it a mockery? Or was she disgusted because she understood that some heterosexual men would actually prefer Holly Woodlawn over her? I wondered.

I was so thrilled when Michael Bruno helped promote Holly's Backlot show in his column for *Nightlife* magazine, but despite the buzz, few people showed up to see her perform. 1988.

Despite all the work I put into promoting Holly Woodlawn's show, her cabaret debut at the Backlot was an abysmal flop. After the musicians were paid and the club took its cut, Holly barely had the money for a pack of cigarettes and cab fare. She certainly didn't make enough money to pay her rent or utilities. And unbeknownst to me, both were overdue.

While hanging out at Holly's apartment one day, I asked how she made a living and she told me she "sold her pussy" in the back pages of the *L.A. X... Press*, a tawdry Los Angeles-based publication that catered to the sex trade. Holly showed me the paper. Porn stars, prostitutes, and a variety of fetishists filled those black-and-white newsprint pages as she turned from one to the next and pointed.

"There I am!" she said. "When I'm hookin', I call myself 'Kim.'"

"Wow," I said. I couldn't imagine doing anything like this myself, probably because I was raised to believe prostitution was immoral and degrading, although I'm not even sure how that topic ever came up during my childhood. I certainly can't imagine my mother ever saying "Don't sell your pussy!" But she probably did because somehow I had a strong, rigid constitution against the sexual exploitation of one's body. And because I was so uptight, I didn't want anyone to know that the Andy Warhol superstar I'd chosen for my film debut was peddling her wares in a sordid sex rag. So I kept that little secret to myself.

"Who are your clients?" I asked.

"Straight guys who want something extra. A gay guy wouldn't be interested in me. But straight guys . . . honey! They can't get enough."

"What are they like?"

"All kinds, hon. Finance guys. Blue-collar construction types. Young. Old. Married. Divorced."

I was more fascinated than I was repelled.

"Aren't you afraid of getting AIDS?"

"No," she said. "I use condoms."

Unfortunately, Holly Woodlawn's "pussy" wasn't yielding much in returns. In fact, her imaginary peek-a-boo snatch had been so oversold, Warren Buffett would have deemed it a catastrophic loss. And that's exactly why she couldn't pay her telephone bill.

"Darling, do you have twenty bucks I can borrow?"

"No, but I can lend you five."

I opened my wallet and gave her my last five dollars.

"Thanks, hon."

I'd never had a friend who was a prostitute before, and I wondered why Holly chose prostitution over getting a regular day job. I never did ask, though, because I didn't want to know. It was none of my business. But for a moment, I wrestled with the moral dilemmas of her profession and my choice to befriend her. To resolve my internal conflicts, I asked myself one simple question that was inspired by my grandmother: *What would Jesus do?*

He'd love her the way she is, I reasoned. So I accepted Holly for who she was and focused on the challenge of raising money for our film project, which I believed was the answer to all of my problems.

Wealth was omnipresent in Los Angeles. Everywhere I turned, someone was flaunting their Rolex, BMW, and Louis Vuitton. But I was clueless as to how one tapped into that vast financial resource, and figured the best place to start was at the top of a major talent agency.

The next day I called in sick so I could spend the day hustling for an agent. I lay back on my Murphy bed and strategized. First, I called General Motors' finance department and deferred my car payment for a month so I could afford script copies, envelopes, and postage. Then I sat down at my typewriter and crafted a thoughtful, heartfelt letter. Each script would include a letter, Holly's headshot, a one-page biography about Holly, and press clippings about her life as an Andy Warhol superstar.

That morning, I typed twenty personalized letters to various literary agents around town. That afternoon, I packaged those letters with the script and Holly's attachments, and then mailed each one out. I knew something good was going to happen from this mailing. I could feel it.

"The script is only twenty-eight pages," I told my friend Keith. "It won't take that much money to get made."

We were wandering Santa Monica Boulevard in hopes of finding meaningful romance instead of one-night stands.

"All I need is ten thousand dollars."

"Why do you want to make a movie?" Keith asked. "Holly Woodlawn is such a unique character. You should write a book."

"A book?!"

I honestly believed this short, black-and-white passion project that starred Holly Woodlawn was going to be my great calling card in Hollywood. Keith was unconvinced.

"The Holly Woodlawn story would make a fascinating book," he said. "Andy Warhol, the Factory, Lou Reed..."

But I wasn't sold. I'd already written two press releases about Holly Woodlawn. What else did the world need to know?

"No, I'm going to be a filmmaker," I said. "I don't know how to write a book."

I didn't know how to focus a camera either but somehow didn't see that as a deterrent. I wanted to tell stories with black-and-white avant-garde images. I wanted to write gritty scenes with desperate characters who spewed dirty, cheap dialogue. I didn't want to spend days on end wrestling with paragraphs. But that all changed one morning when I cheerfully answered the phone, "Newt Mackleberry's office."

"I'd like to speak to Jeff Copeland, please."

"This is Jeff Copeland."

"Hi, my name is Robert. I'm calling from the Tonya Waddell Agency. You sent us a script—"

"Oh, hi, Robert."

I was so excited I almost screamed. Finally, after nearly four years, I was getting a call from a literary agent.

"Did you read my script?" I asked.

"Uh . . . well..." And then he paused. A pause is never a good sign.

"It's not for us," he said.

My heart sank. But Robert continued to speak, and I came to find out that he wasn't an agent at all. He was actually an agent's assistant who spotted Holly's photo in his boss' trash. When he fished it out, he found my screenplay and Holly's bio attached.

"We can't do anything with the script because we're not in that kind of business. We don't represent screenwriters. But I think Holly's story could

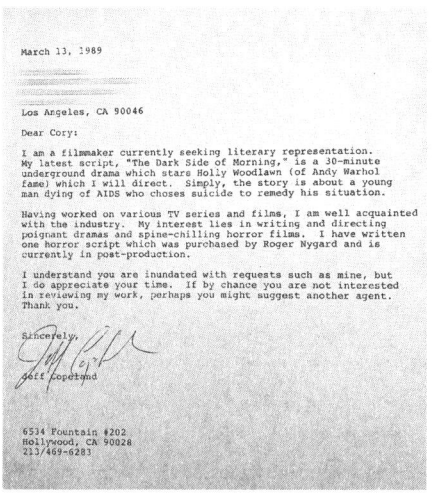

March 13, 1989

Los Angeles, CA 90046

Dear Cory:

I am a filmmaker currently seeking literary representation. My latest script, "The Dark Side of Morning," is a 30-minute underground drama which stars Holly Woodlawn (of Andy Warhol fame) which I will direct. Simply, the story is about a young man dying of AIDS who choses suicide to remedy his situation.

Having worked on various TV series and films, I am well acquainted with the industry. My interest lies in writing and directing poignant dramas and spine-chilling horror films. I have written one horror script which was purchased by Roger Nygard and is currently in post-production.

I understand you are inundated with requests such as mine, but I do appreciate your time. If by chance you are not interested in reviewing my work, perhaps you might suggest another agent. Thank you.

Sincerely,

Jeff Copeland

6534 Fountain #202
Hollywood, CA 90028
213/469-6283

This is the actual letter that I sent to lit agents. I look at it now and I cringe. It's wrong on so many levels and when I think back to those days, my heart goes out to the poor kid who wrote it.

make an interesting book. Can you give me her contact information?"

I thought about my friend Keith, how he encouraged me to write a book about Holly, and how I refused. Perhaps he was right all along.

I didn't give Robert Holly's phone number. Her phone had been disconnected because she hadn't paid the bill, but I told him I'd swing by her place after work and have her get in touch.

By the time I'd arrived at the Park Cherokee Apartments that evening, I'd convinced myself that writing Holly's life story was better than not writing it. So what if it wasn't a screenplay? It was still a story, although I had no idea what kind of story it was or how to go about telling it. Regardless, it was an opportunity, and as the saying goes, beggars can't be choosers. Sometimes you have to take what you can get.

The sun had started to set and the apartment house was bathed in golden light. Since Holly's phone didn't work, there was no way for me to call her from the front gate. So I shouted her name several times with the hope that she'd hear me, but she never answered. Finally, after about five minutes, I saw an old heavyset man exiting one of the apartments.

"Excuse me," I called out to him. "I'm trying to reach my friend Holly Woodlawn. Can you please knock on her door for me?"

He came to the gate and grumbled, "Holly Woodlawn's gone."

"What?" I said in a panic. "What do you mean she's gone?"

"She left."

"Where did she go?"

He shrugged. "Don't know, don't want to know, and good riddance. Skipped out of here two months behind on the rent."

I couldn't believe it. Holly Woodlawn had vanished and so had my shot at getting a literary agent. The mystery of her sudden disappearance baffled me. Where did she go? Why didn't she say goodbye? And how was I ever going to find her?

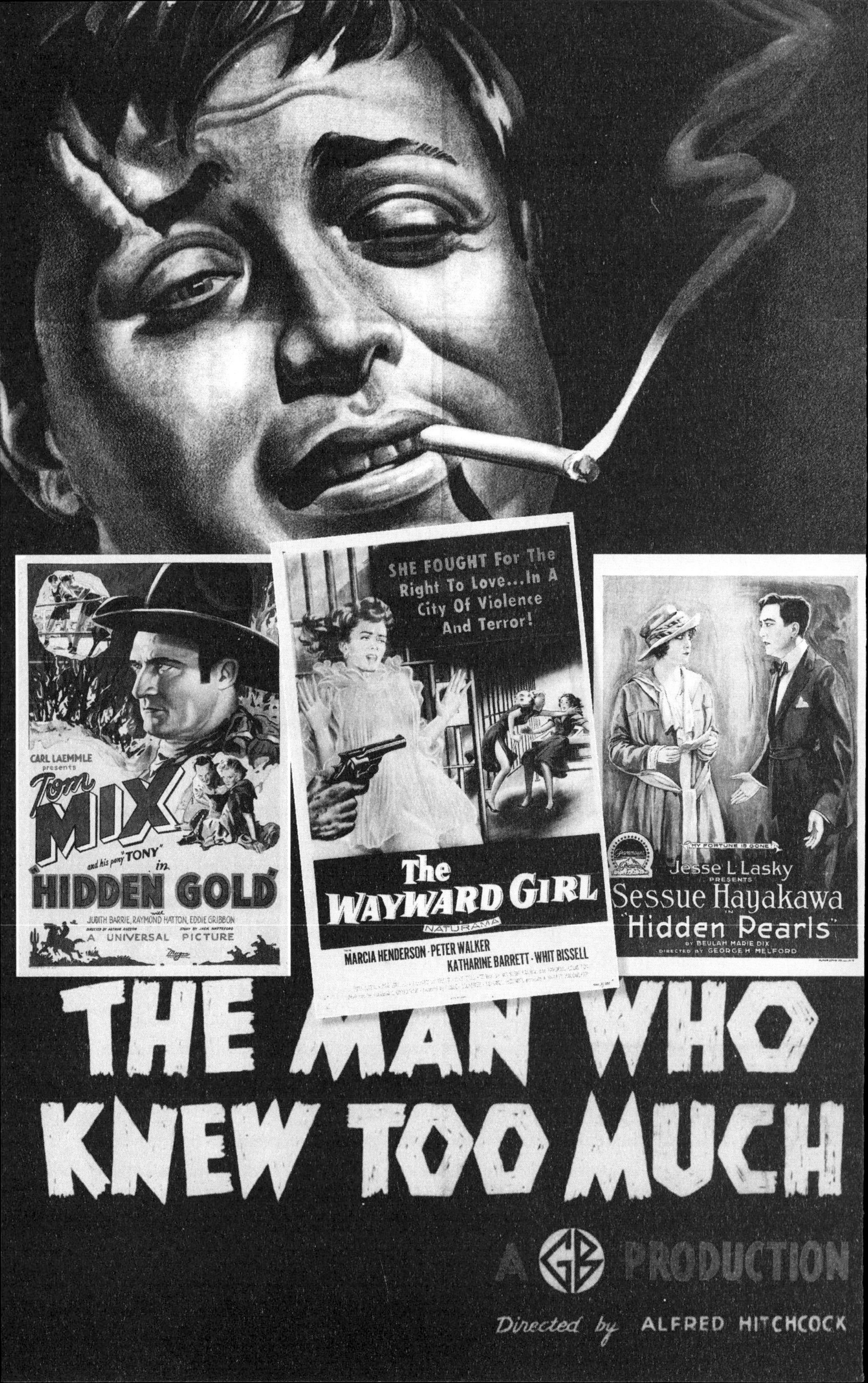

CARL LAEMMLE presents

TOM MIX

and his pony "TONY"

"HIDDEN GOLD"

JUDITH BARRIE, RAYMOND HATTON, EDDIE GRIBBON

A UNIVERSAL PICTURE

SHE FOUGHT For The Right To Love...In A City Of Violence And Terror!

THE WAYWARD GIRL

NATURAMA

MARCIA HENDERSON · PETER WALKER

KATHARINE BARRETT · WHIT BISSELL

JESSE L LASKY PRESENTS

Sessue Hayakawa

"Hidden Pearls"

BY BEULAH MARIE DIX

DIRECTED BY GEORGE H MELFORD

THE MAN WHO KNEW TOO MUCH

A  PRODUCTION

Directed by ALFRED HITCHCOCK

CHAPTER 7

THE NIGHT I DISCOVERED HOLLY HAD DISAPPEARED, I just assumed she had made a rash decision to run away. I imagined she was under financial pressure and fled in the night. I never once thought her departure was premeditated and that she had led me on. All I knew was that I had some good news and I had to find her. In 1989, the world wasn't connected via social media like it is today. In order to track someone down, a person had to do it the old-fashioned way: knocking on doors and talking to people.

The north side of the Park Cherokee Apartments had a row of units that faced the street. Unlike the apartment Holly lived in, those apartments were not behind a gate and the front doors were easily accessible. So I knocked on doors, hoping someone would answer and have some information. No one answered the first door I knocked on. A small African American man answered the second one. His name was Percy. I recognized him from Holly's show at the Backlot. I asked if he knew where Holly had gone and he said he had no idea.

"Does she have any friends in the area who I can call? Maybe they'll be able to help."

The Park Cherokee apartment house, where Holly lived when I first met her.
Photographer unknown.

I pressed Percy for details, and he hastily jotted down a telephone number. Moments later when I got into my apartment, I grabbed my phone and dialed the lead. The person who answered didn't know where Holly had gone, but he gave me another number to call. I dialed that number and spoke to another clueless person who gave me yet another phone number to try. This connect-the-dots-let-your-fingers-do-the-walking fandango went on for a few days until I finally reached someone at the Backlot in West Hollywood, who gave me the phone number of some know-it-all in Las Vegas, who laughed when I told him I was trying to track down Holly Woodlawn.

"Does she owe you money?" he asked.

"No," I said.

He chuckled some more as if I were a stupid dope unwittingly setting my own trap.

"Just give it time," he said, then suggested I try calling Holly's parents who lived in Miami, F-L-A. He gave me their number.

Holly had parents? I couldn't believe it. And I couldn't help but wonder what kind of parents would have Holly Woodlawn for a child.

That night, sitting on the edge of my Murphy bed, I called them. The phone rang a few times. A man answered.

"Hello, my name is Jeff Copeland," I said. "I'm calling from Los Angeles and I'm trying to reach Holly Woodlawn."

"Hold on," he said. I listened to the other end of the line and heard faint voices say, "Who? Somebody in Los Angeles." And then I heard a familiar cough to clear the throat followed by an upbeat voice that almost sang, "Hello."

It was unmistakably Holly Woodlawn.

"Holly!" I said excitedly as if I'd won a jackpot. "This is Jeff Copeland."

"Who?"

"Jeff Copeland. The guy who wrote that script for you to star in—"

"Jeffrey! What are you doing calling me here? How did you get this number?"

"It wasn't easy, but the reason I'm calling is I sent my script to an agent—"

"Oh, you know, Jeffrey, I can't help you with your movie. I need to make money. That's why I left town. My father gave me a job."

"Oh . . . What are you doing?"

"My father is an accountant. I'm helping him with his bookkeeping."

"Well, how would you like to write a book about your life? That's why I'm calling. I've got this agent . . . well, he's sort of an agent. He's like a junior agent and he works for this literary agency and he thinks your life story would make an interesting book."

Pause. Never a good sign.

"You're joking," Holly said.

"No, I'm serious. He wants to speak with you. Can I give him your number?" I was excited, like I was on the verge of something big, even though I couldn't quite define it. But I knew it was good, and intuitively, I knew it was important for Holly and Robert to chat.

Holly agreed to speak to Robert, so the next morning I called and gave him her number. That afternoon, while typing my missives for Mack, Holly called.

"Jeffrey, I'll come back to Los Angeles, but I need a few weeks to save up some money. Can you find me an apartment?"

"Sure," I said. "That's not a problem."

"Something cheap, though. I can't afford much."

"That's okay."

"And it has to take dogs. I have my little daughter, Honey. I can't live without her."

"Holly, don't worry about it. I'll find you a cheap place that takes dogs."

Well, that was easier said than done. Finding Holly Woodlawn an apartment was more difficult than finding Holly Woodlawn! It was a time-consuming challenge, not just because she had a dog, but she also had bad credit and a horrible rental history. And to make matters worse, she didn't have a job. But despite the obstacles, I pushed forward and was determined to find her a home.

I had four weeks to secure Holly a place to live, and I scoured the city on lunch hours and on weekends in search of the impossible. Even Babe Yancey said, "Hell no!"

After two weeks, I called Holly and told her it was too difficult to find an apartment that was cheap and accepted pets.

"Would your dog Honey be able to stay with your parents?" I asked.

Holly was horrified, as if I suggested we toss Honey into a meat grinder and turn her into a hot dog.

"But she's my daughter!" Holly wailed over the phone. "I can't leave her in Miami! I can't live without my baby!"

"All right, Holly," I said, just to calm her down. "I'll do the best I can."

That damn dog was now the bane of my existence.

Three weeks had come and gone, and I'd looked at every low-rent fleabag joint I could find that would suit Holly's needs. The property managers all turned me down, so I ventured into some of the sketchier parts of downtown. No dice. Even the slumlord plugs who didn't speak English said, "Estás loco? Diablos, no!" I was shit out of luck finding Holly an apartment. I couldn't even find her a storage unit. The only option left was to share my Murphy bed with her and Honey-the-dog, or stick her in a tent on the roof of my building and hope Babe Yancey didn't catch on.

As I drove back to work after an exhausting but fruitless lunch-hour search, I was deep in thought, trying to figure out my next move, when I made a wrong turn. I wasn't paying attention until I realized I was driving down an unfamiliar street. When I braked for the stop sign, I was at the corner of Waring and Las Palmas. In a moment of lost confusion, I turned to my right and glanced out the car window. A "For Rent" sign was haphazardly staked on the raggedy yard that had more dirt than grass. It was divided by a long concrete walk and had a broken-down jalopy parked on one side.

I pulled over quick, parked and grabbed the manila envelope containing Holly's press clippings and publicity photos. I got out of my car and took in the whole four-story structure. It looked like something out of a Raymond Chandler novel, an old foreboding brick monster with dark windows, a fire escape up the front, and decorative Dutch gables on the roof. The building had seen better days, as had most houses on the block. But it was in a good, central location and it looked cheap. The address was 800 North Las Palmas.

The glorious Las Palmas Apartments... after it was spruced up. When Holly first moved in, the place looked rundown and neglected. 1990.

The building's old black double doors were ajar, so I went inside and found the unit marked "manager." I knocked, heard some rustling and then a raspy voice called out, "Who is it?"

"Hello, I'm inquiring about the apartment for rent."

Silence. My eyes wandered as I waited. Stairs were to my immediate right that led to the second floor. The front lobby had a white marble floor with a large crack running through it. Old-style plasterwork and grand crown molding imbued the foyer with an old-world charm, but the hideous, light green paint and the suspended fluorescent lighting grids gave it a strange and surreal dinginess.

The manager's door opened to reveal an older man staring at me. I smiled and introduced myself.

"Three-fifty. Utilities included," he snapped.

His name was Bob. He had a full head of light brown hair and a long, drawn face that was probably quite handsome in his youth. He wore large square-framed glasses with thick lenses and waddled from a leg injury he sustained in a war, or so he said as he guided me down the main hallway to a narrow door painted high-gloss brown. He yanked the door open and revealed an old elevator gate. He pushed it aside and we stepped into the contraption. When

A few articles from Holly's press kit. A lot of rave reviews and a photo of her with Rock Hudson. Who wouldn't be impressed?

the door firmly closed, he pressed the button and the elevator started up with a jolt and a boom. The grinding gears turned and clanked as the wooden box ascended to the fourth floor, then came to a jarring, abrupt stop, punctuated with another loud boom.

"It's a single," he said as he opened the door and led me into the white, light-filled room that had two large double hung windows overlooking the sprawling Hollywood landscape. The view was spectacular. The kitchen was nice with old-fashioned wood cupboards that went all the way up to the high, nine-foot ceiling. The refrigerator looked new; the stove was from the 1950s with chrome accents. The apartment also had a large walk-in closet with a vanity, and an old-fashioned 1920s bathroom with a deep porcelain tub.

"This is perfect," I said, captivated by the majestic picture-postcard view and the iconic Hollywood sign in the far distance.

"You want an application?"

"Yes, but the apartment isn't for me. It's for a friend of mine who'll be moving here at the end of the month. Her name is Holly Woodlawn."

I pulled one of Holly's glamorous publicity photos out of the envelope and gave it to him.

"She's an actress, mostly famous for movies that were produced by Andy Warhol. You know Andy Warhol. The artist."

"Andy Warhol," Bob said as I handed him copies of Holly's press clippings.

"Anyway, she's coming to Los Angeles to work on a book about her life. Isn't she beautiful?"

I could tell he was impressed.

"Why would she want to live here?" he asked.

"Because she's discreet and very private. No one would ever think to look for her here."

"She's that famous?"

"Oh, she's more than famous. She's infamous."

For not paying her rent! But I sure as hell wasn't letting that cat out of the bag, particularly since I had to bring up Honey-the-dog. As he gazed over Holly's press clippings, I gently took the photo out of his hand and said, "You're going to love having her live here. And she's got the cutest little dog."

He sneered. "No dogs!"

"Oh, it's so small, it's more like a kitten. The cutest little fluff ball you ever saw."

"I've never seen a dog that looks like a kitten."

"You haven't seen a lot of things, my friend. But wait until you meet Miss Holly Woodlawn. She's a sight to behold. And when she moves into this building, she's going to light it up with a flair of international celebrity."

His eyes flashed.

"Fuzzy Knight lived here once. You remember him?" he asked. "He was an actor. Westerns mostly. Lived on the third floor."

"It's so nice having a celebrity around, isn't it? How much did you say it would cost for Holly to move in?"

"First month's rent plus two hundred security."

"She'll take it!"

A little fast talk, some razzle-dazzle, and a photo of a beautiful woman can do wonders when one needs to skirt around the rental application process. Before he knew it, I had made plans to bring Holly by on Sunday and was shaking his hand and walking out the door.

Finally, Holly had a place to live. I was feeling quite proud of myself for having secured her an apartment without having to submit prior landlord references and a credit check. It was a miracle! But little did I know a potential disaster loomed on the horizon.

That Sunday afternoon, I revved up the Pontiac Fiero and sped off to the airport to pick up Holly and Honey-the-dog. I was very excited to see Holly, but when I pulled my car up to passenger loading, Holly was nowhere in sight. The first thing that came to mind was that she'd missed her flight. We didn't have cell phones in those days, so there was no way to communicate with her. I just had to wait. After a few minutes, I wondered if I'd been stood up. The thought that Holly had blown me off caused my heart to sink. Surely she would have called and let me know if she had changed her mind about coming. Did she call and leave me a message on my answering machine? Or was this another disappearance act? She never called me to say goodbye when she'd fled town. She just ran off. Maybe she was just stringing me along. I felt like such a fool and was so disappointed. Now what was I going to do?

A man yelled at me across the way. I'd never seen him before, yet he waved to me in the distance. He started to approach, and as he got closer, I realized he'd mistaken me for someone else. And then I heard his voice call my name.

"Jeffrey!"

I looked down and saw a dog carrier on his luggage cart. I looked back up and saw he had stubble on his face.

"Holly?!" I was shocked.

"What's wrong?" she said.

"You got a crew cut."

"So?"

"There's hair on your arms and chest."

Holly's androgynous features had been erased and I felt overwhelmed and anxious. As we drove away from the LAX airport and headed to Hollywood, I explained the predicament.

"Holly, I showed the apartment manager your publicity photos. He thinks you're a glamorous woman. That's why he agreed to rent you the unit."

"I am a woman," Holly said, offended that I'd insinuate otherwise. "I just can't look like one when I'm living with my parents. They don't get it."

"Getting it" could be a challenge, even for me at the time. Holly was a gender-fluid chameleon, and I was concerned whether Bob, the manager of the Las Palmas Apartments, would accept that concept.

"Well, what are we going to do?" I asked. "This guy is expecting a woman and you're going to show up looking like a man."

"Jeffrey, what do you want me to do, change into a fabulous gown on the side of the road? What I'm wearing is all I've got, except for a couple of shirts in the bag."

Holly was wearing Bermuda shorts, a polo shirt and sneakers. I let out a big sigh of frustration. I didn't have the cash or a credit card that was necessary to solve this problem, and neither did Holly. This was possibly the worst mess I'd ever been in, and suddenly I felt like a fraudulent bait-and-switch schemer.

We hightailed it down Las Palmas and skidded to a halt in front of the old brick building with the broken-down Mercury parked on the dirt-patch lawn.

"Good Lord!" I hollered, so nervous I wanted to throw up. What was Bob going to say when he saw Holly looking so manly? Where was that glamorous, international celebrity I promised? Even Honey-the-dog didn't look that small to me now, or even that cute. I was so fucked! The only plausible explanation could be summed up in one word: menopause. It turned Holly into a man and caused Honey-the-dog to swell.

Holly got out of the car, glanced up at the building and frowned.

"This is it?"

"It's a top-floor apartment with a spectacular view," I said, pulling her bag out of the Fiero's trunk. "You're going to love it."

I led Holly into the marble entryway and knocked on the manager's door. In that moment, I prepared for the worst-case scenario: Bob opening the door, taking one look at Holly, and grousing, "That's not a woman!"

I was second-guessing the menopause excuse and thought perhaps I should simply apologize and explain, "She's a little butch today, but she dolls up real nice when she puts on her wig and shaves."

Luckily, as fate would have it, the door flew open and a surprise blessing changed everything. Bob was drunk! He was so crocked, he didn't seem to notice Holly's masculine features. If he did notice, he never mentioned it. In fact, the entire time Holly lived in that building, whether Bob was drunk or sober, he always referred to Holly as "she."

The next day after work I took Holly to meet Robert, the apprentice agent, to discuss his idea for a book. His office was a few miles away from Las Palmas on Melrose. It was housed in a modern two-story red brick building with storefronts downstairs and offices upstairs. I'd never been inside a literary agency before and was excited to see what it looked like. When Holly and I opened the office door and stepped inside, we were in a corner unit that had windows on both sides. It was light and airy, so different from the dog-eared office where I worked. I noticed three white lacquered desks that were piled high with books and manuscripts. The ambience was hip and attractive, and the energy felt good.

Robert greeted us. He was a friendly, handsome young man with brown hair and eyes. He led us to a white overstuffed sofa, where we sat down and became acquainted. Robert explained the process of selling a memoir. He

Las Palmas Apartments. My sister, Tina, meeting Holly for the first time. Holly is wearing her favorite orange silk thrift shop blazer. Teresa Conboy is sitting in the background. 1993.

said it began with writing a book proposal, which involved writing a two-page pitch, a sample chapter, and a brief summary of each additional chapter.

"Does that interest you?" he asked Holly.

"Yeah! Oh, honey, I would love to write a book. Andy Warhol told me I should write a book. But the problem is I can't write."

"That's okay. We can get you a collaborator," he said. "Someone who can capture your voice. And you'll probably want to go into therapy."

"Therapy?!" Holly scoffed.

"Writing an autobiography can be a hard process," Robert explained. "It can be very emotional and challenging. You might need a therapist to help you through it."

Later, as we drove back to Las Palmas, Holly huffed, "Therapy! I don't want to go to therapy!"

There was a tense moment of silence. Holly was frustrated. I was curious as to why she was so defensive.

"Why are you upset?"

"I'm not upset," she snapped.

I stayed quiet. In Holly's agitated state, it was better that I just listen. Eventually she would tell me all that she wanted me to know. But as we continued our drive down Melrose Avenue, I couldn't help wonder about the possible childhood traumas that contributed to a person deciding to work as a transgender prostitute.

"Honey, I don't want this book to be a dull, heavy, woe-is-me drag," Holly said. "I want it to be Auntie Mame on speed."

The idea of writing a straight biography about Holly Woodlawn never appealed to me, but creating a character's voice that reminisced about her madcap romp through New York's underground scene was incredibly rich. If a writer was going to be brought in to helm the project and craft the voice, I felt I'd earned the right to request first crack at the opportunity.

"Holly, I want to write your book," I said, parking in front of the Las Palmas Apartments. "I know I can do it."

It was 1989. I'd worked four years in Hollywood and had taken enough dictation to earn a master's degree in secretarial drudgery. I needed a mentor, someone who believed in me, someone who would take me under a wing and nurture my talent. I was never going to get where I really wanted to go without that kind of support. I needed a break.

"Jeffrey, of course you're going to write it," Holly said. "Honey, I can't think of anyone I'd rather work with."

I was genuinely touched by Holly's sincerity. But at the time, neither of us knew that another writer, a real writer, had already been lined up and was ready to take over.

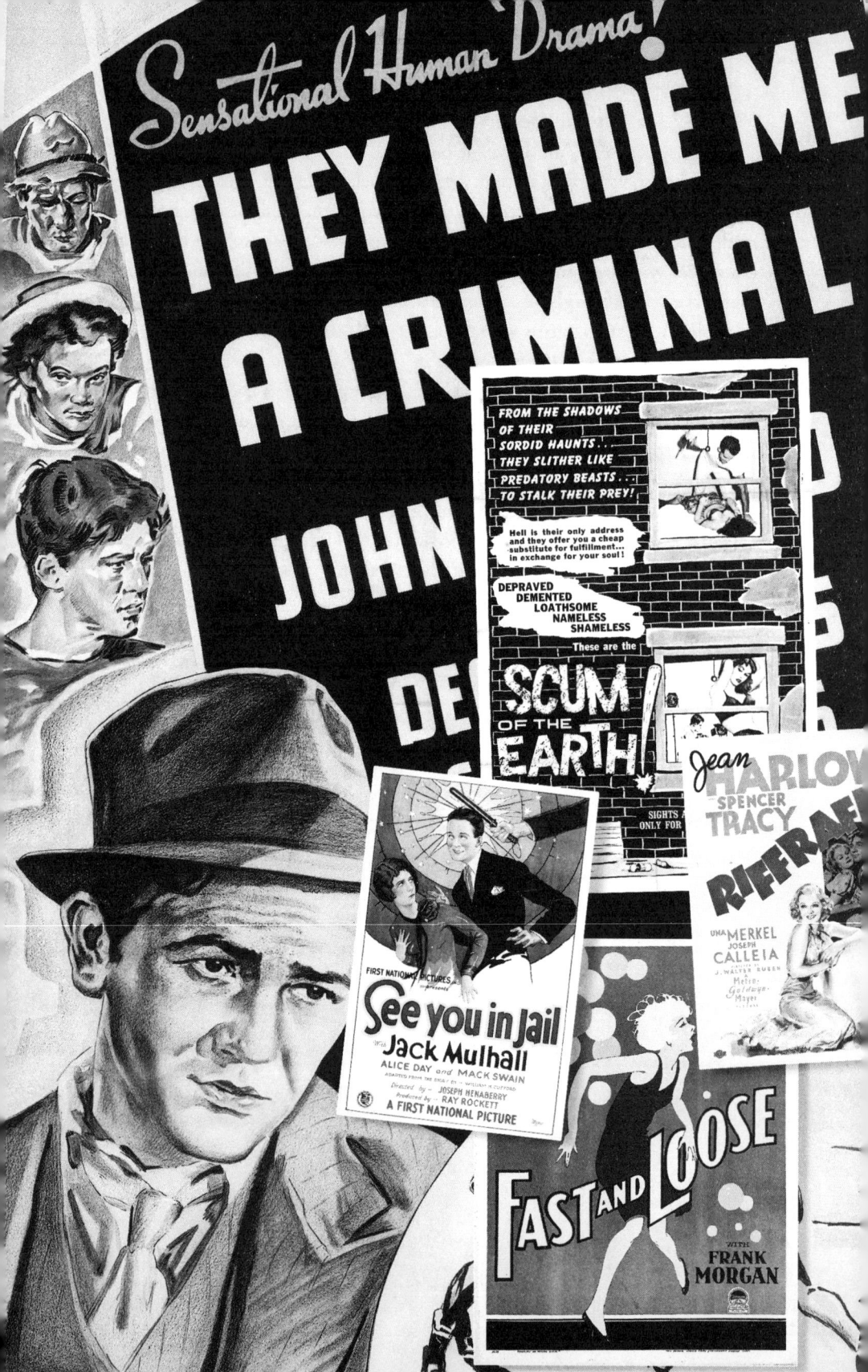

CHAPTER 8

S HORTLY AFTER HOLLY MOVED BACK TO LOS ANGELES, Robert invited her to a small soirée being thrown by one of his friends, a writer whose work he was developing. Holly wanted to arrive in a Ferrari, so she asked me to take her. Holly didn't have the wardrobe to arrive as "Holly Woodlawn - Superstar," but she did have an orange nubby silk blazer she'd found at a thrift shop for only three dollars.

"Honey, feel the quality of this fabric," she said. "And I love the color. It's so LAH-ooooood!" "LAH-ooood" was Holly's playful way of saying "loud."

It was eight o'clock when we arrived at a nice, contemporary apartment in Hollywood. White walls, modern furniture, clean lines, and books everywhere. Hundreds of books.

Robert introduced us to the hostess. She was a young, attractive, fair-haired woman with an easy smile.

"Robert tells me you're a writer," I said. "What do you write?"

"Mysteries mostly," she said.

"Oh, wow." I marveled at all the hardbound books behind her. She was a real writer and I was nervous and intimidated. There was a moment of awkward silence. I didn't know a thing about mysteries or the people who wrote them, and in an effort to keep the conversation going, not knowing what else to say, I blurted, "Did you write all those books?"

She looked at me, taken aback. I couldn't believe I had asked such a stupid question.

I expected her to snap, "Who the fuck are you? Gomer Pyle?" But she had too much class and simply responded, "No."

I felt like an idiot.

"She's really good," Robert interjected. "Very talented."

"Robert is a huge champion of my work," she smiled.

She was confident and poised, and I felt inferior and threatened. Was she the writer Robert had lined up as a possible collaborator for Holly? Was my sole purpose reduced to that of a chauffeur?

"So what do you do, Jeffrey?" she inquired.

"I'm a screenwriter," I said, then wished I hadn't said it at all. I wasn't a screenwriter and she knew it. I was just a wannabe toiling in the secretarial trench, trying to feel a little better about myself, and now felt like all the other Hollywood phonies I'd grown to detest.

"That's how we met," Holly spoke. "Jeffrey wrote a fabulous script for me to star in. A tortured drama about a drunk who just keeps getting drunker. Which reminds me, honey, where's the bar? Oh, there it is."

"Please, help yourself," the hostess said. "There's plenty."

Holly grabbed my arm and guided me to the all-you-can-drink buffet.

"What we need are a couple glasses of wine," Holly said. "Maybe even a jug."

We grabbed two plastic cups filled with white wine, then we stood back and took in the crowd.

"I can't believe I told her I was a screenwriter. What a joke."

"Oh, who cares?" Holly said, handing me a cup. "Free vino, honey. Down the hatch."

We both toasted and gulped. Holly sighed.

"Isn't the wine buttery this evening?" she crooned.

"I like it."

"Me, too."

Holly reached over to the bar and covertly grabbed another cup.

"And who are you?" whined a voice that grated. I looked up to see a pinched-faced, pompous gentleman staring at me over his reading glasses. He held the plastic cup of wine as if it were a jewel-encrusted chalice. I smiled. He did not.

The meeting of the downtown film underground and the uptown exhibitor establishment, which culminated Mon. (5) with the opening of Andy Warhol's "Trash" at Don Rugoff's Cinema II theatre in Manhattan under the auspices of Rugoff's Cinema V distribbery, was not without its bizarre angle. Apparently unbeknownst to Rugoff and press rep John Springer who were planning the opening last week, "Trash" costar Holly Woodlawn was languishing in prison awaiting arraignment on bad check charges.

Woodlawn, a zealous transvestite with a voice like an auto accident, has been the subject of trade speculation since the Warhol pic began screening for critics some weeks ago. Even some super-sophisticated showmen exited "Trash" without realizing Miss Woodlawn was actually Mr. Woodlawn, a fact director Paul Morrissey finds very amusing while hoping some highbrow critics make the same mistake.

Woodlawn (who's real name is suitably shrouded in campy mystery) worked for approximately eight days on the Warhol pic and has emerged with surprisingly good notices. Since he is not really a part of the Warhol Factory family, details about his whereabouts since shooting was completed have been difficult to come by.

Word began to circulate two weeks ago in the underground's sub-basement that Woodlawn was indeed behind bars in the Tombs, New York's oft-troubled clearing house for those awaiting court appearances. Apparantly he had been

(Continued on page 53)

What bothered me about this newspaper article is that the reporter describes Holly as a zealous transvestite with a voice like an auto accident. He couldn't be more wrong, and it made me wonder if he ever saw the movie at all.

"My name is Jeff Copeland and this is my friend Holly Woodlawn," I said.

"Hollywood who?" he whined.

"Holly Woodlawn," Holly said, enunciating the syllables.

"Holly is an Andy Warhol superstar. She's come to Los Angeles to work on her autobiography," I explained.

"Oh, really?" He smirked and gave Holly the once-over. I recognized that nasty look in his eyes. I'd seen it before from strangers on the street whenever Holly and I were out. It wasn't a look of curiosity but one of scorn, and it hearkened back to the days of junior high, when the cruel early bloomers picked on those of us who looked like shit.

"I'm writing a critical analysis on the works of Marcel Proust," he said. I found it curious that someone so arrogant and intellectual didn't have the social grace or common sense to introduce himself.

"Oh, yay, honey!" Holly chirped. "Here's to Miss Proust and all her literary glory."

Then suddenly, almost purposely, the toffee-nosed queen fluttered his eyes and got distracted.

"Oh, Mindy," he called. "Yoo-hoo!"

He waved to a woman in the distance and ran off to catch up with her. I was so happy to see him go.

I turned to Holly. "Who the hell wants to read a critical analysis of Marcel Proust?"

"Yuck! Blah! Pah-too-ey!" Holly laughed. "That little asshole can kiss my *chocha*."

I might not have been polished or as accomplished as some people at this party, but at least I knew how to treat people with kindness and respect. And that, along with driving a flashy car, went a long way with Miss Woodlawn.

"Darling, I am going to be your Auntie Mame. The Roz Russell version," she said, referencing the 1958 film adaptation of a novel written by Patrick Dennis. "I'll teach you about the more important things in life."

Pouilly-Fuissé was my first lesson. It was Holly's favorite chardonnay.

"Poo-weee fwooos-say, darling! Repeat after me: Poo-wee fwoos-say! It's the only French you need to know."

The following day, Holly met with Robert and persuaded him to give me a shot at writing a chapter. It would be my audition. I had one week to pull it off.

That weekend, on a Saturday morning, I took Holly for a long walk with a small tape recorder in hand. We walked from the St. Kat's Apartments on Fountain and Wilcox and headed north to Hollywood Boulevard. As we walked, I fired off questions about her life, trying to get every detail about her childhood as a little boy, what caused her to run away from home as a teenager, and how she hooked up with Andy Warhol.

"And then I got arrested and wound up in prison."

"Prison?! How did you wind up in prison?" I asked.

"Well, the drugs ran out. And we needed money to get some more," she explained. "So I impersonated a French diplomat's wife, went into the U.N. building, and withdrew two thousand dollars from her account. Twice!"

"You did it twice?"

"Yeah. The first time was a success. The second time I got caught. Oh, boy. Was that a fiasco! You should have heard the prison matron scream after they did my strip search."

"WHAT?!"

I stopped dead in my tracks. I knew the Andy Warhol superstars were a wild, rambunctious bunch . . . but Holly impersonating a French diplomat's wife and embezzling money from her bank account was far more outrageous than anything I'd ever read. The Warhol superstars I knew about were Ultra Violet and Edie Sedgwick. They were wealthy heiresses hungry for attention.

In 1970, when Holly skyrocketed to fame, she was a transgender ex-con! Until this moment, I had no idea that Holly had been incarcerated. But as I soon discovered, there was a lot I didn't know about Holly. During our three-hour walk, I learned that Holly had been a street urchin in New York, a speed freak, a thief, a housewife, a go-go dancer, a beauty queen who was crowned Miss Donut in Amsterdam, New York, a floor model at Saks Fifth Avenue, a rioter at Stonewall, an Off-Broadway star, and a celebrated cabaret performer.

The more memories Holly shared, the more excited I became because I instinctively knew her story was rich material, and it was probably going to be the most outrageous, craziest tale I'd ever write. This was a story that would leave my family aghast, shock my English teachers, and offend the entire Republican party. And for a moment, I thought, *Do you really want to go down this road?*

And then I thought about all the TV writers I'd worked for . . . all well-paid hacks who churned out one sitcom joke after another. They all had their BMWs and WGA pensions. What did I have? I had Holly Woodlawn. She was my one bird in the hand, and while she may have been an odd duck... sometimes you just have to take what you can get and make the best of it.

Though many of Holly's antics went against the grain of my own moral code, I was intrigued and curious, and I always wanted to know more. At the core, her story was about a misfit who rejected the social norm and struck out to create her own reality. That in itself was inspiring, and that was the hook that resonated with me.

When the tapes finally ran out, I went back to my apartment alone and sat at my kitchen table, where I listened to the recordings and hammered out the notes on my typewriter while nursing a two-liter bottle of Pepsi.

When I'd finally gotten through the tape and had all my thoughts organized, I took the stack of pages to my Murphy bed and spread them across the mattress. Holly's memories were haphazard and disjointed, so I cut and pasted paragraphs together to create a chronological order. This was before the computer revolution, so cutting and pasting involved real scissors and real paste, or, in my case, Scotch tape.

It took the rest of the afternoon to get the chapter organized. I had to come up with a beginning, middle, and end. Once I had the structure, I had to figure out the voice. I sat at the kitchen table and stared at the blank white page . . . flummoxed. Now what?

I was stumped. I didn't know how to write a book. I could barely write a press release. What made me think I could pull this off?

Concentrate, I told myself. Focus. Put your mind to it and just do it. Fake it. Who cares?

"I write characters and dialogue," I loudly proclaimed. "I don't know how to write a book! I don't even know where to begin."

All the sugar and caffeine in that two-liter bottle of Pepsi made that blank white page glare even brighter. And then the nagging voice of negativity chimed in about all the wrongs I'd been forced to endure, like bad acne in junior high and getting beat down by the snarky Hollywood system for trying to make something of myself. Fuck writing. I closed my eyes and threw myself onto the Murphy bed. Fuck it all.

I rested on the lumpy mattress, eyes closed, floating in darkness. I wanted to fall asleep, but the sparks of my imagination kept firing. My mind was now a black-box theatre. A light came up on Holly Woodlawn. She sat on a stool, puffed on a cigarette, and looked fantastic.

"So there I was! Stuck in the goddamn hoosegow with all the other queens behind bars, who were singing and carrying on. They would sing 'Ain't No Mountain High Enough,' and fight over who sounded more like Diana Ross," she laughed at the memory. "Jeffrey, don't worry about writing this book. It's not *To Kill a Mockingbird*. It's a cheap thrill with me looking fabulous throughout. Just imagine me sitting on a stool, talking to the audience like I'm doing now. I'm the star. You're the writer. Go!"

And that's when it clicked. I'd write this chapter as a theatrical monologue.

I leapt off the Murphy bed, sat down before the typewriter, and typed one word. F-A-M-E.

Fame was the aphrodisiac that attracted most underdogs to Hollywood. We believed it was the answer to all our prayers, the solution to all our problems, the magical snake oil that would ease our pain. And fame was the driving force behind Holly Woodlawn. She was like a strange flower that bloomed only in the nocturnal glow of an adoring moon. She craved the limelight. She longed to be extraordinary. Look at me! I matter, too! The desire to be somebody was all so superficial yet oddly so important. Without that validation, I would soon discover, Holly Woodlawn was lost.

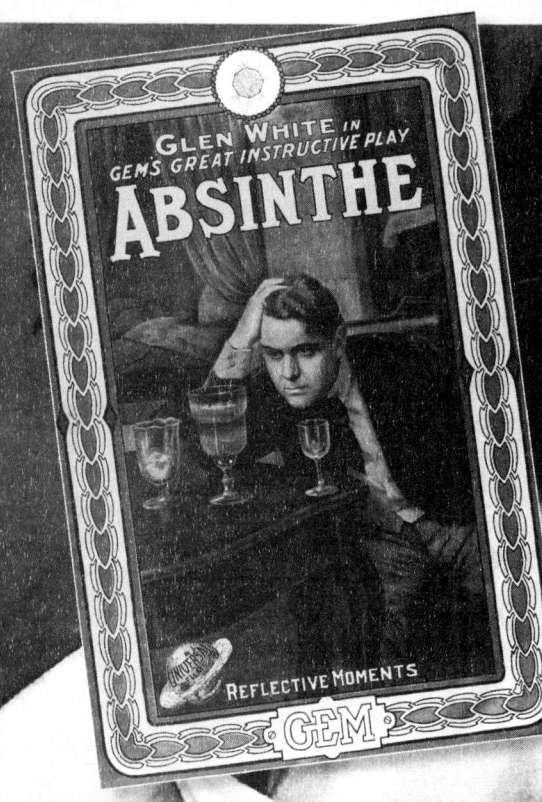

GLEN WHITE IN
GEM'S GREAT INSTRUCTIVE PLAY

ABSINTHE

REFLECTIVE MOMENTS

GEM

FIRST NATIONAL
PICTURES INC.
Present

Compromised

L

"Ho blew up the house -
is what they say of JOE MARTIN

A PROHIBITION MONKEY

COMING SOON
A WILD NIGHT
JOE MARTIN COMEDIES

"COCKTAIL HOUR"

CHAPTER 9

"**N**OW WHY THE HELL DO YOU WANT TO WRITE A story like that?" asked my mother.

After banging out ten pages on my typewriter, I took a break and gave her a call.

"Well, I think the Holly Woodlawn story could make a great movie, Mom," I said. "Maybe even an Off-Broadway musical."

"Is she a *real* woman?"

"Physically, she's a man."

"Who's a man?" my father asked, picking up the extension in the other room. "Dottie, who is Jeff talking about?"

"He's talking about Holly Woodlawn, Denny."

"Hollywood who?"

"Holly Woodlawn, Dad," I said. "She's an Andy Warhol superstar."

"Andy Warhole?"

My father never could pronounce Andy Warhol's name correctly.

"It's not War*hole*!" my mother laughed. "Get your ass off the phone!"

My father hung up. My mother sighed.

"Holly is still a man anatomically," I said. "But he did have hormone injections about twenty years ago, and now he has little man boobs."

"Well, I don't know how the hell we're going to explain that to your father."

Deciphering Holly Woodlawn's gender for my dad was the least of my worries. I wrestled with a bigger challenge: writing a chapter that would land us a book deal. Organizing jumbled memories into a cohesive structure that compelled a reader to turn the page wasn't easy. Trying to identify an audience was even harder. Who cared about Holly Woodlawn? Why was this story important? What purpose did it serve? This chapter had to answer all of those questions and it had to be hilarious.

The first chapter set up the New York underground scene, the drugs and debauchery, the Andy Warhol superstars, Holly's rise to "superstardom," and the insane crime that landed her behind bars. It was a fun ride, and as I pecked out one sordid paragraph after another on my humming typewriter, I remembered the advice of Suzanne Beauchamp, my creative writing teacher in high school: Revise. Revise. Revise. And the more I polished my sample chapter, the more excited I got because I knew I was working on something special. This story was a jewel that only got brighter every time I did a pass.

By the seventh day, I was ready to give Holly and Robert copies of what I called my first draft. It was really the tenth draft, but what they didn't know wouldn't hurt them. I took the day off from work, feigning stomach flu, even though it was May and flu season wouldn't start for a few months.

I delivered Holly's draft to her Las Palmas apartment. She didn't have a telephone yet, so I wasn't able to call to see if she was home. I left the package at her front door, then drove to the literary agency, where I found Robert at his desk.

"I hope you like it," I said, handing him the envelope that contained twenty-three pages. "I put a lot of work into it."

Pure and wholesome, and much more fun than going to a doctor.
Courtesy of the Missouri History Museum.

There were two literary agents sitting at their desks in that small office: a man and a woman. Neither looked up or said hello. They were preoccupied with their own tasks. The atmosphere seemed so cold, so different from the first time Holly and I met Robert there.

Robert took the package.

"Okay, thanks," he said. "I'll get back to you."

I sensed a coolness in his tone and suddenly felt wary and insecure. No one in that office would ever know how much of my own heart was poured into those pages. I walked out the door and regretted ever hearing the words "I'll get back to you." It sounded like a blowoff to me. Suddenly my "audition chapter" seemed to be nothing more than a polite ruse. I was just a hurdle in the way of some other writer's success, a writer who happened to be their client. I wondered if I'd even get a thanks for bringing Holly to the table in the first place. Probably not.

"Well, hon, I tried my best," Holly said in my mind as I walked down the narrow stairs that led to Melrose Avenue. She did all she could. She went to bat for me, and that's all I could expect. If those pages were trite, contrived, and without any emotional depth, that was my fault.

It was all my fault.

I walked outside the building, lost in thought, fending off the imagined goblins of self-doubt and failure that circled me like voracious, insidious, red-eyed piranhas. Those omnivorous, ubiquitous, shit-faced little trolls, with gnashing jaws and nasty criticisms, taunted, needled, and cackled with glee, pulling at every goddamn tenuous string that manipulated and undermined my every move through the abyss of Hollywood hell. Oh, how they savored every bite.

I felt terrible. I needed a drink to shut those little fucks up and retreated into my apartment, where I downed four cheap canned beers while petting the dark teal mohair of my Art Deco sofa, a souvenir of a golden moment, when I was actually paid for all the time I worked. Now I was drunk, grasping at straws, groveling to write someone else's story. Was I really that pathetic? Four years of hard work and all I had to show for it was an old sofa, four empty beer cans, a stack of screenplays, and a wave of depression. There was only one way out of this funk: Pearl Bailey! I'd just pulled out the record of *Hello, Dolly!* when my 1940s rotary dial telephone rang. The shrill sound of its bell startled me. It rang again. I wasn't in the mood to talk and forced myself to answer.

"Hello?" I said when I really wanted to say, "Fuck off."

"Jeffrey!"

It was Holly. I didn't care. I was tired, I was soused, and I just wanted to be alone.

"Hi Holly," I said in a feigned cheerful tone, wondering where she was calling from because she didn't have a telephone.

"Darling," she said. "This lunacy you've written . . . it's out of control."

I sighed.

"I'm sorry, Holly," I said. "I thought it was funny."

"Funny? Honey, it's fucking insane," she said. "I love it."

I had already accepted the worst possible outcome and was not prepared for this unexpected twist.

"What are you talking about?" I asked.

Holly laughed and raved over her favorite parts. "I love the part where I'm the Venus de Warhol, carrying on in the back room of Max's Kansas City. It's hilarious!"

"Are you kidding? What did Robert say? Have you spoken to him?"

"Have I spoken to him?" Holly said. "Darling, I'm with him right now. Can you meet with us at his office tomorrow?"

I supposed that was a good thing. I had beaten myself up so hard I didn't know what to think anymore.

The following evening after work, I drove to the literary agency to meet with Holly and Robert and sat on the plush white couch near the windows. Holly sat down beside me.

"Great job, Jeff," Robert said, pulling up a chair. "This is good, and it's really funny."

"Thank you," I said with incredulous apprehension, waiting for him to spring on a "but."

"Isn't it fabulous, darling? We're going to write a book!" Holly was excited.

"It's going to make a wonderful movie," I said. "You know that, don't you? This story has got all the makings of an award-winning independent film."

"Well, there's a lot more work to do before we get to that," Robert said. "But I think you're right."

Robert had some minor notes on the first chapter, which were easy fixes. Then he gave me a sample book proposal to study and explained I had to write one-paragraph summaries for the rest of the chapters and create a marketing proposal. By the end of the meeting, I realized there was no bait-and-switch: I was the writer on this project, and I was excited and confident that this opportunity would launch my career. But not everyone shared my optimism. When I confided to one of the publicists at Rosenbaum/Finnegan/ Blithe that I was working with Holly Woodlawn on a writing project, he said I was wasting my time.

"I remember her when I was living in New York," he said, and then recalled seeing Holly in a crazed, Off-Broadway musical production. "She ran around screaming 'Eat my pussy!'"

That evening, when I recounted the memory to Holly, she rolled her eyes and scoffed.

"I never screamed *that*!" she snapped, irritated and defensive. "I screamed 'Free pussy!'"

And then, to demonstrate the inflection so I would not misunderstand, she yelled, "Fah-reeeeeee puuuusseeeeeey!"

How vulgar and rich this tawdry melodrama is going to be, I thought.

Working with Holly Woodlawn, whether a mess or not, was a lot more fun and interesting than taking dictation from a crabby old fart who didn't have the decency to call me by my first name. I was sick of being called "the secretary" when I wanted to be "the writer."

One morning, while trying to make sense of a mess of dictation, my desk phone rang.

"Newt Mackleberry's office," I answered.

"Jeffrey?" The voice was slurred. "It's Holly."

Something was wrong.

"Holly, are you okay?"

"Darling, I'm faaaabulous," she said, but from the sound of her voice, I could tell she was drunk.

"Holly, where are you?"

"I'm at the Voom Voom," she said.

"The what?"

"The Voom Voom!"

I had no idea what she was talking about, but I could hear traffic noise in the background so I could tell she was on a busy street.

"What is the Voom Voom?" I asked.

"The donut shop on Highland."

"Holly, it's called Yum Yum."

Holly was at the pay phone outside the Yum Yum donut shop, but she was so drunk she misread the Y's as V's.

"Yum Yum. Voom Voom. Whatever!" Holly said, and then she started to cry. "Jeffrey, I can't do this. You go to work every day and I'm home with

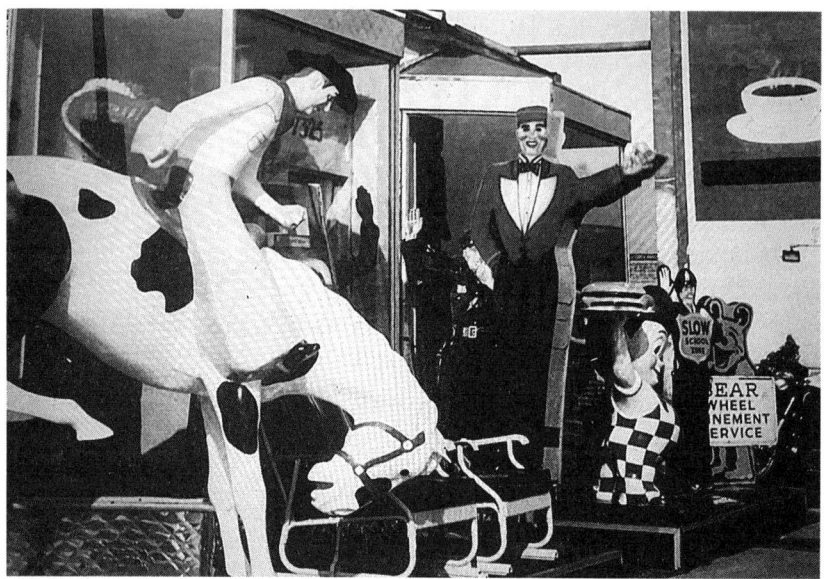

Off The Wall Antiques, one of the hippest stores on Melrose Avenue in the 1980s.
Courtesy of Off The Wall Antiques.

nothing to do."

We had a book proposal to write and Holly was bored because she didn't write and she didn't want to write. That was my job, but because I was writing for free, I still had to work during the day.

"I can't stay at home and do nothing," she cried.

Now that the first chapter was finished, Holly didn't have much to read except for the chapter outlines, which were only a few paragraphs in length. She got restless and started to drink. Now I was faced with an even bigger challenge: Holly was an alcoholic.

"Holly, I want you to calm down. It's going to be okay. Do you hear me? Everything is going to be okay. Just go home and take a nap. I'll come over tonight right after work."

That night I went to Holly's apartment. She was sober now, but on the floor were two empty bottles of chardonnay beside her makeshift bed. Honey-the-dog, who usually walked up to me whenever I entered, was nowhere in sight.

"Where's Honey?" I asked. I looked around the apartment. Honey was gone. "Holly, what happened to your dog?"

"My daughter?" Holly looked at me with tired, bleary eyes.

"She didn't fall out the window, did she?"

Paul Reubens clowns around with a stuffed monkey outside Off The Wall Antiques on Melrose Avenue. June 27, 1984.

Photo by Mike Edward, courtesy of The Los Angeles Times *Photographic Collection at the UCLA Library.*

I looked out the fourth-floor window and thankfully didn't see a dead dog on the ground. Holly was despondent.

Holly replied, "I gave her away."

"You what?!?!"

Holly frowned. After all the trouble I went through to find an apartment that would take that dog, and the big fuss Holly made about keeping her . . . I was flabbergasted.

"You called her your daughter!" I responded in a heated tone. "How could you do that?"

"Well, hon, you know..."

Holly shrugged and explained that Bob, the apartment manager, told Holly his wife loved Honey so Holly said she could have her. I couldn't believe it was that easy for Holly to let go of something she loved so much.

"I couldn't afford to buy her food anyway."

"No, but you could afford to buy two bottles of wine."

"Don't yell at me!" Holly shouted.

I was upset. Writing this book proposal took commitment, discipline, and hard work. And now I was afraid Holly's drinking would jeopardize the entire project. I refused to let that happen.

"Holly, you're getting a job!" I yelled.

The shock hit her like a bolt of lightning.

"A job?!" Holly shrieked, horror-stricken.

"Yes, a job," I said firmly. I felt like a parent scolding an insolent child.

"I don't want a job!" she howled.

"You're getting one. Now get your ass up and get dressed."

In that moment, with so much at stake, I would not accept things as they were. Holly Woodlawn was not going to be a mess, not on my watch. Those days were over. Within minutes, Bronski Beat's "Smalltown Boy" blasted over the Fiero's loud speakers as we ripped down Melrose Avenue on a journey that would change Holly's life for the better . . . or so I hoped.

Alice WHITE

SHOW GIRL IN HOLLYWOOD

The kind of woman most men want...but shouldn't have!

Mildred Pierce

JOAN CRAWFORD
JACK CARSON
ZACHARY SCOTT

EVE ARDEN · ANN BLYTH · BRUCE BENNETT

Margaret **SULLAVAN** · James **STEWART**

The ERNST **LUBITSCH** *Production*

with

FRANK **MORGAN**

JOSEPH **SCHILDKRAUT**

A *Metro-Goldwyn-Mayer* Picture

THE **SHOP AROUND THE CORNER**

Warner Bros. **READY WILLING and ABLE**

CHAPTER 10

I N THE 1980s, MELROSE AVENUE WAS THE HIP destination in Los Angeles. It was a vibrant, colorful scene of trendy cafés, vintage shops, and fashionable boutiques that attracted movie stars, pop stars, and anyone who was interesting, offbeat, and creative. But more importantly, Melrose celebrated diversity and I knew Holly would feel comfortable working there.

Driving down Melrose was a fun experience because there was always something beautiful or unusual to see in the lighted store windows. One of the most interesting shops was called Off The Wall. Its large storefront windows featured eclectic finds like a 1940s bubbling jukebox, salvaged neon signs from old motels and gas stations, and a life-size mechanical fortune teller.

The people on Melrose were also a visual treat. Pink leopard-print pants, fluorescent green fur coats, and triangular-shaped sunglasses were just some of the fashion choices that caught my eye. But my favorite sight to behold was an older, tall, thin woman who wore what looked to be a tailored brown jumpsuit with bell-bottom legs that fit snugly over high platform shoes. She had a long face, high rouged cheeks, and strange narrow eyes. Her dark hair was pulled tautly upward and wound into a rod that stuck up from her head like an antenna. With her hands elegantly folded over her torso, she floated down Melrose with slow measured steps and carried herself with majestic grace.

I never saw her up close, only from afar while I was driving. She was a woman of great mystery and a Melrose legend of sorts. Some people called her "The Venusian" because she looked like she came from outer space. To me, she was an urban Sasquatch, a strange yet benevolent being who was always talked about but seldom seen. When I did see her, which was rare, I always felt a tickle of excitement.

Holly and Gorilla Rose, the former Cockette who managed Wacko. Shortly after Holly started working at Wacko, Gorilla moved into the Las Palmas Apartments and became our neighbor. 1990.

"There she is!" I yelled out and pointed.

"Who?" said Holly.

"The lady from Venus!"

Holly craned her neck to see, but our view was suddenly blocked by an old outrageous car that pulled up beside us. It was a most unusual sight, decorated with film cans, headshots, and a huge sign that read, "ACTOR DENNIS WOODRUFF SEEKS HIS BIG BREAK."

"Oh, mon Dieu!" said Holly.

"Shit! You missed her."

"Who is Dennis Woodruff?" she asked.

"Another local legend, famous for wanting to be famous," I said.

"Oh, he's cute. Free pussy, honey!"

Melrose was stylish and irreverent, and many of the businesses had outrageous and creative façades. One of the most unusual was a restaurant called The Burger That Ate L.A., which looked like a giant cheeseburger eating City Hall. Even the local adult bookstore, Drake's After Midnight, had a stylized front that featured a bolt of green neon lightning tearing through the building's center. It was fantastic! Only on Melrose could a sex shop, with all its rubber toys and S&M accoutrements, be esteemed with sublime chicness. And thank goodness! After eight years of having Ronald Reagan in the White House, America needed a place where shopping for a dildo was as ordinary as buying toothpaste.

The most spectacular landmark on Melrose Avenue was a stucco corner storefront imbued with Spanish Churrigueresque ornamentation. It was boldly painted with bright colors and patterns like a giant funhouse. One side of the building housed a store called the Soap Plant and the other side featured a wild neon sign that read "Wacko," which was the name of an eclectic collectible shop that sold battery-operated tin toys, Pee-wee Herman dolls, vintage Frankenstein models, thousands of fun postcards, and anything else that was kitschy and retro-cool. It also had a quirky staff, which included rockers, punks, goths, gays, and a vampire-like ghoul who worked the cash register.

I parked the Fiero on a side street called Martel.

"Where are we going?" asked Holly.

"My dear, we are going to Wacko."

"What's Wacko?"

"Don't worry. You're going to love it," I said. "Just let me do the talking."

I hustled Holly into the store to the vampire standing behind the cash register.

"Hi there," I said. "My friend would like to apply for a job. Can we have an application, please?"

"You have to talk to Gorilla," she said.

"Who's Gorilla?" I asked.

"He's the store manager."

"Oh, great. Is he here?"

"Hey Joey," she called to a co-worker. "Is Gorilla here?"

"No," Joey responded. "He's gone for the day. You can probably catch him at the bus stop."

I hustled Holly to the bus bench outside where a tall, bald, middle-aged man stood. He wore conservative black-framed eyeglasses and a dark trench coat. He didn't look like a gorilla at all. In fact, I could have mistaken him for a straitlaced accountant . . . or a character actor named Richard Deacon, who played Fred Rutherford on the TV show *Leave It to Beaver*.

"Are you Gorilla?" I asked as I approached him.

"Yeah," he said, eyeing me suspiciously.

"Hi, my name is Jeff Copeland and this is my friend Holly Woodlawn, who is an Andy Warhol superstar."

In the '70s when Gorilla was living in New York, he worked as a writer and editor for the *Naked News*. So much more fun than slinging hash at the *New York Times*! The opposite page is a feature story he wrote about Jackie Curtis.

Gorilla looked at me like I was crazy. I pretended I didn't notice and continued with my pitch.

"Holly just moved here from New York and needs a job. And Wacko is so hip and cool, I thought WOW! What better place for an Andy Warhol superstar to work! And Holly would love to work for you, wouldn't you, Holly . . . Holly?"

Holly was dumbstruck because never before had she seen such a desperate pimp. Gorilla just stared at Holly in disbelief.

"Gorilla!" I snapped my fingers to get his attention. "Imagine having an Andy Warhol superstar working at Wacko. She could be a tourist attraction!"

Gorilla looked at me, dazed, as if he'd just been accosted. Then he turned to Holly and said, "Can you start tomorrow?"

I was stunned. I thought Holly was going to pass out.

"Uhhh..." Holly didn't quite know how to respond.

"What time do you want her here?" I asked.

"How about eleven?"

"Sure," said Holly.

"Great. Come in tomorrow at eleven and I'll get you started," Gorilla smiled and I was so relieved.

"Thank you, Gorilla," I said, shaking his hand.

When I drove Holly back to Las Palmas, she was genuinely pleased.

"Jeffrey, you just got me a job."

"I know. I can't believe it myself," I said. "But Hol, you're going to love it. You'll have a fun place to go during the day. You'll be around fun people. And you'll make some money. It's going to be great."

And it was.

Holly's minimum-wage job at Wacko was a godsend. First and foremost, it gave her something to do. She liked Gorilla and the staff, she took the job seriously, and it helped curtail her drinking. Secondly, Holly was now earning money. It wasn't a lot of money, but it was enough to cover her rent and food, and it instilled in Holly a sense of independence and self-respect. She seemed happy at Wacko. As far as I knew, she was no longer prostituting herself in the back pages of sex rags to make ends meet.

Gorilla liked Holly a lot, and surprisingly, they had a great deal in common. Later, after Gorilla and I became friends, I learned that he had performed with two outrageous, irreverent drag groups in 1969: Ze Whiz Kidz in Seattle and the Cockettes in San Francisco. His stage name was "Gorilla Rose." In the 1970s, Gorilla lived in New York City and worked as a writer for an adult magazine called *Naked News*. He was very familiar with the New York underground scene, and he knew all about the Andy Warhol superstars, which is why he looked so shocked when I introduced him to Holly at a bus bench.

"I was blown away," he told me later. "I couldn't believe I was meeting Holly Woodlawn and you were asking me to give her a job."

The artistic kids who worked at Wacko embraced Holly as a gender-fluid person. It didn't matter if she was a man or a woman. In their eyes, she was super cool because she was an underground icon who'd been immortalized in a Lou Reed song, and that alone was awe-inspiring. In turn, Holly loved being around them. They were carefree and fun, happily working part-time while studying to be musicians, actors, makeup artists, and designers. Their dreams were fresh and sweet, like well-ripened plums, and their impact was profound and inspiring. For a while Holly stopped drinking and quit smoking. She even listened to subliminal audio tapes about positive thinking that she played on a headset at night while she slept. So in the few months Holly was back in Los Angeles, her life turned around in a dramatic way.

Meanwhile, I wallowed in a mire of disillusion, slogging through the muck at the Rosenbaum/Finnegan/Blithe fame factory. That racket was nothing more than a meat grinder. It sucked in young hard-working souls, ground their spirits into pulp, and hurled the quivering, tortured remains onto cold, hard Wilshire Boulevard. I saw how the publicists were racked with stress, how they struggled to meet deadlines, and clamored to get their clients press. And I saw how mean-spirited Sol Finnegan could be when the pressure was high, swearing at the top of his lungs, barking at Ickity and Kookity. And then there was Dorie Clark, who pussyfooted into his office and calmed him down. It all seemed so sordid to me now.

Writing for Holly Woodlawn was fun and exhilarating, and the world of entertainment public relations lost its panache. I'd grown tired of the nasty celebrity managers who made everyone's life a living hell, all for the sake of what? A sensational headline or a story that didn't contain an ounce of truth? I despised the inflated egos and detested the ridiculous publicity stunts. Those shiny brass stars on the Hollywood Walk of Fame were bought, not given. It all seemed so vapid and meaningless.

While most of the R/F/B clients were A-list superstars, some were bottom-of-the-barrel sludge. That firm would represent a turd if it paid the $10,000 monthly retainer, and one of the worst was a pompous "star" of low-budget crap that went straight to video. He bragged about his prowess in the sack and publicly proclaimed to have the biggest dong in town.

One afternoon I answered the phone and a young woman on the other end of the line said she was calling to verify this dope's "celebrity status."

"He's one of our clients," I confirmed.

"He said he's famous. Is he really famous?"

"Who is this?" I asked. "Why would you even ask that question?"

"He invited me up to his hotel room," she said. "He said he'd help me become an actress. I just want to make sure he's legit and he gave me your number to find out."

"Look," I said, lowering my voice. "If I were you, I wouldn't mess with that guy."

"But he said he'd help me get a part on a movie he's working on."

"Are you kidding? That's not how it works in this town," I said.

This poor kid was just like me, clinging to hope that one day she'd make it in Hollywood, and somehow that would make everything better. Poor baby. I'd seen her type. Those gals plastered their glossies in the print shops and delicatessens up and down the boulevard, clamoring for attention, waiting to be discovered, only to wind up abandoned and disgraced like a used toy with its legs spread wide and its dreams crushed. It was more than I could bear.

The ugly R/F/B game had run its course. Now that I was working at night on Holly's book proposal, I wanted an easier job, one that didn't suck the life out of me and leave me exhausted at the end of the day. I found it that week in the classified ads of a gay community news magazine:

<u>Photo Assistant Wanted</u>

I submitted my résumé and got the job. No more taking ridiculous dictation or typing up bullshit missives for me. Instead, I was getting my hands on some of the best ass in town.

Constance BENNETT
WHAT PRICE HOLLYWOOD

Popular MAN

YOUNG
PHYSIQUE
STARS

ARE
MUSCLEMEN
OVER-SEXED?

Trim

VITALITY
STRENGTH
MANLY VIGOUR

HERMAN
HAMILTON
GREGORY RATOFF
Directed by George Cukor
RKO PATHE PICTURE
DAVID O. SELZNICK, Executive Producer

CHAPTER 11

SKIPPY PERKINS LOOKED MORE LIKE A KINDLY grandfather or a well-respected Beverly Hills antique dealer than he did a producer of skin flicks, but in fact, he was one of the most successful producers and distributors of hardcore gay pornography in the country. By the time I met him, he had stopped producing hardcore porn because of the AIDS crisis. Now he was focused on greeting cards and magazine layouts, and I was hired to assist on a series of beautifully photographed male nudes. My job was to set the lights, load the film, and help with the models' makeup. Since I'd worked as a production assistant at Paramount, Skippy thought I was the best candidate for the job. Little did he know.

As I drove over the Hollywood Hills to Skippy's studio in North Hollywood, I heard my mother's voice.

"All my babies are blue bloods," she often said when I was a little boy. "You're not like that trash living down the street."

That trash was anyone who didn't have style, class, good taste, and a strict moral code. Drinking beer, chewing gum, and using the "F" word were just a few of the code violations that my mother frowned upon. As a child,

I fancied myself as a prim and proper mama's boy and did whatever I could to make her proud. But the L.A. gay culture was so different from the five square miles where I was raised. I was negotiating my way through a unique and unusual world now, a glittering universe that glorified sex, drugs, and gratuitous nudity. These boys played by their own rules, no matter how reckless, and the rampant hedonism challenged my own values and direction.

In 1989, North Hollywood looked wretched. The street I traveled down was lined with ugly low-rise commercial buildings. The landscape was dry and barren. The trees were short, scraggly, and unkempt, like hopeless dirty-faced children whose growth had been stunted from years of neglect.

I pulled up to the drab building where I was going to start my new job as a photo assistant.

"Don't do porno!" my mother screamed in my mind as I shifted the Fiero into park.

"This isn't porn," I reasoned aloud, then got out of my car and walked inside the studio.

When I entered, I met the assistant I was hired to replace. His name was Gary. He looked to be in his mid-thirties and was All-American handsome. Dark hair and eyes with a warm smile and a charismatic personality. So much personality, in fact, that he also worked in front of the camera during Skippy's hardcore heyday. I'd never met a bona fide porn star before, and I was struck by his kind, gentle nature.

Gary told me he was quitting his job because he was moving back to Oklahoma to be closer to his family. He said he missed his parents, and on his last trip to visit them, he bought his mother a new washer and dryer. He liked doing nice things for his folks and I got the impression he was trying to do as much as he could for them before he got sick and died of AIDS.

Gary was a nice guy. I sensed he had a good heart and he loved his parents, which I found endearing. Then, out of the blue, he changed the subject from his plans to return to Oklahoma to the movie star he banged, which I found hard to believe. But Gary said it was true, and that the beautifully chiseled actor was just as much a superhero in bed as he was on the screen. I found it curious that he would tell me something so personal on the first day we met, but I supposed people who starred in porn films didn't feel the need to be private or discreet.

Shortly afterward, the model arrived. He was a muscular, blond Adonis who disrobed and sat before a lighted makeup mirror. Adonis didn't have much to say. He was the smart cerebral type, an engineer from Bakersfield,

Bomba The Jungle Boy… just for fun. 1949.

which shattered another misconception. I thought the reason people took their clothes off on camera was that they were desperate for cash. It never occurred to me they might do it for fun.

Gary demonstrated how to do the model's makeup, and I was surprised at how much this blond guy needed to look good on camera. He was stunning in real life, but under the hot white lights, his facial features were washed out. So everything had to be enhanced with bronzers and rouge. Even his blond eyebrows had to be penciled in; otherwise, they wouldn't photograph.

I followed Gary's instructions as best I could, and when I was done, Skippy came over to inspect.

"Jesus Christ!" he snapped. "What did you do, color those eyebrows on with a Magic Marker? He looks like Joan Crawford. Gary! Can you fix those, please?"

I could load the camera and set the lights, but working with the eyebrow pencil took more skill than I anticipated.

Once the makeup was corrected, Adonis retreated into the bathroom with a stack of *Playboy* magazines. What I was surprised to learn is that many of the bodybuilders who posed nude for the enjoyment of gay men were actually straight, and some of them were recruited by scouts in other parts of the country and flown in for the shoots. I wondered if these guys knew what audience they were posing for, and if not, would it make a difference?

I worked four hours that day and made $150. That was some good cabbage, much more than I ever made taking dictation. It was a good gig for a writer, if I could hang on to it and make it work.

The shoots were easy, for the most part. The most unpleasant experience involved a strikingly handsome model who arrived carrying a TV script for *The Young and The Restless*. His arrogance was as sharp as his cheekbones and chiseled jaw.

I finished his makeup and Skippy sent him to the bathroom with some girlie magazines so he could muster up some motivation. When he emerged a few minutes later, he was fully erect and entirely naked, except for the black motorcycle boots that covered his feet. He clomped across the studio floor like he was king of the hill.

He swaggered under the hot lights, straddled a Harley-Davidson motorcycle, and jerked himself with bold, tantalizing strokes.

"Oh, that's great," Skippy said as he angled the camera. "Keep doing it."

This guy's performance was raunchy, pure carnal filth. I could see he reveled in being dirty. He was one big tease, and as I stood on the sidelines, holding a powder puff, I felt a rush of conflicting and complex emotions. This handsome muscle stud embodied everything gay men idolized. He was the beautiful fantasy everyone wanted, the son my father dreamt of having, and an ugly reminder that I'd never been good enough. Because if I were good enough, I'd be the one under those hot lights getting all the attention. But no one gave two shits about what I had to offer. No one except Holly Woodlawn.

The camera strobe flashed wildly. The longhorn stud's penis drooled so much pre-cum that it dripped onto the concrete floor. Skippy got on his knees, moved in for extreme close-ups, and covered every possible angle. The flashes were frenzied and ravenous now. The meat was raw and pungent. And the camera devoured it whole like a starved hyena.

Suddenly, and surprisingly, the longhorn unleashed a torrent that was so voluminous it nearly ruined the camera lens.

"Can someone get me a tissue!? Please!" Skippy yelled in frustration. As his assistant, I should have jumped in with a box of Kleenex before he had to ask, but I'd gotten distracted by the lurid performance.

Working with beautiful men posing nude was one thing. But having to endure an arrogant asshole jacking off and blowing a wad all over the place for me to mop up later was something entirely different. I tried to hide my contempt, but I was disgusted with the entire scene, which I recounted to Holly later that night at the French Quarter restaurant.

"Oooh, darling, did he have a big fat cock?" she asked. When Holly said the word "cock," she really emphasized it so it sounded like "KAHHH-k."

"It was an elephant's trunk."

"Economy-sized! How fabulous! You could have swung on that like Bomba the Jungle Boy."

"He was straight, Holly. There was no swinging on that."

"Jeffrey, you get to put your hands all over these beautiful straight naked muscle men. Darling, that's the best job in the world . . . and you don't like it!"

"It's porn, Holly. I don't want to work in porn."

"You're not on camera. But I know what you mean. That's where I draw the line, honey. It's one thing to act like a pig on screen. But *being* a pig on screen is a whole other story. And do you know there are people who think I actually stuck a beer bottle up my twat in *Trash*? Darling, I would never do such a thing! I mean, look at poor Divvie. She ate that dog shit in *Pink Flamingos* and never lived it down. That's all anyone ever wanted to talk about."

Before I had the chance to fully contemplate the lifelong impact of Divine's most infamous scene, a young, handsome waiter arrived at our table to take our order. He was a beautiful distraction from all that was bothering me, tall and lean with dark shiny hair that contrasted beautifully against his creamy white skin.

"Where are you from?" I asked.

"Colorado," he said.

"Are you an actor?"

"No, I'm a photographer." His smile was sweet and he looked fresh and pretty, like a baby lamb, all precious and dewy-eyed . . . before it's eaten by wolves.

"Oh, we were just talking about photography," Holly interjected. "Jeffrey loves photography. Don't you, Jeffrey?"

"I can't get enough of it."

Sometimes Skippy rented houses in the Hollywood Hills for poolside shoots. The most interesting was a mid-century modern house that was the former home of Vera-Ellen, whom I didn't know from Adam.

"She was in *White Christmas*!" Skippy snapped. "Haven't you seen *White Christmas*?"

"No," I flatly answered.

"Ugh!" he cried out and threw up his hands in despair. "Have you seen *Auntie Mame*?"

"Of course," I said. "I love Lucille Ball."

"Oh, never mind," he said in a persnickety tone, then stomped off in a huff. "Lucille Ball. Hah!"

I thought Lucy was pretty good myself, but when I revealed this later to Holly she nearly had a fit.

"Darling, no!" she exclaimed as if I'd committed blasphemy. She insisted we go to Video West immediately and rent the Rosalind Russell version. We watched it that night, and OH MY GOD—what a life-changing experience that was! Only then did I fully understand the difference between *Mame* and *Auntie Mame*. Now I got the joke whenever Skippy referred to the model as the B-O-Y.

One morning, I was called to a shoot at a Balinese-style home in the Hollywood Hills. As we entered the house with all the camera gear and lights, I was surprised to see a giant framed poster of Holly Woodlawn and Jackie Curtis in the entryway. The poster promoted *Cabaret in the Sky*, a show they performed at Manhattan's Lincoln Center in 1974. Holly looked beautiful, like a 1940s movie queen. Her face stopped me dead in my tracks.

"Oh my gosh," I said. "I can't believe it. That's my friend, Holly Woodlawn."

"*You* know Holly Woodlawn?" Skippy asked, emphasizing the "you" with a cynic's whine.

"Yeah," I said. "I'm helping her write her autobiography."

"Oh, dear," he said with a snicker and a roll of his eyes. "That's just what the world needs. A book about Holly Woodlawn."

His tone was belittling.

"Why do you say that?" I asked, biting my tongue because I really wanted to say "FUCK YOU!"

Skippy scoffed and looked at me as if I were an idiot.

"Because she's a mess! Now put those lights over there," he snapped.

I thought Skippy's criticism was ill-thought and unfair. After all, having George Cukor petition the Academy of Motion Picture Arts & Sciences to nominate Holly for an Oscar for her performance in the movie *Trash* was very impressive, and if Skippy thought Holly Woodlawn was a mess, what did he think of me? I didn't say any more about it that day, but I knew he was wrong. They were all wrong. And I was determined to prove it.

A few weeks later, Skippy decided to do a shoot in Palm Springs with a college boy who had flown in from Alabama. Skippy rented a classic, mid-century house that had been decorated in 1969 and hadn't been changed since. Shag carpets, bright geometric wallpaper, and swag lamps imbued the place with a retro charm that reminded me of my little sister's Barbie Dream House.

The night before the shoot, I had a hard time falling asleep. I was anxious and felt out of place in that strange house with people I didn't really care to know.

"You're not like that trash living down the street," my mother's voice called out in my mind.

But I needed the money. That's what got me on this tightrope in the first place. Now I was teetering on the edge of indecency, struggling to justify my involvement, and wondering how long this charade would last. I had nothing in common with Skippy Perkins. I didn't even like him. He was hifalutin and persnickety, and he exploited people, paying them peanuts while he raked in a fortune. That's what Andy Warhol did to Holly. He paid her $25 a day and never gave her a dime in residuals.

And then there was the beautiful boy in the room next door, who was to be photographed the next morning. He was a nineteen-year-old college kid. What was he getting out of this experience? A one-time payment of two hundred bucks so his image could be sold in magazines, calendars, and greeting cards. Did that little bit of money really mean that much to him? Or was it the adulation that he really craved? Maybe it was both, a double-whammy jackpot. I wondered if he would regret it. What if his friends found out? Or worse yet, his mother? Or perhaps she already knew. Maybe she even encouraged it. After all, not every mother tells her son he's a blue blood and then backs it up with a twelve-hundred-dollar bet.

After a quick breakfast the next morning, the lights were set and the kid was oiled, erect, and ready to go. Skippy had him squat on a leather sofa and arch his back. I held a silver reflector that illuminated his fine, powerful musculature that was God-given and so easily shared.

"That's great," Skippy said, setting off a few strobe flashes. "Now stick out your butt and spread your cheeks."

The boy did as he was told. Skippy frowned, stood back from his camera.

"There's a shine on that butthole," he announced. I repositioned the reflector, thinking that solved the problem. Skippy got frustrated.

"No," he growled. "Powder it!"

"...What?" I was shocked.

"You've got to powder his butthole."

Good Lord, I thought. *I can't believe it has come to this!*

I was mortified. I grabbed the powder compact, approached the model and got down on my knees so that his glaring pooter was inches from my face. I raised the puff and tentatively dabbed around it quickly.

"There! That looks better," I said as I stood back and tried to feign pride in my work, well aware there was no change whatsoever.

"It's still shiny," Skippy barked.

I started to go through the motions again, when he suddenly grabbed the puff out of my hand.

"Give me that," he said. "I'll do it!"

He powdered that butthole with gusto.

"There!" Skippy tossed me a look of haughty disdain and stomped back to his throne behind the camera. I couldn't believe I'd gone from working at Paramount to taking dictation to now this absurdity . . . and I failed at it!

"That stupid ass can't even powder a butthole!" No one said it, but I imagined Skippy thought it, and I suddenly felt hot. The sun's incoming rays poured through the sliding glass doors and I resumed my position to catch them. I held the reflector high and warmed the boy's lean athletic build with a golden light, while he rolled onto his back, playful and carefree, looking as happy and content as a stretched-out cat.

BULLETS! WOMEN! -- CAN'T HOLD A MAN LIKE THIS!

EDWARD SMALL presents

RAW DEAL

starring
DENNIS O'KEEFE · CLAIRE TREVOR · MARSHA HUNT
with JOHN IRELAND · RAYMOND BURR
CURT CONWAY · CHILI WILLIAMS

Directed by ANTHONY MANN

William Fox presents

MARY THURMAN

Does It Pay?

A DRAMA OF DOMESTIC
RELATIONS OF TODAY

Directed by
CHARLES HORAN

Screen Version by
HOWARD IRVING YOUNG

with
HOPE HAMPTON
AND A NOTABLE CAST INCLUDING
FLORENCE SHORT   PEGGY SHAW
ROBERT T. HAINES   MARY THURMAN

FOX FILM CORPORATION

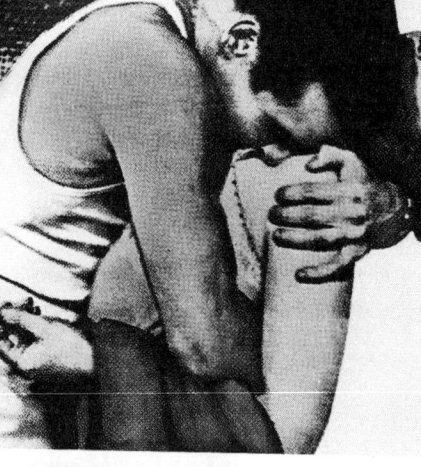

20th Century-Fox presents

PAUL NEWMAN
in ROBERT ROSSEN'S
THE HUSTLER
starring PIPER LAURIE · GEORGE C SCOTT
JACKIE GLEASON
AS "MINNESOTA FA

Ernest Hemingway's

"To Have and Have Not"

WALTER BRENNAN · LAUREN BACALL

DOLORES MORAN · HOAGY CARMICHAEL
A HOWARD HAWKS PRODUCTION

HUMPHREY BOGART

WARNER BROS.

ROBERT ROSSEN

CHAPTER 12

ON MEMORIAL DAY, 1989, THE BOOK PROPOSAL WAS finally finished. We called it *On the Wild Side*, and it included one chapter, twenty chapter outlines, a synopsis, and a marketing proposal that had been written, rewritten, polished, and completed. Our agent, Robert, oversaw the entire process and served as our editor and proofreader, spotting typos and fixing sentence structure. He even punched up the humor. His contribution was immeasurable, and we were so fortunate to have him as our agent because he was smart, creative, and intuitive. He knew we were on to something special. He knew it when he spotted Holly's photo in the trash, which is how this ball got rolling in the first place. It was all so serendipitous and odd, yet terribly exciting because I knew this whole experience was being driven by a bigger cosmic force.

While Holly played cashier at Wacko, I spent the holiday alone inside our agent's heat-scorched office, stripped down to my underwear, typing the first chapter into the agency's computer. The air conditioner wasn't working, but I didn't care. Not even a Los Angeles heatwave could keep me from one last opportunity to revise and revise. The one thing that bothered me was the way the first chapter ended. Holly gets out of jail . . . which was okay, but instinctively I knew it needed to pack more of a punch.

Fuck the truth, I thought as I paced the floor. Just make up something! Paint a crazy-ass picture. Throw in some Judy Garland! She's always a good time. And bring in the dancing monkeys. The ideas cracked and roared, and my brain sparked with a dopamine rush as a storm of inspiration took hold and the final line struck like a bolt of lightning.

"FREE PUSSY!"

Oh, Lordy! It might have been offensive, but it made sense to me. What else would she scream now that she was sprung from the clink? Holly thought it was a hoot.

Later that week, Holly and I celebrated the milestone in Robert's apartment and finalized our formal collaboration agreement. If the book sold, Holly would get sixty percent of the proceeds and I would take forty, which (I was told) was the standard split for these types of partnerships. When it came to our byline, I liked "by Holly Woodlawn with Jeff Copeland." I could have had "and" but preferred "with" because I thought it elevated Holly. I wanted her to look like she was more of a writer than she actually was because I wanted to prove that she wasn't a mess like so many people had said. Also, I wasn't aspiring to have a career as a book writer. I wanted to be a screenwriter, and because of that, I was holding out for something far more valuable than a byline on a book jacket.

"I'm very grateful for this opportunity," I said. "But there's one thing I want more than anything."

I'd mentioned this interest in casual conversation before, but now it was time to put it in writing.

"I want to write the screenplay," I said. "This story is going to make a great film. That's the only reason I'm writing this book."

Those screen rights were the ultimate jackpot and my just reward. Holly screamed with excitement.

"Honey, I can't wait for the premiere!"

We were all excited, but this was an important term, and it was the only reason I was working on spec. The screenplay rights were the one golden carrot I held out for, and I made that clear so there were no misunderstandings.

"The only reason I'm writing this book is so I can write the screen adaptation," I said.

"Darling, of course, you'll write the movie!" Holly agreed. "It's going to be fabulous!"

HOLLY WOODLAWN
writing with
Jeffrey Copeland

The original cover that I drew for our book proposal. While much of Holly's story took place in the '60s and '70s, the title graphic was wacky tacky '80s. It made no sense whatsoever...but it was fun! 1989.

Our agent did not disagree and I requested a provision about screenplay rights be added to our agreement. But what I got instead was this: "Neither of us may enter into any agreement for any of the rights in and to the work without the written consent of the other party." Well . . . that didn't say a darn thing about screenplay rights! But in my heart, I knew I had nothing to worry about. Holly was my best friend. I knew she'd look out for me, and I was so excited about becoming a *real* writer, I didn't want to spoil the high by making demands, appearing difficult, and ruffling feathers. I just wanted to move forward.

I'd spent years feeling like a "have not" in Hollywood, and this collaboration agreement made me feel like I was on the brink of being a "have" . . . even though it was a deal that still paid no money. The money would come later, if and when the book sold to a publisher. I believed it would, but that didn't matter to my apartment manager, Babe Yancey. She wanted to see those hard-earned greenbacks that I could only get from doing "real work." According to Babe, the only job that mattered was the one that paid. Anything else was just "fiddle-farting around."

Shortly afterward, my job as a photo assistant came to an end. Apparently, my lackluster enthusiasm for the work had impeded my performance, particularly when it came to working with a powder puff. By the end of June, I was struggling to make it on wooden nickels, sour grapes, and a glimmer of hope. Through a temp agency, I found work as a secretary on a television western called *The Young Riders*. It was a good gig, but when they asked me to join the show full-time as a writer's assistant, I declined because the hours were long and it would leave no time for late-night writing adventures with Miss Woodlawn, once our book sold.

Then I got a call from Paul Reubens' office, asking if I'd be interested in working as his assistant on *Pee-wee's Playhouse*. I liked Paul Reubens a lot, but I wanted to be a writer. I didn't want to be an assistant again. That was a twelve-hour-a-day commitment. I couldn't start working for Paul Reubens and then quit in the middle of his show to write a book with Holly Woodlawn. Writing is a lot of work, and I didn't have the energy to do both, so I put all my chips on Holly Woodlawn, betting, in the long run, she'd have the greater payout.

"Sounds like a crock of horse shit to me," Babe Yancey grumbled when I told her the reason I was late with the rent. For once, I agreed with her. I tumbled from one temp job to another that summer, eagerly anticipating a publishing deal, but it never came. As the months dragged on, Holly's patience began to wane. She was bored. The whole reason she came back to Los Angeles was to work on a book about her life, and now the project had stalled.

"What's going on with that book proposal?" Holly asked almost daily only to get the same frustrating answer. Nothing!

So when a friend of hers asked if she'd like a free trip to Europe, Holly jumped at the chance. This friend was named Harriet and she was a musical theatre powerhouse who blew in from New York to work on a TV series. I first met her when I drove Holly to her apartment on Hawthorne Avenue in Hollywood.

Harriet was a portly little troll with a big round head and long, thin stringy brown hair. She didn't look or act theatrical at all. In fact, she looked frumpish, like a middle-aged hausfrau who spent all day scrubbing floors, and she spoke with a deep, almost monotone voice.

"Oh, darling, she's a real hot mama," Holly told me later. "She's into leather, bondage and all that S&M stuff."

"You're kidding," I said.

"Oh, no, honey, she's a hardcore diva," Holly laughed. "A bona fide, tried-and-true dominatrix dyke, stomping around in her leather boots, cracking her whip, showing her pretty young girlfriends who's boss."

"How do you know?" I asked as I visualized a scenario that tickled more than it shocked.

"We're sisters, honey. She told me all about it. Oh, that Harriet! She's got more kinks in her wig than a closeted Presbyterian. And wait until you see her in drag."

It never occurred to me that a biological woman could do female drag. In my mind, the concept of "drag" was reserved for a man impersonating a woman or a woman impersonating a man. But Harriet didn't disappoint when it came to the art of transformation. When Holly and I went to see her perform at an AIDS benefit in West Hollywood, I was curious as to how this homely, stringy-haired gal would carry off a live performance on stage. I was not only surprised, but I was literally astounded. Harriet was a force and she looked fantastic. Painted face, huge hair, and a thunderous voice that gave me chills.

But despite her tremendous talent, Harriet, like a lot of actors in Hollywood, never hit the big time. She hopped from job to job, had a few good TV gigs, made a disco record in Europe, and performed at cabarets while hustling antique jewelry and vintage tchotchkes on the side. But all that hard work wasn't enough to sustain her during the down times when she wasn't working, and by the end of summer, Harriet was belly-up financially. Knee-deep in debt, she decided to fuck all and take Holly to Europe for an all-expenses-paid vacation.

"How does that make sense?" I asked Holly upon hearing of the scheme.

"Hon, you do what you gotta do," said Holly as she sorted pennies from a jar of change. "Harriet's going broke and I'm going to help her."

"What?!"

"We're maxing out her credit cards, darling. We're going to spend every bit of credit she's got. All her cash, too. Honey, by the time she gets back to America, she'll be flat busted. Then she'll claim bankruptcy and the bill collectors won't be able to touch her."

"But I don't understand. Why?"

"Because she doesn't have enough money to pay her bills. So before they take away her credit, she's going to live it up and blow through it. That way when she comes back, she'll be so poor she'll get welfare and food stamps."

I couldn't even wrap my head around that logic.

"But Holly, what about your job?"

"Oh, they know I'm going."

Holly had worked at Wacko for only a few months and was already taking off on a two-week vacation!

"Miss Lawn needs to convalesce," reasoned Harriet, who always truncated Holly's last name. We were sitting in her dimly lit 1920s apartment and I was admiring her collection of framed vintage Maxfield Parrish prints that adorned her darkly colored walls.

"The respite will be good for us both," Harriet continued. "You know, darling, it's not good for a person to work too hard."

"And don't I know it," chirped Holly. "That Wacko cash register is wearing me out!"

The truth is Holly could barely work the cash register at Wacko. She always pressed the wrong buttons and was lousy at counting change. A friend of mine told me he tried to buy a two-dollar postcard once and Holly got so flustered with the register buttons she threw her hands in the air and said, "Oh, honey, just take it!"

Then one day, Harriet showed up. Holly told me she came in with a shopping bag that was the size of a wheelbarrow. When she got to the register and dumped her take onto the counter, Holly was beside herself. Harriet reached into her pocketbook, pulled out five dollars, and handed it to Holly.

"Harriet, what are you doing?" Holly asked.

"I'm paying my bill," said Harriet. "Here's five bucks."

"Honey! You've got at least two hundred dollars' worth of stuff here."

"I know," said Harriet. "Take the five bucks."

"No!" Holly was aghast. "You can't give me five dollars for all this! I'll get fired."

"Oh, all right!" huffed Harriet as she crammed all the stuff back into her shopping bag. "Here's twenty."

She begrudgingly slapped two tens on the counter, grabbed her shopping bag, and walked out the door.

"Honey, I was plucked," Holly told me afterward. "The nerve of that broad. She robbed us blind!"

But now Harriet's nerve was paying off in ways Holly never imagined, and within a few weeks, I received a postcard from Paris that read:

> "Bonjour from La Tour Eiffel! Paris is flawless. The people suck!
> See you soon. Love you madly, Holly."

While Holly and Harriet cavorted from Paris to Amsterdam to indulge in an all-you-can-smoke hashish buffet, my temp job came to an end and my beautiful Fiero broke down. I was out of work, out of a car, and down to my last can of corn in the cupboard. My rent was due in two days, and no matter how hard I hustled for work, nothing materialized . . . except for a job interview in the bowels of the San Fernando Valley that turned out to be an awful ruse staged by a hidden camera TV show called *Totally Hidden Video*. It was just one more slap in the face, one more shitty indignation . . . except for those who were on the opposite side of those hidden cameras, making six figures a year and driving Porsches.

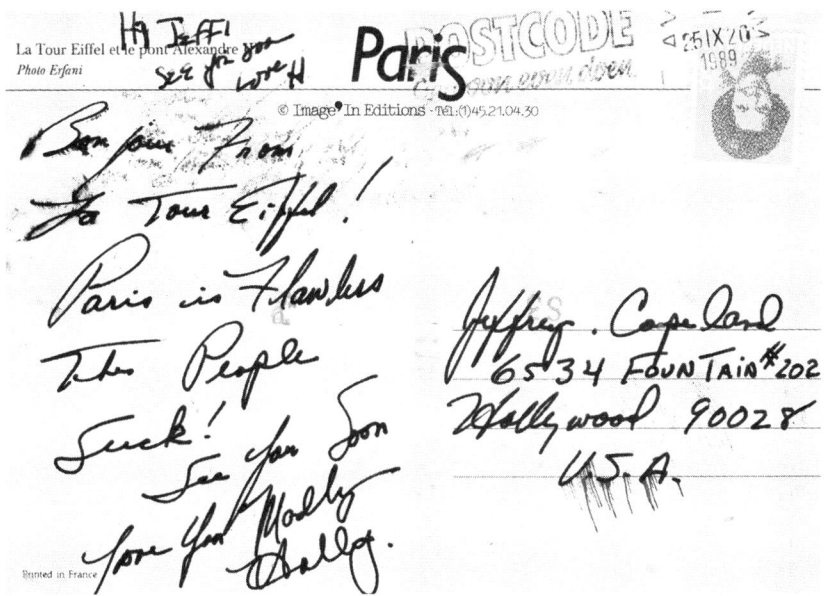

The postcard Holly sent to me while she cavorted around Europe, blowing through Harriet's line of credit. 1989.

That night, I sat on my Murphy bed and sorted my bills. I had enough money to make my monthly car note, but I only had half of the rent. I knew that wouldn't go over well with Babe Yancey.

"All you writers are full of shit," Babe growled when I told her of my plight. "If you worked a regular job and stopped fiddle-farting around with that Holly Woodland, you wouldn't be in this mess. Shit!"

Then she slammed the door in my face. I'd spent four years trying to make it in Hollywood. Always hustling, always hoping, hungry to be a winner. Just once. But I was still lost in a labyrinth of grand dreams and twisted realities, and while I was persistent and tenacious, pushing to forge my way to the golden statue in the center, I only dug myself deeper into a strange, inescapable hole.

I didn't have a credit card to bail me out of this mess, and I refused to call my parents and ask for a handout. This was my shit to shovel, my problem to solve, and I needed some fresh ideas. So I called my friend Jean, whom I'd met two years earlier on the Paramount lot.

Jean was the salt of the earth. Coincidentally, she was also from Missouri and had driven by herself from St. Louis to Los Angeles to pursue a career as a comic actress. Jean was quirky and fun with short dark hair, bright expressive eyes, hilarious facial expressions, and a black two-piece permanent press business ensemble that she wore every day.

"This suit is the best investment I ever made," she said. "All I have to do is flip up the collar and change my blouse, and it's a whole new look."

Jean was the quintessential American everywoman. She could play the nice mom next door, the Avon lady, and the friendly grocery store checker . . . if granted the opportunity. She was also grounded and responsible, and her moral principles and values were the very antithesis of Holly's crackpot lunacy. I could count on Jean; we looked out for each other. When she was out of work, I helped get her jobs. When I was low on cash, she made me dinner. A couple of months earlier, when Jean told me she wanted to move because she found a dead drug dealer in her apartment building's Jacuzzi, I took her to the Las Palmas Apartments where a one-bedroom unit next door to Holly had become available.

Jean was a good friend. In a moment of despair, I called her.

"Jesus, Mary, and Joseph!" Jean exclaimed. "Jeff, come to Las Palmas and move in with me. You can have the bedroom. I'll sleep in the living room closet."

Problem solved! It would cost $250 to rent Jean's bedroom, and that's exactly what I had. By the time Holly blew in from Europe, I was her neighbor and we shared a common wall.

The biggest challenge of living with Jean wasn't a lack of space or a lack of privacy, it was a shifty, bug-eyed cat named Booter. Whenever I left my bedroom to go into the kitchen, that gray short-haired asshole would dart out of nowhere, swat at my ankles, and scare the hell out of me. But despite those aggressive shock-and-awe attacks, I enjoyed living next door to Holly and sharing a common wall. If either of us wanted to chat, we knocked on the wall and stuck our heads out our windows.

"Hey, Lola!" Holly called out. "I'm making Puerto Rican pork chops. Come on over!"

Holly loved to cook and introduced me to the joy of cilantro.

"Darling, I took the bus to East Hollywood today and loaded up on Latin spices. That's the only way to do it, hon. Latin-style!"

Then she pulled out a big bottle of Glen Ellen chardonnay and filled a cup.

"One cup for the recipe," she said, tossing the wine into a hot mid-century electric skillet. "And two cups for Mama."

She tipped the bottle into a tall glass tumbler.

"I thought you quit drinking."

"Oh, what's a little sip every now and then? Where's Jean?"

"She's at the Groundlings studying improv. She won't get home 'til around nine."

"Improv classes!" Holly scoffed. "What's she wasting her money on that for? A couple glasses of wine is all it takes. Honey, if I was stacked like her, I'd have a million bucks by now. She needs to know how to work it. I'll give her some lessons on how to be a real woman."

"I'm sure she'll appreciate that," I said, smiling to myself at the irony.

Holly had her own ideas of what a "real woman" should be, and those could usually be summed up into two words: Lana Turner.

"Have you seen her in *The Prodigal?*" asked Holly as she minced fresh garlic on a plate.

"No."

"Oh, honey! She's fabulous! Lana Turner plays a beautiful high priestess who glides across the screen in these fabulous gowns with glamorous beading down to there and tits up to here, and that face looking all blonde and gorgeous. Oh! Mon Dieu! Jeffrey, when I saw that movie I plotzed. I said, 'Vera! If you're gonna be a woman, be one draped in beads and chiffon.'"

Holly threw the garlic into the simmering sauce and threw back another glass of wine. Then she chopped up a mess of cilantro and added that to the broth.

"Who taught you to cook?"

"I used to live with a chef," she said. "He taught me the importance of having good knives. Don't ever let them soak in the dishwater! You have to hand-wash them separately, one at a time."

It sounded like good advice to me, even though neither of us could afford good knives or a pair of scissors, for that matter. We were so poor, we had to cut the meat with our teeth.

CHAPTER 13

THE INEQUALITIES OF HOLLYWOOD ANNOYED
Delores Francine. Her displeasure was evident in the way she squinted
and frowned, and I wondered if this unhappiness was perhaps genetic
because at times it seemed deeply rooted in her DNA. As luck would have
it, I was now working as her assistant at a low-rent advertising company that
could barely pay its bills. Of course, I didn't realize the company's financial
troubles until after I was hired. That's also when I came to understand
the depth of Miss Francine's torment. She was really miserable, and, quite
frankly, so was I.

Every morning when she walked into our office, I'd cheerfully say, "Good
morning, Miss Francine." The tortured look on her face said it all, but to
make sure I knew just how awful coming to work was for her, she let out a
heavy groan, too, just like a dying hippopotamus.

One of the worst things about being a creative person was having to
conform to non-creative environments in order to eke out a living. The
drudgery of office work seemed to make the clock tick slower and was
probably another reason Miss Francine was so depressive. At times I was
depressed, too. My job was boring, but it paid and gave me health insurance,
which was more than I could say for the Holly Woodlawn book proposal.

I remained focused on my typing tasks until Miss Francine got settled behind her desk. Then she called me into her office and we'd have our morning meeting, whereupon she confessed to me all that was wrong with her life. Like me, she longed for an exciting career in show business and fell into advertising the same way I had: by mistake.

Over time, I learned that Miss Francine was brought to Hollywood by M.G.M. in the 1960s to be an actress and somehow wound up in Las Vegas as a lounge singer. In the '70s, she returned to Los Angeles and became an ardent follower of the "est" personal transformation program which changed her life for the better and satisfied most of her material needs. Thanks to est, she had a respectable career, fabulous designer clothes, a beautiful dining set that was too big for her apartment, and a new car that she chose because its lines were very similar to those of a Mercedes. But even with all that, she was still discontent because what she really wanted more than anything was to write comedy.

I liked Miss Francine but felt sorry for her because there were so many mishaps and aggravations that irked her. She divorced the same man twice. Her neighbors fucked all night so she could never get a wink of sleep. The El Pollo Loco fast food joint next door to her apartment house attracted the "wrong element." She had a yappy little dog named Stinkypoo that chewed up her panties. The Italian deli on the corner never did get her lunch order right, which she inferred as being anti-Semitic, even though she confessed she wasn't really Jewish. And, if that wasn't bad enough, she suffered from chronic exhaustion and terrible gas. The happiest I'd ever seen her was when she was describing scenes from her favorite sitcoms that she had watched on TV the night before and she'd laugh aloud and then dream about writing those scenes herself.

"Oh, I'd love to write for that show," she said time and again, staring into space with dead eyes and a longing smile. I could hear the joy of canned laughter running through her mind and I flinched because I'd witnessed sitcom writing first-hand at Paramount, and I thought it was more painful than fun.

"Writers would work until two in the morning, only to have all their jokes tossed out the next day," I said. But that didn't deter Miss Francine. Not only had she an abundance of storyline ideas for *The Golden Girls* and *Roseanne*, she also had ideas for her own shows as well. She was a combustible plethora of creativity, and she could have had her own production company if Grant Tinker or Norman Lear would have given her a chance. Those assholes!

"No matter how hard I tried, I could never crack those nuts," she said.

"Tough nuts are the worst," I said.

Insert canned laughter here.

"We should write a show together," she said. "I have plenty of ideas. If you can use your contacts at Paramount to get us in the door, I'll cut you in on the profits."

"Nahhh," I said, causing the permanent frown on her face to deepen. "I don't want to write a sitcom. It's not my thing."

The humor in a sitcom script would never compare to the ballsy, outrageous high jinks and irreverent drug-induced revelry found in the Holly Woodlawn story. I dared not say a word about that to Miss Francine, though, because other people had reacted negatively when I mentioned the project, so I thought it best to keep it a secret. Then one morning, Miss Francine told me she was reading *The Andy Warhol Diaries*, and I made the mistake of telling her I knew Holly.

"Holly Woodlawn?" she asked.

"Yeah, she's my neighbor," I said. "I'm taking her to the Bel-Age tomorrow after work for a shoot with Chuck Workman. He's interviewing her for his new documentary about Andy Warhol."

"Really?" Miss Francine's mouth twisted to one side as she pondered a thought. Of all the questions she could have asked, the one thing Miss Francine wanted to know was, "What bathroom does she use?"

Holly hated that question.

"Well, when he's dressed as a man, he uses the men's room. And when she's dressed as a woman, she uses the ladies' room."

Miss Francine's mouth dropped open. I could see that the thought of Holly Woodlawn inside a women's room stall, with her cock and balls flopped over the edge of a toilet seat, did not sit well. After that conversation, Miss Francine would occasionally ask about Holly, but curiously whenever she spoke Holly's name, it always had a negative tone.

"So how's *Holly*?" she frowned.

"She's doing great," I said.

"Still working at Wacko?"

"Oh, yeah. She loves it."

Miss Francine groaned and I sensed a bit of envy. After all, Miss Francine worked hard to have a respectable station in life. How could it be possible that a washed-up, ex-con has-been like Holly Woodlawn, who never had any money and worked a shit job, got invited to better parties?

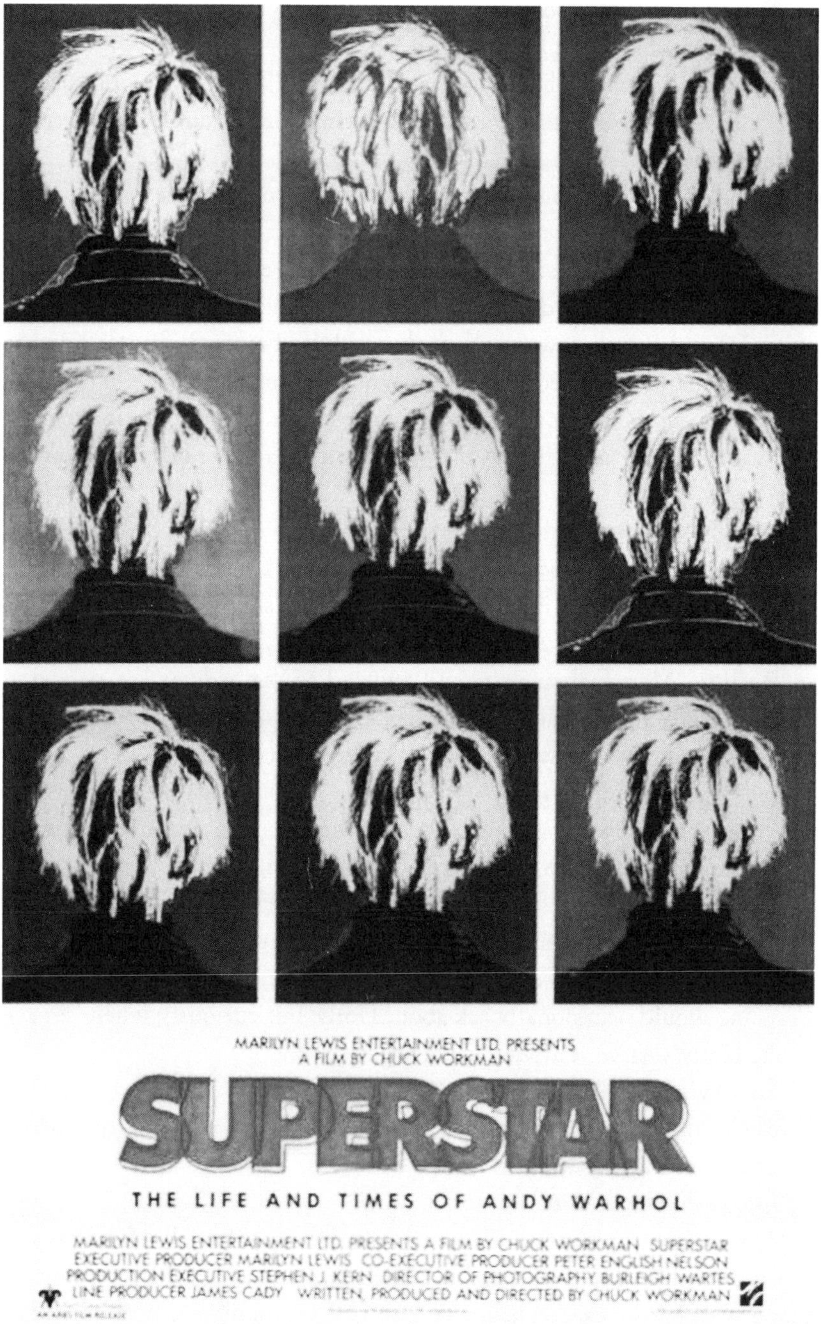

MARILYN LEWIS ENTERTAINMENT LTD. PRESENTS
A FILM BY CHUCK WORKMAN

SUPERSTAR

THE LIFE AND TIMES OF ANDY WARHOL

MARILYN LEWIS ENTERTAINMENT LTD. PRESENTS A FILM BY CHUCK WORKMAN SUPERSTAR
EXECUTIVE PRODUCER MARILYN LEWIS CO-EXECUTIVE PRODUCER PETER ENGLISH NELSON
PRODUCTION EXECUTIVE STEPHEN J. KERN DIRECTOR OF PHOTOGRAPHY BURLEIGH WARTES
LINE PRODUCER JAMES CADY WRITTEN, PRODUCED AND DIRECTED BY CHUCK WORKMAN

AN ARIES FILM RELEASE

When Holly was asked to appear in the Chuck Workman documentary *Superstar: The Life and Times of Andy Warhol*, we were both thrilled. Chuck Workman was a highly respected, Academy Award-winning filmmaker, and being invited to appear in his film was a major coup for Holly.

Holly didn't have cosmetics, hair, or a fabulous gown, but she did have a friend from New York named Conrad, who now lived in a small hacienda on Willoughby, several blocks west of Las Palmas. On the day of the shoot, Conrad helped Holly pull together a "look" that stopped me dead in my tracks. With hair that was too big and a dress that was too short, Holly looked like a cheap dime-store floozy who'd gotten a ninety-nine-cent makeover at the Pic 'N' Save on Vine, but that didn't stop us from valeting the Fiero at the posh Bel-Age Hotel's main porte cochère and making a grand entrance. If Holly's manly, well-proportioned legs didn't confirm something was awry with this illusion, her wide feet and gorilla toes crammed into a pair of vintage gold Spring-o-lator mules did.

The double takes and stares were quickly intercepted by Robert, who escorted us to the large banquet room where a small film set had been built. It was a wall and a large makeup mirror, so it looked like Holly was being interviewed in a dressing room. That was an interesting choice. Instead of documenting Holly in her real environment, she was put in a fake, manufactured one. How L.A.! But it made sense financially because it was cheaper to shoot many interviews in one location and alter the backdrops.

Chuck Workman greeted Holly and brought her over to the set. A portrait of Andy Warhol was positioned behind her so it loomed overhead in her reflection, like he was God. It was so perfectly stylized and contrived, yet so symbolic of Warhol's impact on Holly's life. He was the force that caused Holly Woodlawn to be created in the first place. The only reason Holly became Holly Woodlawn is because she wanted to be an Andy Warhol superstar like her friends Candy Darling and Jackie Curtis. She saw all the fun they were having and she wanted to get in on the action, too. Even though Holly wasn't close friends with Andy, her association with him was the gift that kept on giving. No matter how penniless or poverty-stricken Holly would become, she would always be celebrated and there would always be fans who were captivated by her presence.

On that day, Robert and I were those fans, and we stood to the side like two dutiful servants. It was exciting to see the crew adjusting lights and the makeup artist touching up Holly's face.

"Holly, do you want some water?" Robert asked.

"Oh, I'm fine, hon. But thanks," Holly answered.

I was impressed and felt important just being there. This shoot was a big deal and a boon to our book proposal. A Chuck Workman film would be marketed to mainstream audiences in all the major cities. It promised national exposure for Holly, and publicity of that magnitude was huge and not easily achieved.

The interview didn't last long, but during that short time, while the lights shined bright and the film camera rolled, I could see Holly was exactly where she needed to be. . . . Viva la célébrité! It didn't matter that she looked like a two-bit hussy who'd just been picked up on the corner of Sunset and Martel. She lit up like a firefly and her delivery and humor were spot on.

The next morning, I told Miss Francine about the Chuck Workman shoot, but she wasn't very interested. She was preoccupied with a new gold treasure that wrapped around her wrist.

"Hey, check out my new Rolex," she said and extended her arm so I could see.

"Wow!" I replied. "It's gorgeous."

I didn't know anything about Rolex watches and was surprised when Miss Francine invited me to see an entire stash of them in her office. She also had an array of Chanel handbags and other wristwatches that bore the names of Gucci and Patek Philippe.

"They're not real," she said, explaining they were fakes that were acquired in some sort of trade deal. She kept them stashed in a cabinet under lock and key as if they were as precious as the real McCoys.

"You can have one for twenty-five bucks if you want," she said. "A real Rolex would cost thousands, so you can't beat that deal."

When I gave Miss Francine twenty-five bucks and purchased a knockoff Rolex, I had no idea that tinny piece of shit was illegal. I thought it was beautiful.

The stability of a 9-to-5 job outside of the entertainment business gave Holly and me enough cash to grab weekly pizzas at Raffallo's, our favorite Italian hole-in-the-wall. As part of my salary, my company also gave me a thousand dollars in restaurant scrip, which was paper currency for free food that the company acquired via advertising barter deals. So even though we couldn't afford to go to nice restaurants, for a while we did and we ate for free! That was one of the perks of "selling out" and working a "normal" office job. But it was a strange pool in which I now swam and the waters felt odd and unnatural. This advertising business was a world that ran on a different kind of creativity that was driven by large-scale media buys focused on numbers and percentages, and everyone around me seemed preoccupied with money, sales, deals, and prestige. Status symbols were necessities. Projecting the right image was of paramount importance, which became apparent one day when a handsome co-worker grabbed hold of my necktie, flipped it over, looked at the label, and frowned.

"I knew it was polyester," he uttered, rolled his eyes, and then walked away.

When I told Holly about it later, she scoffed.

"Oh, don't even bother with that pretentious asshole, honey! That says more about him than you. People who have real money don't rub it in your face."

None of those people had real money. They had restaurant scrip! But despite their widespread pomposity, I actually liked my co-workers. They were nice people who opened my eyes to things I didn't care to see but were important to understand. In this odd wonderland, those who weren't up to par got snubbed. The car a person drove, the designer clothing a person wore, the neighborhood a person lived in were all very important. Even the thread count of a person's bedsheets mattered.

I took a trip to Bullock's department store to educate myself on these finer necessities. While admiring a display of Lalique crystal, an arrogant sales queen approached.

"Is there something I can help you with?" he inquired.

"No, I'm just looking."

"I figured that's all you could afford to do," he sniggered and walked away.

"Oh, the nerve of that snotty queen!" Holly snarled when I recounted the episode to her later. "As if she can afford Lalique on her salary. Don't you worry about it, hon. One day you'll have Lalique. One day when we get a book deal."

If we ever got it. That pie-in-the-sky book deal was the one great hope I counted on to change my life for the better. That horror film I wrote didn't do anything. Even after it won the Gold Award at the Houston International Film Festival, it amounted to nothing more than a fleeting thrill. For a moment, I was excited. I won! Finally! But then as I read the letter of congratulations further, I was shocked to learn I had to pay fifty bucks to actually receive the award. How did that make any sense? I won an award . . . and now had to pay to get it! That sounded more like a bait-and-switch scam than an actual honor. The only winner on that deal was the guy who owned the trophy factory.

They take the PARK AVENOO LAFF by LAFF
...and give you the LOWDOWN on HIGH SOCIETY!

Leo GORCEY
Huntz HALL
and THE BOWERY BOYS

HIGH SOCIETY

AN ALLIED ARTISTS PICTURE

with Amanda BLAKE

JAMES CAGNEY
JOAN BLONDELL
RUBY KEELER
DICK POWELL

FOOTLIGHT PARADE

A WARNER BROS.
& VITAPHONE PICTURE

FRANK SINATRA
ANN MILLER

They Paint The Town With Joy!

ON THE TOWN

M-G-M's BIG TECHNICOLOR MUSICAL!

JULES MUNSHIN   VERA-ELLEN

CHAPTER 14

THE VIBRANT LOS ANGELES RESTAURANT SCENE WAS quite the sham in 1989. The only reason I knew anything about it was because I read L.A. *Style,* which was an oversized glossy magazine that focused on anything and everything beautiful and hip. The fashionable folks didn't care about value. They wanted to be dazzled by a glorious presentation, which was usually a large white plate with a smidgen of this and a dollop of that drizzled in fancy sauce and sprinkled with whatever. Food was art, and that justified minuscule portions and outrageous prices. I experienced it once. For thirty bucks, I got four bites and wound up at Astro Burger afterward.

One day, when my co-workers were comparing notes on places they liked to eat, I casually mentioned a place Holly and I discovered called Ida's, which was on Santa Monica Boulevard next to a gay hustler bar known as Hunters. When two of my colleagues decided to check it out, they were expecting white linen tablecloths and bottled Pellegrino. What they got was a cheap dump in a sketchy part of town where an old gal who looked like Ma Kettle was slinging hash.

Upon their return from their lunch hour adventure, they told me how awful the place was and how horrified they were that I actually ate there! I was embarrassed. When I told Holly about it later, she laughed.

The legendary French Quarter restaurant in West Hollywood. Everyone's favorite hangout.
Photo by Alan Light. Courtesy of The Lavender Effect.

"Oh, who doesn't love a good meatloaf?" Holly replied. "What's wrong with those people?"

While I knew about Muse on Beverly, Le Dome and Spago on Sunset, and The Ivy on Robertson, Holly and I couldn't afford to go to those places because they didn't serve a six-dollar blue plate special. So when we had to foot the bill with our own hard-earned cash, the French Quarter restaurant in West Hollywood was where we dined most, mainly because the wait staff learned of Holly's superstar status and sneaked her free glasses of wine on the side.

Holly was a hustler. She knew how to wheedle free wine out of the tightest box. But sometimes, her hustle went a bit too far. One night we were taken to dinner by a former work colleague of mine, who had become one of my favorite friends. Her name was Angela, a high-cheekboned Italian beauty from Queens, New York, and you knew it the moment she spoke.

"This is on me," Angela said. "Get whatever you want."

Angela was a fun broad, and the minute she confirmed she was footing the bill, she became Holly's new best friend.

"I'll take a carafe of chardonnay, darling," Holly told the waiter.

"And for your appetizer?" he asked.

"Oh, an appetizer!" Holly thought for a moment. "Two carafes!"

It was a great evening, we had a wonderful time, and Angela generously picked up the tab. As she drove us home, Angela and I were chatting in the front seat when Holly lunged forward from behind, interrupted, and said to Angela, "Hey hon, you got five bucks on ya?"

I was stunned. Angela laughed.

"Well, yeah, I got five bucks," she said. "Why?"

"I need some cigarettes. Can you pull over and buy me a pack?"

I was mortified. Angela chuckled, seeing the humor in the situation.

"Sure," she said as she pulled into the Gelson's grocery store parking lot and gave Holly the cash. I would've given Holly the money myself, but I didn't have any.

"Thanks, hon," said Holly, then jumped out of the car and ran inside while I profusely apologized. I couldn't believe Holly hit up Angela for five bucks after she'd just spent a fortune on dinner. But that's how Holly's mind worked. She was an opportunist. Angela was well dressed. She drove a nice car. She had a good job. And Holly was going to milk her for everything she could get.

"She's an executive," Holly reasoned later. "Why can't she pay our rent?"

"Why should she?"

"Because she's rich. She has the money."

"She's not rich—"

"Oh, honey, please. I know money when I see it," Holly snapped.

I don't know where Holly got the notion that her friends who earned more money than she should pay her rent. Perhaps that was carried over from her days in New York, when she ran with the elite Studio 54 crowd.

"Holly, it's not Angela's responsibility to pay our rent."

"Who said anything about responsibility? I could care less about responsibility."

Now I saw a side of Holly that I didn't like. I loved her as my knockoff Auntie Mame. But I didn't care for her as an irresponsible leech who wanted to freeload. I just couldn't relate to her on that level. All I knew was that Holly was troubled in ways I couldn't even comprehend. There were many sides to her, and like a Rubik's cube, she wasn't easy to figure out. But I tried. She ran away from home at the age of fifteen, which probably contributed to some form of arrested development. Holly was childlike. She didn't want to be responsible. She wanted other people to take care of her. During those formative years when teenagers learn to be responsible adults, Holly was on the streets of Times Square, turning tricks to survive. No wonder her moral compass had gone awry.

Her drive to mooch and grift seemed as inherent as her sexuality. She did it without even thinking, like the times we were chatting or writing and she would unconsciously put her hand in her shorts and start playing with her cock. Oddly, it made the strangest noise... TCH! TCH! TCH! Like a turtle's mouth smacking on some lettuce.

"Holly, what are you doing?"

"Nothing," she said, quickly removing her hand.

"How are you making that noise?"

"I don't know. I just squeeze it and it makes a noise."

Like a party favor. Holly loved having a cock. She told me so herself. The only reason she ever considered a sex change in her youth was because the man she fell in love with wanted her to have it.

"If I got a pussy, then we could get married," Holly explained.

Holly's soon-to-be-husband gave her several thousand dollars for a sex change, but when it came time for the operation, Holly had a change of plans.

"So instead of buying a pussy, I bought a fabulous new wardrobe. Oh honey, I'm so glad I came to my senses. I can't imagine putting myself through all that pain. And what if I didn't like it? There was one person I knew who went through the surgery and regretted it. She was so miserable, she committed suicide. And darling, I wanted no part of that. So I just shot hormones, grew some tits, and called it a day."

"What about the guy who wanted to marry you?"

"He was not very happy. In fact, he was furious. He called me a liar and a cheat, and then he kicked me out of the house. The nerve!"

While Holly's integrity may have been dubious at times, the aura of her celebrity was indisputable and more powerful than I ever imagined. Even though she was financially broke, living hand to mouth, there were people who catered to her. When I asked about the scars that were behind her ear that ran along her hairline, she told me those were from a New York plastic surgeon, who gave her a face lift for free.

"Why did he give you a face lift when you were only thirty-eight?" I asked.

"Why not?" she answered.

It was just another example of how Holly's connection to Andy Warhol entitled her to many perks and privileges. She partied with the rich and famous at Studio 54. She was photographed by some of America's best-known photographers. When the film *Trash* was scheduled to premiere while Holly was in jail, artist Larry Rivers paid her bail. And when Holly needed a dress for a swanky event, Halston invited her to his showroom so

that I moved in with him immediately! It lasted a while, until
we both became bored and I packed up and left. *with a new winter coat!*

One night in that after hours club, I ran into Libra and
Josie. Libra was still getting over her boyfriend behind bars and
just the mention of his name would send her into a ~~tearful tizzy!~~ *hysteria · you'd think*
we would throw herself open un neart wall & beat her breast.
By now, Libra had left his mother's flat in Brooklyn and was *cute little hovel* *& guy, it was awful. right in the middle*
living in a little ~~dump~~ on 38th Street. She was so lonely I *of the garment district with trucks jain, by at 4 & 5 in the morning delun children!*
decided it was my duty as a friend to move in and occupy her

lonely nights. And I did!

Miss Loper →

Libra was working as a hair dresser and encouraged me to
pursue a career in the art of beauty. Afterall, I had to do
something with my life and why not do hair! Why, the thought of
making the world more beautiful by becoming a professional
beautician sounded thrilling. Oh, I was so excited about this
new adventure, but there was one thing. It cost a fortune to go
to beauty school and I was lucky to hustle up ten bucks! It
would take years before I could hustle up the five hundred dollar
tuition fee! There was only one thing for me to do, and the
thought of it made me very nervous. For the first time nearly
five months, I was going to call my parents.

~~As it turned out,~~ My parents sent me a bus ticket ~~to return~~ *home.*
~~to Florida. And~~ When I arrived, my father leveled with me. He *said*
he understood that I would ~~told me I wasn't going to~~ be happy *living* at home and he asked what I
had planned for myself. I told *him & my book* ~~them~~ about my ~~idea about going~~ *plan to go*
to beauty school and they encourged ~~me~~ *pursuit idea.*
I stayed with the & work & it WAS a time I'll never forget. Which
~~It was a week to remember. I was~~ soaking in the bathtub
listening to The Beatles sing "I Wanna Hold Your Hand", ~~when~~ an

A very rough draft from Chapter Four. Holly always wrote her notes in pencil while I preferred ink. This eventually became Page 61 in the book. 1990.

she could pick one out. No amount of Lalique or bedsheet thread count could ever top that breadth of experience. Holly enjoyed the best of everything and the worst of nothing, and I didn't know of anyone else who lived in such an extreme paradox. Her celebrity status, no matter how minor, was a magnet to those in higher positions who were always willing to lend a helping hand, or so it seemed. What I didn't know or anticipate is how her magnetism and opportunism would ultimately become a threat and betray me in the end.

During that time, my grandmother got deathly ill. My parents flew me back to Missouri so I could say goodbye, but I couldn't afford to stay for the funeral because I had to get back to work. Like most working-class folks,

I was on the proverbial hamster wheel, always running but never getting anywhere. I didn't have the time or money to take a leave of absence from work or go on a vacation. If I wanted an escape, I'd pick up a book or go to Lizards coffeehouse in the dregs of Hollywood, where the 1920s French jazz lulled me to another place and a different time.

Lizards was created by John Gonzales and Clinton Oie. John was a Vietnam veteran and Clinton was an actor and writer who had worked with the Goodman Theatre in Chicago. They decided to open a late-night coffeehouse in Hollywood's crummy "Theatre Row" so patrons would have a place to hang out after the show. The name Lizards was inspired by the dry Arab landscape, where Arabica coffee originated.

In 1989, there were only a handful of European-style coffeehouses in Los Angeles, which included the Onyx next to the Vista Theatre in Los Feliz, the Pik-Me-Up on 6th Street, and Deja Vu on Hollywood Boulevard. But Lizards was my favorite because it had a vibe I couldn't find anywhere else, probably because of its unique space, the music, and its location along a tired stretch of Santa Monica Boulevard where male prostitutes peddled their wares. It was located under the second-story studio of a world-famous photographer named Herb Ritts, who shot every major star in Hollywood and directed some of Madonna's black-and-white music videos. There was always somebody interesting hanging out there.

One day as I walked down the sidewalk toward Lizards' entrance, Herb Ritts and another man rounded the corner with Elizabeth Taylor between them. Because I resembled a street urchin in old ripped jeans and a wife-beater T-shirt, they looked at me with leery apprehension . . . like I was going to hit them up for five bucks! Well, I should have, but I wasn't that fast-thinking.

Lizards had an unpretentious vibe, even though it attracted a cool crowd. Its long narrow space was decorated with a large old Persian rug and vintage furniture. An eclectic assemblage of chairs were arranged in stylish vignettes. There were pink iron-framed 1960s butterfly chairs, old Queen Anne wing-back chairs, a vintage bar against the wall with two stools, and two low-backed mid-century sofas. Paintings by local artists decorated the stark white walls and were lit by track lighting.

The place was rarely crowded. Only a handful of people were generally there, the most striking being a cool dark-haired beauty with fair skin, large painted eyes, and vivid red lips. Her name was Merle Ginsberg. The most beautiful was a young actor named Brandon Lee, who was appearing in a play

HOLLY WOODLAWN

Dear,

I've always thought autobiographies were written by people with
one foot in the grave and the other on a banana peel. But with
mortality being what it is these days, I figured now is as good
of a time as any! With so many friends gone and so many voices
silenced, now I can tell the filthy truth about all of them!
After all, I've been hit by lightning once already and as they
say, lightning never strikes the same place twice.

Funny how things finally get done, or begun. How many lifetimes
ago was it when I said to Andy, "I'm still writing my book." And
he said, "Oh, Holly, you must. Nobody has had a life like yours,
being a woman and a man and all. Just think of all the people
who'll read it...and maybe you find a rich publisher to marry!"

I'd be happy with a good editor.

Love you madly,

Holly Woodlawn.

SUPERSTAR

While digging through dusty old boxes, searching for lost photos, I was surprised to find this letter
from Holly to prospective publishers. 1989.

The Lizards Coffeehouse Gang: John Gonzales, Tom Cunningham, Manuel Sanchez, Clinton Oie, and Ed Evans. 1990.

at the Fig Tree Theatre next door. And the sweetest was a young, handsome, porcelain-skinned bodybuilder named Ron-Jon, whom I only admired from afar and never got to know. I assumed he was in college because he was always studying. Clinton told me he had a boyfriend, though I never saw him. It didn't make any difference. Ron-Jon was always a nice distraction.

Lizards soon became my favorite place to write, and Holly and I would go there often. Its menu was simple but very carefully planned. The warm, homemade chicken pasta salad was delicious, and the "Artist's Lunch," which consisted of soft Brie cheese and a French baguette, was a flavorful contrast to the bold rich coffee. The first time I tasted that coffee, the flavor was so strong it nearly knocked me over.

"Jesus! What the heck is this?" I asked.

"It's a Sumatra roast," said John.

I'd never tasted anything so horrible. The flavor was just so overwhelming, not anything like the coffee they served at the French Quarter. But oddly, the more I sipped, the more I craved, and by the time I finished the mug, I was hooked.

I didn't have cash or a credit card, so John let me run a tab that I paid off weekly. Sometimes Teresa, my friend from R/F/B Public Relations, would join us. Teresa was a big fan of the book proposal and offered encouragement when others expressed doubt.

"It's a good story," Teresa said as we noshed on Brie cheese and French baguettes. "I hope it sells because I want to publicize it when it does."

"Yay, honey!" Holly squealed excitedly, toasting us with her coffee mug and then taking a sip. "Jesus Christ, this coffee has more kick than a chorus line."

"It's a dark roast, Hol. It's called Sumatra," I said.

"Oh, that Nancy Sumatra, always kicking up her boots," quipped Holly. "No wonder this coffee is so loud. Laaa-hooood!"

Lounging with Teresa and Holly in those old wingback chairs, savoring that hot rich elixir, munching on Brie and baguettes while Charlélie Couture sang "Parlez-Moi D'Amour" in the background became a much cherished memory. Those moments were pure nirvana. Even though I was broke, basking in that faux Parisian ambiance with friends I genuinely liked made me feel like the richest person in the world.

CHAPTER 15

IN SEPTEMBER, HOLLY'S MOTHER FLEW OUT TO California for a visit. She stayed with Holly's cousin in Anaheim and we drove down to meet them for dinner at a Mexican restaurant. Holly dressed as a man and wore the same shorts, shirt, and sneakers she usually wore, almost on a daily basis.

Holly, Holly's mother, and Holly's male cousin bore a striking resemblance to one another. They all had the same almond-shaped eyes. Holly's cousin was straight and very masculine, and meeting him was like being introduced to a butch version of Holly. Holly's mother was dignified, well-coiffed, and very reserved. They both referred to Holly as Harold, which threw me at first. Even though Holly looked like a man, she was always a woman to me.

As we sat in a booth and Holly chatted, Holly's mother stared at me, almost incredulously, like I was an odd puzzle piece she couldn't quite fit into the allotted space. Her watchful eyes made me uncomfortable. "Jeffrey, tell me, this book you're writing," she said with a faint Puerto Rican accent.

"Oh, Mom, it's going to be fabulous," Holly interjected.

"But what's it about? I don't understand," she said.

"It's my life story, Ma. And Jeffrey's writing it. What's there to understand?"

Holly's mother frowned.

"But why?" she pressed.

Our waiter came with our food and Holly threw him a look of despair.

"Can I have a glass of chardonnay, please?" she asked.

"And I'll take another margarita," Holly's mother said.

As the waiter distributed the hot plates, Holly turned to her cousin and changed the subject.

"So what's it like living in Anaheim?"

Life in Anaheim was a snooze. It was mundane and acceptable, but I could see that's the story Holly's mother preferred. Her nephew was handsome, respectable, and hard-working. He had a normal, ordinary job. He was responsible and presentable . . . a son that would make any parent proud. Perhaps that's the reason Holly's mother chose to sit closer to him.

I admired Holly's mother because she immigrated to the United States, made a better life for herself, and achieved the American dream. She and her husband worked hard, owned their own home, and had investments and security. By comparison, Holly's life was a contrast to the environment in which she was raised, and her choices caused her parents much frustration, disappointment, and grief. There were even a few times when Holly referenced "the hell" she put her parents through and expressed shame for all the trouble she caused them. But on this night, any morsel of guilt was overridden by angst and disparity.

For me, the dinner with Holly's mother and cousin felt awkward. To make conversation, I asked about their family in Puerto Rico.

"Our bloodline is a hodgepodge," Holly said. "Spanish, Brazilian, Black—"

Holly's mother bristled.

"We do not have Black!" she announced and seemed angered by the insinuation.

"Oh, Ma, what do you mean—" started Holly.

"We do not have Black in our blood. We don't!" she insisted.

Her hostile reaction gave me pause and I wondered why she was so staunch in her denial. Perhaps it was because she immigrated to the United States during a time of segregation when people who were identified as Black were denied civil rights and opportunity.

After dinner, Holly's mother graciously paid the tab and we parted ways. As we drove back to Los Angeles, I thought it odd that Holly's mother didn't want to come up to Hollywood. When I mentioned it to Holly, she didn't seem to mind. Perhaps it was easier to keep her mother in Anaheim where she couldn't ask too many questions, like what kind of book is this going to be? Who in their right mind is going to publish it? And haven't you embarrassed us enough?

Despite her mother's misgivings, Holly was hell-bent on telling her story. The Chuck Workman shoot reaffirmed the notion that people were genuinely interested in what Holly had to say. She was a pop curiosity with an extraordinary past, and she appealed to the counterculture rebels who revered art, music, and the New York underground. Their intrigue and fascination were seemingly endless, so it was plausible that a book about her life would find an audience . . . if we could find a publisher. But for some reason, that wasn't happening.

Holly and I were still very excited about our book proposal. We believed we were on to something big, and we were looking forward to the response from publishers . . . until we got our first rejection. I was in Holly's apartment when Robert called to give us the news.

"Don't worry about it," Robert said. "We have other options."

"Well, what didn't they like?" asked Holly.

"It just wasn't for them," he said.

"Huh," said Holly. She was sensitive to rejection, and this didn't go over well.

"There are other publishers," he said. "Don't let this upset you."

But we were upset. It was a funny story. We didn't understand how a person couldn't like it. What was the problem? Was it too absurd? Was Holly not relatable? Was it not well written? Was it my fault? Perhaps I should have taken that job on *Pee-wee's Playhouse*. Maybe my decision to write Holly's story was nothing but a mistake.

"Jeffrey, let's go get a bottle of wine," Holly suggested. We drove to the grocery store and saw our favorite red-haired checker, Miss Melons, who was stacked like the bumper of a 1955 Cadillac.

"Honey, what's up with those knockers, that's what I want to know. They keep getting bigger," said Holly as we exited the store with an economy-sized bottle of Glen Ellen chardonnay.

"I didn't notice that," I said.

"Well, pay attention! Her tetas are so big she can't see to count change. I'd like to grab on to those casabas and smack them in my face."

I stopped dead in my tracks.

"What?!"

"Oh, yeah," she said. "Big beautiful tits bring out the mad lesbian in me every time. I'm like a pig in a honeypot."

I didn't know anything about Holly's "lesbian" proclivities. This sexual revelation came as a surprise, only to be followed by a bombshell a week later, when Holly was sued for breach of contract by a woman in New York, who claimed to be Holly's former lover.

We sat in Robert's office while Holly explained the situation. She said she and her lover, who also worked as her manager, had been working on a large coffee-table book of photographs. Then something went awry. As Holly paced Robert's floor, wrung her hands, whined, and carried on, it was Honey this, Darling that, and Oh, what a mess we're in now! As I sat back and listened, I wondered if anything Holly said was true. Was she the victim in this case? Or was she just a spoiled brat who didn't want to live up to her end of the bargain?

The book proposal I'd written was now in jeopardy and we weren't able to move forward until this legal mess was cleaned up. What publisher would buy the Holly Woodlawn story if it was mired in litigation?

"Well, she can kiss my twat!" Holly cried out in anguish.

Holly could scream, yell, hoot, and holler, but it didn't make any difference. Whether she liked it or not, she was going to court.

Holly's good friend Jimmy Yasky, an attorney in Manhattan, volunteered to take her case. Like magic, Holly got the money to fly to New York City for the court date and the case was settled. Once again, the power of her celebrity prevailed. Whatever Holly needed, Holly got, and if feelings were hurt in the process, well . . . that was just too bad.

In the fall of 1989, *Andy Warhol's Trash* played at the Beverly Cinema, a run-down movie theatre that showed classic old movies and art films. It was located on Beverly Boulevard just west of La Brea.

On the night of the screening, I called the Beverly Cinema and told the manager that I was bringing Holly to the theatre. I thought he'd like to know one of the stars of the film would be in attendance. Then I went to Holly's apartment next door and knocked on her door.

"Come in!" she yelled.

I entered her apartment. To the immediate right was the bathroom, where Holly stood at the old wall-mount sink, fixing her face. By now, she could afford cosmetics and a new wig because her parents were helping pay her rent.

"Hi Hol," I said. The bathroom was small, so I stood in the hallway.

"Hello, you divine boy."

Holly with her good friend Jimmy Yasky, a highly respected NYC attorney and gay rights activist who came to her defense more than once. 1990.

"The movie starts in an hour so we should leave in about forty minutes," I said.

Holly's face was entirely covered in foundation, even her mouth, which surprised me. I'd never seen my mother or Jean put foundation on their lips.

"Why do you cover your mouth with foundation?" I asked.

"Why not? This is where the magic begins. It's got to be full and complete," she explained.

"Oh."

Somehow that made sense. Holly leaned into the medicine chest mirror and worked the cream foundation into the edges of her hairline.

"This reminds me of when I was a little boy. I used to love watching my mom put on her makeup," I recalled.

"How's Dot doing?" Holly asked. "Good ol' Dot!"

"She's fine. She loved the book proposal. My father's excited, too. Although he doesn't understand what it's about . . . which is probably a good thing."

"Honey, I can't wait for that book to sell," Holly said. "But Robert keeps dragging his feet. I don't get it."

"It's going to be fine, Holly. He knows what he's doing."

Well . . . at least I hoped he did. I didn't know that for sure. In fact, we didn't know much of anything about that literary agency when we signed our agreement. We were just happy to be signing something.

"Darling, can you pass me that brown eyeshadow?" she asked.

Holly pointed to a small plastic compact sitting on the dresser in the adjacent closet.

"Sure," I said, grabbing the clear container and noticing it held three shades of brown. I was mesmerized by the artistry that went into creating Holly's eyes. As she colored her eyelids with varying shades, she talked about Greta Garbo's eyes and how she had the "creased look."

"That creased look is nothing but a pain in the ass," Holly said. "Hon, hand me that liner over there, will ya?"

I loved watching Holly's transformation process because it was so dramatic. The "after" was always astounding. That night, Holly wore tailored black slacks and a simple black blouse that was entirely covered in black buttons. She looked fantastic.

In 1989, the Beverly Cinema was a dump. But it was also fun and interesting because of the types of films it exhibited and the kind of audience it attracted, which was mostly cinephiles who studied and cherished the art of film.

Teresa met us at the theatre, and when we arrived, I was surprised and impressed to see a small crowd mingling outside. We parked down the street and walked to the box office. As we got closer, people turned and gawked, curious and somewhat starstruck. Many of them were smiling, eyes lit up with curiosity and excitement.

While I bought our tickets, people came up to Holly and said hello. She was thrilled. Holly was warm and gracious, and she was genuinely touched by the enthusiastic reception. She loved it when people came up to chat. This was the first time I'd seen Holly engage with fans. I didn't know she had any because when she performed at the Backlot a year before, nobody showed up . . . except a few friends. So to be with Holly and see her attract attention from a small crowd was pretty exciting.

After a few moments, we made our way inside the theatre and sat in awful, lopsided seats that were so rickety my butt dropped to the floor.

"Jesus Christ!" I groaned.

"Jeffrey, what on Earth—"

"This seat is a little wonky," I whispered.

"Wonky?" Holly said. "Mine just goosed me with a loose spring. The nerve!"

Holly squirmed in the chair and tried to get comfortable, when suddenly it thrust backward with such a force, she nearly got whiplash.

"Obviously they're not making much money on art films," I whispered.

"Tell me about it," Holly snapped. "That's the story of my life."

The theatre darkened and the film played. Seeing it with a live audience on the big screen was so much better than watching it on video. When Holly's infamous masturbation-with-a-beer-bottle scene played out before our eyes, Holly dropped her face in her hands and said aloud, "Oh God!" The crowd roared with laughter at hearing her response. Holly was embarrassed by her onscreen shenanigans, even though film scholars lauded her acting for its poignance.

Despite the rickety seats and their broken springs, we enjoyed the movie. Sitting next to Holly, watching her act, and hearing the audience respond favorably was thrilling. It was also powerful because it validated Holly in a way that was important for me to see. It gave me a whole new perspective on Holly's superstar status, and Teresa was impressed as well.

After the movie, in the theatre lobby, people came up and told Holly how much they enjoyed her performance. This was the first time I'd seen people fawn over Holly, and she was friendly and humble, and her alluring stardust was infectious. It radiated my way and made me feel special, too. In moments like these, I was so proud to have her as my friend.

I use men the way other women use makeup...

Gilda

CHAPTER 16

THE LAS PALMAS APARTMENTS WAS HOME TO MANY colorful and creative characters, some of whom worked or aspired to work in entertainment. One of the most prolific was a middle-aged blonde woman named Sheila, who slept all day and wrote all night. She was a singer, songwriter, poet, and novelist who lived on popcorn and faith that one day her dreams would come true. We were all knee-deep in the bullshit and glitter, yearning to be rich and famous, an aspiration that was now beginning to feel more like a horrible curse.

Still, I envied Sheila's easygoing, do-as-you-like lifestyle, supported by public assistance, and I wondered what it would be like to live on SSI and have the freedom to be creative all day. When I mentioned this to Holly, she said it was easy to live off the system in the '70s.

"Oh, it was fabulous," Holly explained. "We were all living on SSI and welfare in New York."

I was confused as to how that could happen.

"I don't understand," I said. "How did you get SSI?"

"Honey, all you had to do was go to a doctor, have some hallucinations, act like a lunatic, and he wrote you a prescription for SSI and welfare."

Well, no wonder the Republicans were in such an uproar over social programs! Holly lived on welfare in the early '70s, when she was a strung-out hedonist who wasted her days playing with heroin and speed and spent her nights partying at Max's Kansas City. She didn't work. Who would hire her, except Andy Warhol, who seemed to encourage her ridiculous lunacy. During that time of her life, Holly pretty much survived as a mooch and a thief. Thankfully, she didn't become a junkie.

"How did you not get hooked?" I asked.

"Because I was smart enough to quit," she said.

Still, her dalliance with methamphetamine took its toll, which I discovered one day as we were standing outside Holly's apartment, about to go inside, when she sneezed. That sneeze nearly broke all the windows! It came on with such force, Holly's uppers flew out of her mouth, bounced off the wall, and hit the floor. She quickly snatched them up, hoping I hadn't noticed, and shoved them back into place.

I was shocked. "What the hell was that?"

"My teeth, honey!"

"Your teeth?! Holly, what happened—"

"I did speed in the '70s, what do you think happened?"

The meth caused the whole top row of Holly's teeth to rot, and eventually they had to be pulled. I was floored. But now I knew why Holly had such a beautiful smile. It wasn't real.

There was a lot of phoniness in Hollywood. That was the one real truth everyone could count on. From Miss Francine's line of fake designer goods to my employer filing for Chapter 11 bankruptcy, even though its founders owned one of the world's most prestigious art collections. Phony baloney was doled out in mass quantities. Today, that's known as soy. In 1989, we called it bullshit.

Because I never seemed to have enough cash, I was always jonesing for money-making opportunities. I was proactive, never complacent . . . like a Gold Rush prospector, trying to find a gold nugget in a panful of turds. And that's exactly how Holly and I got mixed up with Chaz and Myrna, a couple of overly tanned boisterous shysters from Las Vegas, who blew into town to have a private, closed-door meeting with Miss Francine. About fifteen minutes later, the door opened. Myrna was all giggles, thrilled over her newly acquired assortment of counterfeit Chanel handbags that were fresh off a boat from China. As they made their exit, I overheard Chaz say they needed a celebrity to help launch a new gay-themed product.

"So if you can think of anyone we should call," Chaz said.

"Will do," replied Miss Francine from her desk, then waved. "Thanks for stopping by."

After they departed, I excused myself to go to the bathroom and caught up with them in the hall. I pitched Holly for their gay project and they were interested.

A few nights later, I took Holly to the Rage bar to meet Chaz and Myrna and discuss their business venture that involved a 976 phone service. In those days, 976 phone lines were used for phone sex, but Chaz and Myrna had reinvented that tawdry wheel and created a 976 multi-line phone system that promoted events and happenings around the city. It seemed like an interesting idea. They explained that the one in Los Angeles could be called "Holly's House," and in Holly's House were virtual rooms that were accessed by pressing numbers. Press 1 for Holly's daily gossip report, press 2 for art gallery openings, press 3 for the hot new restaurants, and so forth. Promoters would pay to have their events listed in the respective rooms and Holly would get a cut of those ad sales.

The details were sketchy, but after a few cocktails and a couple of laughs over Myrna's tips on how to falsify tax records and scam the IRS, it all sounded like a fun idea that could help promote Holly as well. That's when Myrna grabbed hold of Holly's hand and held it tight.

"Oh, we're going to have such a good time," Myrna slurred after one too many Manhattans. Chaz agreed.

"It's gonna be great!" he said, flashing a broad white smile and patting me on the back.

Hugs and handshakes all around, and then Holly and I walked back to the Fiero, excited and proud, believing we were on to something good. Chaz and Myrna walked in the opposite direction and disappeared into the night. We never heard from them again! It was just one more disappointment, one more indignation in the Hollywood charade.

When Jean finally landed a part in a play at a small theatre in North Hollywood, we knew she was headed for the big time. To celebrate, Jean blew some of her hard-earned cash on headshots. Every actor needed them. They were a vital part of the Hollywood game, as were the photographers who took them, the print shops that cranked them out, and publications like *Faces International* that showcased them for an astronomical fee.

When Jean needed makeup tips, I knocked on my bedroom wall and heard Holly yell, "Beulah! Is that you?"

I stuck my head out the window and Holly did the same.

"Jean is having headshots taken. Can you give her some makeup tips?"

Holly lit up.

"You're darn tootin'! I'll be right over with my hammer and chisel."

Within moments, Holly was sitting with Jean at her desk in the living room and taking an inventory of all of Jean's cosmetics, which were strewn across the desktop.

"Darling, it all starts with a good foundation," Holly instructed. "And you've got to slap it on like plaster, hon. Hides all the hideous imperfections, like warts and stubble."

Holly & Jean: two clowns who were so much fun to be around. October 1989.

Holly showed Jean everything she needed to know about transforming herself from a gal into a goddess. Later that week, when Jean showed me her new headshot, I was impressed.

"Fingers are crossed this headshot lands me a good agent," she chirped.

"Darling, I can't wait for you to become a movie star so you can pay our rent," Holly said, and she was serious.

Jean worked hard to be an actress. She did temp jobs during the day and studied at night with two reputable comedy troupes: Second City on Santa Monica Boulevard and the Groundlings on Melrose. She was funny and talented, and I hoped this play would land her some proper representation so she could audition for TV shows and movies . . . or at least a Wisk detergent commercial. There were so many roles available for Jean to play, but she needed an agent to get her those auditions.

But surprisingly, after the play completed its two-week run, Jean didn't land an agent. She was crestfallen, back to square one, working in the secretarial trench during the day, studying with the Groundlings and Second City at night, and hustling for another audition with a stack of five hundred headshots that were going nowhere.

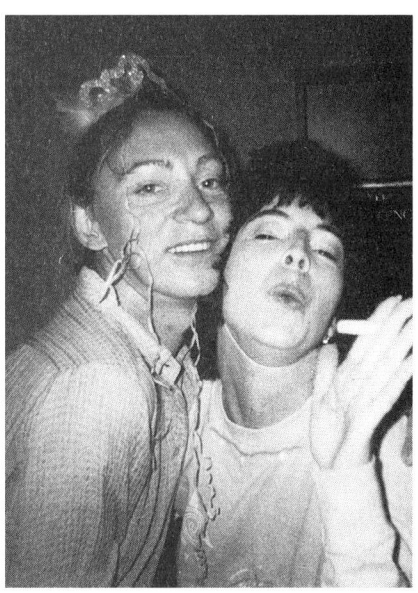

Holly and Jean at Holly's impromptu birthday soirée in Holly's Las Palmas apartment. October 1989.

"Cheer up, Jean," said Holly one night as we gathered in the kitchen and sat on folding chairs we had found in the basement. "Things could be worse. At least you're not in prison."

"Working as a temp in accounting sure feels like it," Jean said as she stirred a cut-up chicken breast in an electric wok.

"Holly, how was your day at Wacko?" I asked.

"Oh! I forgot to tell you. Michael Jackson came in today wearing a disguise. He had on a baseball cap and buck teeth. It was kind of ridiculous."

"Wow! That must have been exciting," said Jean as she doused the brewing concoction with soy sauce. "How did you know it was Michael Jackson?"

"Because he had bodyguards. And he looked like Michael Jackson with buck teeth. Not nearly as cute as Freddie Mercury, by the way. Now that boy had some choppers!"

"How did you meet Freddie Mercury?" I asked as I set the ironing board with three plates.

"I met him in England once when I was performing at a cabaret called Country Cousins. Jean, that stir-fry smells fabulous!"

"It's all healthy," Jean said. "Fresh broccoli, carrots, peppers."

"Oh, yay! Loaded with antioxidants," quipped Holly. "Almost as good as cigarettes."

Jean filled our plates and the three of us sat around the ironing board, which wasn't very sturdy. Water glasses nearly threw the whole thing off balance, and dining on the tapered end was quite precarious. One false move and our dinner would be on the floor. But I loved eating on that ironing board because it was so absurd. It was also a testament to our "can do" spirit and resourcefulness. No one ever groaned, "Ugh! We have to eat on the ironing board again!" We made do with what we had and were grateful to have it.

Holly, me, and Jean getting ready to enjoy a stir-fry feast. It was delicious! 1989.

But the winsome lark of transforming an ironing board into a dining table wasn't for long. Shortly afterward, Jean inherited a table and chairs when her Aunt Tilly, who was chasing a storm on a riding mower, got swept away by a twister. That son of a bitch picked her up in Missouri and threw her all the way to Oklahoma! Well . . . that could be an exaggeration. But regardless, Aunt Tilly croaked, and before I knew it, we had a beautiful antique oak table and four matching chairs in our kitchen. After that, we never ate off the ironing board again.

"Did Jean inherit any money?" Holly inquired, and I knew exactly what she was thinking.

"Jean inherited a table and chairs, and she's not paying our rent."

If that wasn't disappointing enough, an even bigger blow came when Robert called and said our book proposal had gotten another rejection.

"Why? Is there a reason?" I asked.

"They just don't get it," he said.

"What's there to get?" Holly huffed. "What's wrong with those people?"

"Don't get discouraged," said Robert. "I have a plan."

Robert explained he would no longer submit our proposal to individual publishers one at a time. Instead, he was waiting until December to present

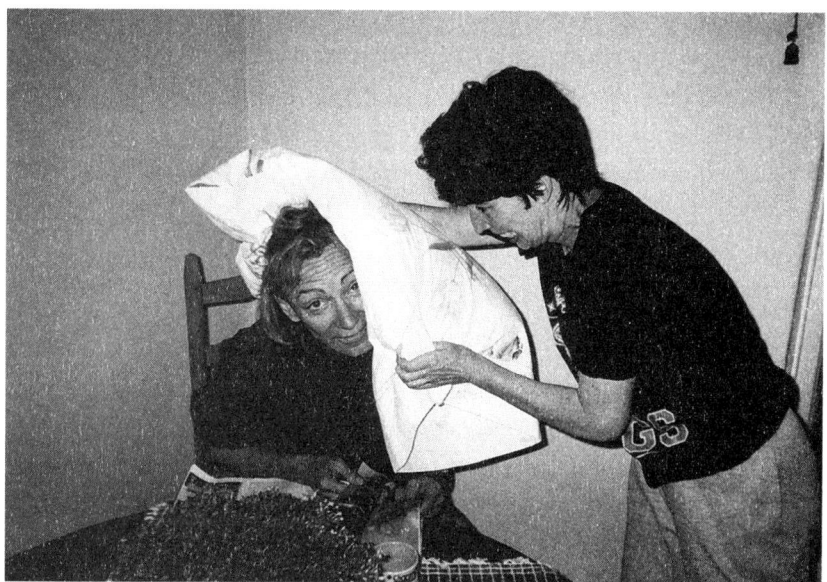

Jean playfully attacks Holly with a pillow. Holly sits at the antique oak table that Jean inherited. Poor in money, but rich in laughter and good times, we were all so hopeful and optimistic that we'd hit the big time. 1989.

it at the American Booksellers Association Convention in New York.

"December!" Holly later ranted to me in her apartment. "I'm out of cigarettes *now*. I can't wait until December. What's he thinking?"

"Holly, he knows what he's doing. Obviously, there's a reason."

She sighed with frustration.

"A bookworm convention!" she smirked. "Sounds like a real gas to me. Oh, who cares! We'll just wait until December. That's all we can do is wait. Wait. Wait for what? Another chance? Another party? Someone to pay my rent? I'm so goddamn sick of waiting I could scream."

Those tense moments gave me a rare, truthful glimpse into the emotional complexities of the real Holly Woodlawn. Deep down, she seemed to harbor a great deal of anger and resentment, but I didn't know why. I wanted to understand her better. When I asked questions, she responded with stories about her life, but oddly even the most traumatic events were regaled as lighthearted follies. If I pressed her for her real feelings, the question was often met with resistance.

"Do you think being sexually abused as a small boy had any bearing on you becoming a teenage prostitute?"

"Abused?" Holly responded. "How was I abused? I liked it."

I tried to dig deeper. "But you were a child."

Holly just shrugged it off.

"Oh, who cares," she responded and then changed the subject. If I probed further, Holly would get angry, so I learned to recognize her limits and backed off. But there was one instance when she totally unraveled, and I was shocked at how something so trivial would trigger such an explosive reaction.

It was a work day, and I had just come home for lunch. When I got to the fourth floor, I found Holly standing outside her apartment. She was at the door, but her head was down. She was staring at the floor. I could tell something was wrong. When I asked what happened, she said her key had fallen down the elevator shaft and she was locked out. She was so upset that she burst into tears. I tried to calm her down, but it only made matters worse.

"Jeffrey! You don't understand!" she screamed at the top of her lungs.

An elderly woman who lived across the hall came out to see what the commotion was about, and Holly was crying so hard we couldn't understand what she was saying. The neighbor hugged Holly and told her it would be okay.

"I'm locked out!" Holly yelled at me. "Don't you get it? Don't you know how many times this happened to me in New York?"

This emotional meltdown seemed so over-the-top and irrational. Perhaps I should have understood, but I didn't. Why didn't she go downstairs and ask Bob, the building manager, to let her in? That seemed like the logical solution, but obviously, she wasn't thinking clearly, so I did it.

Bob came upstairs, kindly opened Holly's apartment door, and called the elevator company to retrieve her keys from the elevator shaft. Problem solved. By the end of the day, Holly was back to her old carefree self.

Later, I tried to understand her extreme reaction to the keys-down-the-elevator-shaft incident. But when I asked her about the times she'd been evicted and locked out of her apartments in New York, the most I could get out of her was, "Darling, I was America's guest."

America's guest? What did that mean? I pressed for details and learned that when Holly got kicked out of one place, she just finagled her way into another. Rarely did she live on her own.

The frustration of waiting for good fortune to come our way was taking an even worse toll on Holly now. The reality of living day-to-day, hand-to-mouth was a grind. In New York, Holly had friends, parties, theatre, and cabaret. In Los Angeles, Holly had Wacko. Sometimes, the huge disparity between the life

Holly all dolled up for the Los Angeles premiere for Chuck Workman's documentary, *Superstar: The Life and Times of Andy Warhol.* She's wearing a red beaded gown designed by Tony Chase, who also made many of Dolly Parton's costumes. 1990. *Photo by Sean Hahn.*

of a menial cashier who could barely afford cigarettes and a celebrated Andy Warhol superstar was just too much. Holly's heyday was over, her fifteen minutes of fame had expired, Chuck Workman's film wouldn't be released for another year, and our book proposal was stalled.

"Jeff, what are you going to do if the book doesn't sell?" Jean asked.

"It'll sell, Jean," I said.

That was my knee-jerk reaction because I didn't want to face the horrible possibility that it wouldn't sell. If that happened, it would be catastrophic, and I'd be lost, just like so many other Hollywood hopefuls who had tried their best and got nothing in return. Not everyone in town got to be a winner. There was nothing wrong with being a loser, I tried to tell myself . . . until the pain of rejection and disappointment was just too much to bear. Peg Entwistle famously proved that point in 1932 when she climbed to the top of the "H" of the Hollywood sign (which, in those days, spelled "Hollywoodland") and jumped to her death.

While I certainly wasn't suicidal, in some ways I felt trapped, tottering atop the Holly Woodlawn sign, grasping for a thread of hope. It was a dicey situation. Holly's life story meant as much to me as it did to her. The waiting game that kept us suspended was nerve-wracking. I tried to distract myself from the foreboding doom by writing a TV script for the horror series *Tales From the Crypt.* Whenever writer's block set in, I'd find something to clean . . . which usually helped unclog my brain's gears.

Meanwhile, Holly surrendered to an ice-cold, jumbo-sized bottle of Glen Ellen chardonnay. When Holly wasn't working, she spent most of her time isolated in her single, sparsely furnished apartment that faced the Hollywood sign. That fabulous view enticed her when she was sober and taunted her when she was drunk.

ACADEMY OF MOTION PICTURE ARTS AND SCIENCES

8949 Wilshire Boulevard · Beverly Hills, California 90211-1972 · (213) 278-8990

Telex: 698-614   FAX: (213) 859-9351   or   (213) 859-9619

March 6, 1991

Jeffery Copland
Fax # 650-2126

Dear Jeffery,

Here is a press release that I found in the files:

    HOLLY WOODLAWN created film history and revolution-ized contemporary cinema. She bridged the gap between underground movies and the legitimate film with her screen debut in Andy Warhol's TRASH. Her performance was hailed by the critics around the world and drew an audience of millions.

    She received an unprecedented and somewhat contro-versial "honorary" Oscar nomination from the renouned director George Cukor. The nomination was denied by the Academy, because TRASH was a non-union film* Nonetheless, actor Ben Gazarra collected signatures from Academy mem-bers in New York, and in Hollywood, Mr. Cukor. Enough signatures were collected to secure the nomination. The following year the rules were changed. Now all films re-leased in the U.S. are eligible for Academy Awards.

    Since TRASH, Holly has starred in Warhol's WOMEN IN REVOLT, SCARECROW IN A GARDEN OF CUCUMBERS, and had a ca-meo appearance in IS THERE SEX AFTER DEATH? She has appear-ed in Vogue, Bazaar, Art in America, The National Lampoon, and countless magazines around the world.

*The real reason that Holly did not get the nomination that year was that the Academy does not allow write-in votes after the nominations have been made. The Academy does not care if a film is union or nonunion. I hope this explains the Holly Woodlawn/Oscar contro-versy.

Sincerely,

Dan Woodruff
Curator

An interesting letter from Dan Woodruff, clarifying the reason Holly didn't receive an Academy Award nomination for her role in *Trash*.

A rare campaign button to nominate Holly for an Academy Award in 1970. A fan gave this button to Holly, and she lost it later at the Gay Pride Parade in West Hollywood. What a fiasco that was!

"Oh, darling, that's faaaaa-ha-habulous," she crooned after taking her first delicate sip of the white wine. Within five minutes, those sips were gulps, and before long Miss Woodlawn was venting every frustration she'd ever experienced.

"Darling, what difference does it make if I'm a man or a woman? I'm Holly! Can't these motherfuckers understand that?"

If she wasn't ranting over the world's inability to come to terms with her gender fluidity, she was yelling about Andy Warhol.

"I never liked that asshole!"

Then she sobbed over how she mistreated her parents.

"After all I put them through, they still love me," she wailed.

By the time Holly reached the half-bottle mark, all her pent-up anger, annoyance, and guilt was unleashed. Fully pickled and feeling no remorse, she cursed the Hollywood sign that glared out her window and all the "haves" who had kept her down and snatched the golden carrots that were rightfully hers.

"Fuck Dustin Hoffman! What does he know about playing a woman? I'm Holly Woodlawn, darling! George Cukor nominated me for a fucking Academy Award!"

True, Miss Woodlawn was one of Andy Warhol's most celebrated superstars, and yes, George Cukor did petition the Academy to nominate her for her performance in *Trash*. And while that might have gotten her some nice party invitations, it didn't land her a spot on *Hollywood Squares*. So while she fumed and cussed, I was on my hands and knees, scrubbing her grimy kitchen floor.

"Superstar, my ass," was the only thing I could say as I slopped more soap and water onto her dirty linoleum.

"I heard that!" she snapped.

"Barbra Streisand is a superstar," I hollered. "Do you think she lives like a pig?"

Well, that shut her up. She sulked as I continued to scrub because I could not in good conscience allow someone I cared about to live with a dirty, sticky kitchen floor, a greasy stove, and a countertop strewn with hairbrushes, dirty dishes, and cosmetics. This was the one thing, perhaps the only thing, in our lives over which I had power. I could not control her alcoholic binges. I couldn't make a publisher buy our book proposal. And I couldn't stop the spread of AIDS that threatened to destroy my hopes, my dreams, and my entire generation. But I could control the dirt on Holly Woodlawn's floor, and I scrubbed it clean with fierce determination. In some strange way, making that floor shine gave me hope that things would ultimately work out.

CHAPTER 17

THE LAS PALMAS APARTMENTS DIDN'T HAVE A GARAGE, and because I parked on the street, I met many of the neighbors who lived in the little houses that lined the block. One Saturday morning as I walked over to my car, I saw that a neighbor across the way was having a yard sale. I went over to check it out, and that's when I got to meet him for the first time. He was an old, jovial fellow with white hair and a craggy face. His name was Edward Ludlum, and from our conversation, I learned that he was a theatre director. Standing next to him was an old woman with high cheekbones and blonde hair that was pulled back from her face. She had a way about her, like an air of grand aristocracy. When I introduced myself, her face lit up.

"My name is Maila," she said, her mouth stretching into a big toothless grin. Her eyes sparkled and I was taken by her charm as I shook her hand.

"Hello Maila," I said. I knew that name. I'd heard it before, but couldn't place where.

"Most people know me as Vampira," she said, and that's when I recognized her.

Vampira made broadcast history in 1955 as television's first horror movie hostess. I discovered her at R/F/B Public Relations when I found her in the pages of the *National Enquirer* after she sued Elvira, Mistress of the Dark, for "stealing her character." I was fascinated with Vampira's offbeat history and loved her in Ed Wood's 1956 cult classic *Plan 9 From Outer Space* with Bela Lugosi.

Coincidentally, Maila lived a stone's throw away in a rented hovel on Hudson Avenue. When I told her about Holly and the book proposal we were hoping to sell, Maila suggested that we all get together for dinner. I was delighted. So we made plans to meet at an Italian restaurant later that week on Vine Street just north of Melrose.

The restaurant was a small café, a cheap mom-and-pop joint decorated red and green, brightly lit by the large windows that overlooked the street. Holly and I showed up and found Maila sitting in a green vinyl booth with two old men, one of whom was my neighbor and the other a loud, flamboyant queen who wore rings on his fingers with big, colorful stones and a pair of oversized brown plastic eyeglasses that were held together by masking tape at the bridge.

Holly and I joined the party and squeezed into the booth. Maila gushed over Holly and told her how much of a fan she was, and Holly gushed over Maila and repeated the same compliments. The flattery struck me as contrived and I wondered if it was sincere or just polite conversation. Maila's friends entertained a brief interest in Holly, but then the loud bejeweled queen redirected the spotlight.

"Oh, honey, if only you knew *my* story!" he chuckled and then yapped up a storm about the fabulous times he had working on the stage in small Hollywood theaters. I wanted to hear more about Maila and her experiences with Orson Welles, James Dean, and Bela Lugosi . . . but she couldn't get a word in edgewise.

"Oh-ho-ho-ho! You should have seen us at the Goody Box Theatre. It was me, Reenie Sussman, Bootsy McNeal . . . Do you remember Bootsy?" the crackpot queen chortled. "Mary! She not only chewed up the scenery, she gnawed through the floor. Like a rabid Shih Tzu!"

He smacked his hand on the table, caused the dinnerware to clatter, and jolted us all into a state of high alert. His high-pitched giggle was so sharp it cut to the rafters.

"Oh, yay, honey! Yay for Bootsy!" Holly blurted.

Then the bejeweled queen burst into tears and bawled up a storm. His friends did their best to console him, and through his garbled sobs, I gleaned that Bootsy was tap dancing on the Hollywood Freeway overpass one night when she lost her balance and fell off.

"She was drunk!" he wailed. "But she died doing what she loved. Shaking her fat can for all the truckers!"

He grabbed a napkin and blew his nose so loud, I thought I was hearing the air horn of the diesel big rig that hailed Bootsy's final hurrah. I squirmed in my seat and felt trapped in that booth, like a kid stuck on a carnival ride that wouldn't stop spinning. So excited to get on . . . and simply horrified when it actually took off, with the ghosts of Hollywood's past leading the way.

I nodded, smiled politely and tried to make sense of all the laughter and tears that were shared. These folks were like clowns without a circus, and from the perspective of a judgmental self-absorbed twenty-six-year-old, they looked like broken-down has-beens. Beautiful and accomplished in their prime . . . only to be cast aside for a younger, prettier, more desirable generation. They seemed so misplaced to me now and it was so sad, so pathetic, and so horribly real. In that moment, the idea that they were a reflection of what I was to become was unbearable.

I was too young and too ignorant to understand that they were the lucky ones. They achieved their success. They made it! And despite the awful passage of time, the terrible ravages of age, and pop culture's ugly disregard, their salad days were rich, their memories golden and cherished. When the ride was over, the fun they experienced and the joy they shared was all that really mattered.

Fame was fleeting! Money dwindled! And so what if their youth and beauty were gone forever. It was their ebullience that remained, and it was bold and incandescent . . . and as bright and vivid as any theatre marquee on Hollywood Boulevard. They were the real winners! But it would take thirty years before I'd truly recognize that.

In 1989 at the age of twenty-six, I didn't understand the precocious brilliance of Maila Nurmi. I didn't know about Edward's work as a noted theatre director and his history with the great Tennessee Williams and *The Glass Menagerie*. The crackpot queen who dominated our conversation was probably just as important and interesting. But at the time, all I knew is that I hated being there in that booth, listening politely, watching laughing red-stained mouths swill cheap house wine and gobble wet spaghetti and dry meatballs drenched in a sloppy, runny sauce.

I listened to their stories and watched the sparkle in their eyes, but all I really wanted to do was escape. When the check came and Holly and I prepared to leave, I presented Vampira with an 8x10 photo that I'd protected in a manila envelope.

"Could you autograph this for me, please?"

A look of shock and disgust came over her face as if I'd asked her to perform in a Tijuana donkey show.

Then she smiled.

"Well, of course, dear," she said.

I didn't realize it at the time, but Vampira was used to being paid for her autograph. To think I had the nerve to push for a free one after an eight-dollar spaghetti dinner with shitty meatballs. No wonder she was insulted!

A striking photo of Vampira. She autographed it for me the night Holly and I met her for dinner. Judging from the signature, I think she was pissed. 1957.

"Darling, those people are crazy!" Holly said as we left the restaurant and walked to the Fiero, and I agreed.

"Do you really know who Vampira is?" I asked.

"Oh, sure," Holly said in a way that wasn't very convincing, so I just dropped it.

I got to know Vampira in a friendly neighborly way over the years. I'd run into her at Lizards coffeehouse and I'd give her rides to and from the grocery store. I always looked forward to visiting with her because she was so delightful, always smiling, and I loved her energy. She was so different from the frightening ghoul she portrayed in *Plan 9 From Outer Space*, an image that was reproduced on posters, greeting cards and T-shirts, an image that was overexposed and exploited by the pop culture machine that just ripped her off, over and over. So famous and yet so forgotten, particularly when it came to sharing in the profits.

Thanksgiving came and went that year with less turkey and more stuffing as we struggled to get by financially. Jean went out of town while Holly and I were invited to spend the holiday at our agent's home, where he staged a small gathering. We were excited because in a couple of weeks, Robert was presenting our book proposal at the booksellers' convention in New York. We'd waited eight long months for this milestone, and it was a big deal for us.

I had never been to Robert's place, and when Holly and I arrived, I was surprised and taken aback. Robert lived in the same building as The Lovely Carol. It was an old white stucco apartment house on the corner of Fountain and Stanley Avenues in Hollywood. I couldn't believe their apartments were only two doors apart and they shared the same porch! It was such an odd coincidence.

"Robert, do you know The Lovely Carol?" It was the first thing I asked when he greeted us at the door.

"Yeah, her name is Beverly," he said. "She's my neighbor."

"She's one of my good friends," I told him. "She's the one who invited me to the party where I first saw Holly."

Robert was just as astounded by the serendipitous circumstances that had played out between us. In that moment, the three of us coming together by mere happenstance seemed like it had been manipulated by a strange, ethereal force. I thought it was magical. As Beverly would say, it was kismet, and I believed it to be true.

The first week of December, Robert called to tell us he'd sent our book proposal to *Publishers Weekly*. It was a very smart and strategic move. On December 15, 1989, a columnist named Leonore Fleischer (an accomplished author in her own right) wrote a glowing review about the proposal that said, "If I had the money, I'd maybe buy it myself." When Robert faxed the article to my office so I could see it, I was amazed. It wasn't a blurb or a paragraph. It was an entire half-page! That kind of publicity was like a spark in a mess of dry brush. Suddenly, curiosity about the Holly Woodlawn story spread like wildfire on the NYC publishing scene.

A couple of days later, after Miss Francine greeted me with her usual morning groan, my office phone rang.

"Darling, are you sitting down?" It was Holly.

"What's going on?" I whispered, watching Miss Francine trudge into her office and drop her stuff onto her desk.

"We got our first offer," Holly said.

"What?" Goose pimples shot up my arms.

"Ten thousand dollars!" she howled.

Ten thousand dollars wasn't much, but for a first-time writer, it sounded like a million. Most importantly, it meant we had an offer on the table. I wanted to scream with happiness, but I had to keep my voice down and keep everything under wraps. I didn't want anyone to know I was moonlighting as a writer, especially Miss Francine. She wanted to be a writer herself. How would she feel if her lackey assistant suddenly got a publishing deal?

"Jeff, are you done with those insertion orders?" Miss Francine asked. Her voice was curt.

"I've got to go," I whispered into the phone and hung up. "One sec, Miss Francine. I'll bring them in."

I tried to concentrate on my menial typing tasks, but I was so happy I couldn't focus. At that moment, I wanted to be with Holly, crack open a bottle of champagne, and celebrate the good news that our hard work had finally paid off. But instead, I kowtowed to my boss like a dutiful employee.

"What's going on?" Miss Francine asked.

"Nothing," I replied. "Why?"

"You just seem to have a lot going on, that's all," she said.

"Oh."

For a second, I thought I should be honest with her, but people who are unhappy in their jobs generally don't want to see others succeed, so I refrained. When my office phone rang again, and Holly screamed with excitement that we'd gotten another bid (we were now up to $15,000) the excitement was almost unbearable. I nearly passed out.

"What's going on out there? Who's on the phone?" Miss Francine inquired.

"It's just Holly," I said, then whispered into the phone, "Holly, I have to call you back."

"Dieu!" Holly squealed and hung up. Dieu is a French word that means God. Holly said it with a Z and sang it out so it trailed: "Dzoooooooo!" It was one of her favorite expressions and she used it whenever she was excited.

"Is everything okay?" Miss Francine asked.

"Oh. Everything's great. Holly just got an audition."

"An audition? For what?"

"*The Golden Girls.*"

"*The Golden Girls*?!" Miss Francine lit up.

Jesus Christ. Of all the shows to mention, I had to pick the one that was Miss Francine's favorite.

"I know," I said. "Crazy, huh?"

I sat at my desk, staring at the IBM Selectric typewriter, and could not help but laugh. Holly Woodlawn's life story, which most people thought was a waste of my time, was now in a bidding war with New York publishers. A little while later, Holly called and screamed, "We're getting forty thousand dollars!"

St. Martin's Press was the highest bidder. Robert called to let me know our editor was going to be Michael Denneny, who was very important and well respected.

"You're in good hands," Robert said. I was overcome with a rush of excitement. Forcing myself to contain my emotions made me physically sick. I got dizzy and almost threw up. While Miss Francine was in the bathroom, I called my mother and told her the incredible news. She was elated.

"Jeffrey, you are going to be a published writer," she said. "No one will ever take that away from you. You can work at McDonald's and you'll still be a published writer!"

Upon Miss Francine's return, she wanted to know why I was spending so much time on the phone, so I quickly hung up on my mother.

"I'm still waiting for those insertion orders," she snapped.

"Almost done," I said.

I finished my paperwork and rushed it into her office.

"I've got good news," I said as I watched her correct my mistakes with a red pen. "Holly got the part!"

"That's great," Miss Francine said with feigned enthusiasm, then her smile went back to its natural frown.

"You really need to spend more time concentrating on your work," she said, handing me the papers. "Here, redo these."

CHAPTER 18

A $40,000 ADVANCE WAS THE BEST CHRISTMAS PRESENT of all, even though it didn't arrive until January 1990. At first, forty grand sounded like a lot of money. But when Robert explained how we would be paid in installments ($20,000 up front, $10,000 upon delivery of the manuscript, and the final $10,000 upon publication), I had a disappointing realization. After everyone took their cut, including Uncle Sam, and after I incurred the expense of a new computer, printer and supplies, there wasn't much left to live on. I had no choice but to doggedly write a whole book the same way I wrote the proposal, at night and on weekends, while I spent business hours chained to a desk job. Thank God for Lizards coffee!

On a crisp Saturday morning, I sat down at my makeshift desk to begin the process. My new Epson computer and printer rested on top of an old black dresser, and the keyboard sat on an old typing stand that stood in front of the dresser drawers. It wasn't a perfect arrangement, but I didn't have space to accommodate a real desk, so this Jimmy-rigged system had to suffice.

Today was a milestone. I was to write Chapter Two. Yay! I had no idea how to even begin. All I knew is that Holly and I were contractually obligated to deliver four hundred double-spaced typewritten pages, so each chapter had to run at least twenty pages to meet our quota. I reviewed Chapter Two's brief summary in our proposal and couldn't believe I had to spin that into twenty pages. So I just sat there, stumped, staring at the black screen and the flashing amber cursor.

OH, SHIT! I typed. NOW YOU HAVE TO WRITE 380 MORE PAGES.

Well, it sounded like a good way to begin Chapter Two to me. Holly, however, had other things on her mind when she banged on the wall a few hours later. I stuck my head out the window to see what she wanted.

"Honey!" she shouted. "Let's go shopping!"

I'd spent four hours working on Chapter Two and was ready for a break. Now that Holly had ten thousand dollars in the bank, she was ready to blow it, and made out an entire list of all the things she wanted. Our first stop was the paint store.

"Darling, those hideous white walls have got to go. I'm Holly Woodlawn! I need color!"

And color she got.

"Bright orange walls with chartreuse molding. How chic!" she declared.

It was certainly something. Then we hit a yard sale where she bought a vintage wire loop vanity with a matching stool.

"Oh, this is going to be so divine spray-painted gold! And I can re-cover the seat in hot pink taffeta. Dieu!"

God knows how we got that home because it wouldn't fit in the Fiero. Then we hightailed it to a bed store on Western Avenue, where Holly ordered a new twin bed that, when dressed with a variety of bright pink, yellow, and green pillows, could double as a lovely chaise.

Holly transformed her bland single apartment into something that was unique and festive.

"Honestly, honey, I've never seen such an ultra-mod riot!" she said.

The final touch was a plaster bust of Nefertiti that she found at a garage sale and spray-painted bright gold.

"A gold Nefer-titty. How did I ever live without one? Now all I need are clothes."

Our loot from St. Martin's Press hadn't been in the bank a week and already Miss Woodlawn was insisting we get makeovers.

"You're going to be a published author and I a published authoress. We can't wear rags," she said.

The following weekend, we revved up the Fiero and blazed a trail to the Los Angeles Fashion District, located downtown, a few blocks from Skid Row. The Fashion District looked anything but fashionable. It was dirty and rough. Hardworking people bustling, hustling, pushing, and shoving. Parking was hell. The shopping was endless. The bargains were insane.

Holly and her sweet neighbor, Betty Lynn (who lived across the hall), pose with the gold Nefertiti. Betty was a sweetheart. She was in her sixties when she left Oklahoma and moved to Hollywood to become a ballroom dancer. She was a delight and imbued the Las Palmas Apartments with beauty and grace. October 1989.

"Silk underwear, darling! That's just what you need!" Holly said excitedly as she added a pair of paisley print boxers to my pile.

Silk boxers, shirts, scarves, pantaloons, whatever—if it was 100% silk, Holly said we deserved it, and so we bought it.

Then we spun ourselves down the street to a men's outlet, where Holly found a navy blue pinstripe suit.

"Look at this suit, Jeffrey," she said, pulling it off the rack, holding it up on its hanger. "It's a classic! I've got to try it on."

Holly put on the suit and admired it in a full-length mirror.

"Oh, it's just fabulous," she beamed, turning this way and that to inspect it from all sides. "I can wear it as a man. I can wear it as a woman. I'll take it!"

Holly bought the suit and got a pair of black suede high-heel pumps to go with it. A few weeks later, I bought a child's violin case at the Goodwill and gave it to her.

"It's your new purse," I said. "Now all you need is a toy machine gun."

Her eyes lit up.

"I've always wanted to be a mob moll!" Holly laughed, then opened the case to inspect the inside. "Oh, I love it! I can fit all kinds of things in here. Cosmetics, dinner rolls, even silverware."

One thing I learned from Holly is that a person didn't have to spend a

Holly stands in front of her picture postcard view of Hollywood, modeling her new curtains. 1990.

fortune to look fabulous. Being fabulous was a state of mind, and if one had good taste, one could make the cheapest things look incredible. Holly proved this after I gave her a fifteen-foot strand of pearls that I bought for $3.99 in the Christmas tree department at K-Mart. When she put on her pinstripe suit without a shirt and wrapped the strand of pearls around her neck five times so it covered her bare chest, the effect was stunning.

"Look at that!" she said, admiring her reflection in the mirror. I was awestruck. She was beautiful. Holly laughed, "Rodeo Drive can kiss my twat. Who needs it? Just because a person has money doesn't mean they have style. Style comes from within, darling. I've always had style. Even when I was in prison."

Then she recalled the time she was in jail, right after she made the movie *Trash*, and how she and the other queens behind bars spit on magazine pages and rubbed the colored ink onto their cheeks and eyes.

"We didn't have makeup, honey. We had to make do with what we had, and we did, too."

"I need to put that in the book," I said, running next door to jot down the note.

Holly and I both experienced our share of hard times but had so much to look forward to now that we had a real book deal. While Holly dreamt her career would catapult her into the mainstream, I dreamt about buying an old house to restore.

"Look at this one," I said, handing Holly the listing sheet that showed a Southern antebellum mansion in Alabama for only eighty-nine thousand dollars.

"Oh, Jeffrey! One day, we'll be able to buy that cash. I'll be Scarlett O'Hara and you can be Truman Capootie."

We had wonderful visions of what our lives would be like after the book was published. The thought of sitting on the porch of a grand old plantation house, sipping a mint julep with Miss Holly, was sweet and idyllic. But it would take a lot more work and a lot more time before those fantasies would come to fruition.

A few days later, I went next door to Holly's orange apartment and brought her some pages to read.

"Chapter Two, hon. Hot off the press." I handed her a stack of papers. "I think you'll like it."

"I can't wait to read it," she said.

The sunlight pouring into her orange apartment made the walls seem brighter. The sky outside was blue and crystal-clear.

"By the way, darling," she said, "I have a little present for you."

She handed me a small wrapped box.

"What's this?"

"It's a little good luck charm," she said. "And a reminder of all the good things to come."

"Thank you, Holly," I said and stood there for a moment, just looking at the package because I felt awkward receiving a present and not having one to give in return.

"Well . . . go on, open it."

"You shouldn't have done this," I said, tearing off the paper to reveal a small white box. I lifted the lid and saw the precious token inside.

"Oh, Holly . . . It's beautiful."

Tucked in velvet was a blue Lalique angelfish. I brought it up to the light of the window and admired its deep cobalt color.

"That pretentious sales queen can kiss your ass, honey," Holly snickered. "You've got your own piece of Lalique now."

That angelfish cost Holly one hundred dollars. It was a sweet gift, but I wished she hadn't spent so much money. I was afraid to display it in my cramped bedroom because I worried I'd accidentally knock it over and break it. So I kept it safely hidden inside its box. Every now and then, I took it out, admired its beauty, and cherished its sentiment.

"...of all the good things to come."

It was around this time Holly got a wild hair to do something really good that could have a profound impact on her future. We were in her apartment chomping on Puerto Rican pork chops when Holly said, "Honey, I think I want to go to fashion school." She told me she was inspired by one of her co-workers at Wacko, who was attending the Fashion Institute of Design & Merchandising downtown.

"Holly, I think that's a wonderful idea."

"I love fashion, I love design, and I figure why not?"

"You should do it. Seriously, Holly. You'll be a great fashion designer."

That week, Holly went downtown and started the enrollment process. She had a few hoops to jump through, like getting her GED and figuring out her financial aid. But within a very short while, Holly was hopping the bus to downtown and attending FIDM daily while working at Wacko on the side. It was such a positive change in her life. Twenty-eight years after she'd dropped out of school, Holly Woodlawn was going back. I was so proud of her. I knew she would do well in fashion school because she'd be studying something she genuinely loved. I was also happy because I knew she was going to prove the naysayers wrong. Holly Woodlawn was not a mess. Her life was turning around now, and it was important that this book provide her with the means to a secure a sustainable future. Soon she would be a published author. In time, with her connections, she could have her own fashion line.

"I'll call it The House of Holly!" she said. "There's a queen in every woman, honey! And I'm bringing her out with lots of tulle, chiffon, sequins, and feathers."

And with that vision in mind, we hopped into the Pontiac Fiero and burned rubber all the way to Sears, where Holly bought a beautiful new sewing machine.

CHAPTER 19

"**O**H, THERE'S ESTELLE ON FIRE ISLAND!" HOLLY SAID and pointed to a funny young man mugging for the camera.

We watched old home movies that were projected on a dining room wall. In those flickering, scratched, sunlit images, I saw an era that was beautiful and golden. Our host, Peter Dallas, smiled and laughed as he watched the footage. He was exactly the type of man I wanted to look like when I was a little boy, strikingly handsome with strong, dark features that were highlighted by the projector's refracted light. I couldn't help but have a crush on him.

Peter lived on Sycamore Avenue in a fashionable Los Angeles enclave known as Hancock Park. He worked an office job at Warner Bros. and wrote screenplays on the side but didn't seem to have much success in selling them. Holly knew him from the old days in New York, back when he worked with Bette Midler on her cabaret act. In 1972, he directed Holly in a black-and-white silent film called *Broken Goddess*. We were writing a chapter about that movie, which was the reason for this visit. While Holly and Peter laughed at the frivolity preserved on celluloid, I took notes and longed to live in those carefree days before the trouble began.

I first heard about the deadly gay virus in 1984, when I was a junior in college. Back then, it was known as GRID [Gay-Related Immune Deficiency]. Rumors circulated that it was gay cancer caused by snorting poppers. Now it was 1990 and AIDS was a global crisis.

The heterosexual ideology that permeated television airwaves and brainwashed me as a child didn't prepare me for the gay culture in which I now lived. While I longed for a monogamous relationship because I thought it would keep me safe from AIDS, all the death seemed to fuel everyone's sex drive. In West Hollywood, a guy could get laid just by walking down the street, and the same was true for the beaches of Fire Island, where Holly and Peter

Peter Dallas exuding boyish charm during his early days in New York City. By the time I met him, he was clean-cut, polished, and just precious. 1974.
Courtesy of the Teresa Conboy PR Archives.

partied that one summer in 1974. While they reminisced and talked about all the friends they'd lost to the virus, I remembered my friend Bobby, who, like me, had also come to Hollywood with the dream of being a writer.

"I just got fucked in the Beverly Center parking structure," he casually mentioned one night before we went to the French Quarter restaurant.

Bobby was only twenty-four years old when we met. He had dark hair, an angular face with a long jaw, and a slight build. He was quite small—barely five feet tall—and had an eye-popping cock that he proudly displayed in blue bicycle shorts while working out at the gym. Oh, those boys with candy and how they loved to show it off.

"I hope you used a condom," I said after he told me about his sexual adventure.

Bobby rolled his eyes, and I was bothered by his reaction. I couldn't understand why he risked his life for an anonymous encounter between two parked cars. Now he was dead. Perhaps he knew he was dying. Perhaps his dream of being a writer didn't mean that much to him. For me, that dream was the only thing I had, and I couldn't bear the thought of an orgasm taking it away.

In the five years I'd lived in Los Angeles, the AIDS crisis had only gotten worse. Sex was dangerous, yet the prevailing motto was "Life is short. Get all you can!" But by now, I'd grown tired of feeling like a piece of chewed gum, tossed aside for another stick. I wanted a safe relationship with someone I could trust, but that seemed impossible to find in a culture where beauty was excessive and distractions were endless. I was as frustrated as a hungry diabetic in Candy Land, taunted by big-knobbed lollipops and all-day suckers. I was so afraid that one careless act would take me down and destroy my life, because by now, I learned that most of the guys I had dated were HIV-positive and many had died.

All of their deaths, including Bobby's, weighed heavily on me as I grappled with the gay psyche and tried to understand the total lack of regard some men had for their lives and each other. Perhaps it could be traced back to the self-hate inflicted upon us during our childhoods. No parent ever wanted a gay child in my world. We were the strange, bruised fruit of society, the outcasts who were damned to hell from the get-go. Perhaps those feelings of inferiority and inadequacy are what triggered the dangerous hedonistic animality that drove so many of us to the edge.

I was surprised that Holly, who had worked as a transgender prostitute in New York, first as a teenager and then later as an adult, never contracted the deadly virus.

"How is it you never got AIDS?" I asked her later.

"Darling! I never had sex with gay men. I'm a woman! They wanted nothing to do with me. And I always used condoms. Just because I was a hooker didn't mean I was an idiot. Back then, I didn't know anything about AIDS, but I sure as hell didn't want to get herpes. You have to be careful, hon."

To escape the horror and despair that was all around me, I immersed myself in the outrageous hilarity of Holly's story. I looked forward to working on it daily and always went to Lizards to sit with a strong cup of hot coffee and pages of rewrites. The surge of caffeine caused my brain to light up like fireworks and made Holly's lunacy all the more madcap. During these spellbinding, imaginative trances, I unwittingly ended every sentence I wrote with an exclamation point.

Sometimes at night when I tried to sleep, my body would be exhausted but my brain was still wired and popping with ideas. I kept a notebook by my sofa, which was where I slept, so I could write down those ideas and incorporate them into the story later. At times my mind was like an annoying, wound-up chatterbox, giving suggestions on how to improve a scene or spewing snappy one-liners. I'd get up, turn on the light, scribble notes, and then lie back down on my sofa. I'd lie there, trying to force myself to sleep, when another idea

"Oh, we're going to make the life of Marlene Garbo. Don't you think I'd be wonderful?" she'd put on her hand to her forehead, looking up to the sky. "Oh, I could be wonderful. I could be so sad. A part for me."

She changed from one pose to the next — like a collage of those portraits. She had one front tooth that was capped & it was always falling off! For photos she'd be minus a tooth! Meanwhile, we were sitting in my bedroom in Queens while Warhol was making these stupid, vulgar films. They were drug addicts + male hustlers — they were junk! Scum o lower East side. Seedy. Inhabited by the last of the immigrants, junkies + welfare recipients.

Holly's bedroom — Vogue Mag w/ Twiggy a cover — smoky cigarettes + drinking Coke, Harper Bazar — played Streisand records — Candy wears a full slip — Hair is fell cut when u fall out to my black — Holly wore panties + [strikethrough], + baby dolls — frilly little pieces of nylon + lace.

CANDY WAS A DEVOUT CHRISTIAN SCIENTIST + tried to convert Holly!   Harlow's mother was Christian Scientist.

Rambling notes about Candy Darling's missing tooth and Andy Warhol making movies with drug addicts and male hustlers. This was years before laptop computers were available, so I always wrote longhand when I was at Lizards. 1990.

announcer abruptly interrupted the song with shocking news. *1964 what a hideous year!*

President Kennedy had been assassinated.

A week later I was back in New York and enrolled in the

Hollywood School of Beauty. That was one horrible winter *to come wit* Libra

and I were huddled up in that little room on 38th Street and 8th

Avenue, trying to keep warm while a deranged latino drag queen

known as Miss Lopez down the hall was banging on the pipes,

Mira You cheep Peego.

screaming, "Turn on the gas!" *in half Spanish & English*

Miss Lopez was the craziest thing I had ever met up to this

time. He was a large, rotund character -- tall with big hips and

tight sweaters + bread from fat. with glasses that held by tape,

a flat ass who stomped around everywhere in house slippers. *And*

pointy hair.

he was big on causing scenes. One of his favorite means of self-

entertainment came by having these unexpected outbursts of sheer

insanity, jumping up and down, waving his arms in the air and

screaming, *Woooo! Wahoooh!* "Whook Whoo!" Those were the loudest, most

frightening whoo-whoo's I had ever heard! But nevertheless, it

didn't keep me from going to Times Square with her on New Year's

Eve and watching the ball fall! *- I figured I was safe in the mob. I be*

was with a crazy person.

I later learned that he was legally declared insane and was

receiving a lifetime supply of Welfare checks from the

government. Some people have all the luck.

+ like two cyclone fences

The apartment *on 38th* was too small and too cold so Libra and

I hightailed it to his mother's place in Brooklyn. It was a nice *neither warm-!*

place, a two bedroom railroad flat in a *in brooklyn* nice neighborhood. *inidgewood section*

Libra's mother was a colorful woman of Irish descent. ~~who spoke~~

~~with a strong brogue. And boy, did she like to drink. If it~~

~~was liquor, she drank it.~~ She was another big woman -- my God!

Holly was left-handed and always wrote her notes in pencil. These are her handwritten notes about the assassination of JFK. "It was as if everything became very still. Sort of like the eye of a hurricane. Everything was so quiet! There wasn't a sound anywhere except the TV telling us the details." 1990.

would dance through my mind. Up I got, turned on the light, jotted down more notes, turned off the light, fell back onto the sofa, tried to sleep again only to have the same pattern repeat itself a few minutes later.

Holly also experienced late-night surges of creativity. Sometimes she knocked lightly on the wall and say, "Hey hon, are you awake?"

"Well . . . I guess I am now."

Then we'd make a pre-dawn trek to the Yum Yum donut shop on Highland to grab some coffee to fuel an impromptu writing session, where we'd discuss a chapter she was reviewing. Holly often had corrections about descriptive details I'd imagined. I loved these spur-of-the-moment get togethers, even though they left me tired and bleary-eyed later that morning, when I was sluggish in my attempt to service Miss Francine's paper-shuffling needs.

I was very happy when I was working on Holly's story. To stay on track with our deadline, I always began a new chapter on Saturday morning and by early Sunday evening, I would deliver a draft to Holly. Weeknights were spent working with her on revisions and then writing a final polish. It was a good routine. But every now and then, I'd have a bout of writer's block and I'd sit at that computer and just stew in frustration. On those occasions, writing was nothing more than a pain in the ass.

One Saturday afternoon, as I tussled with a paragraph, my concentration was broken by a soft, irritating knock at the door. I ignored the knock. I was too busy slaying the dragon that had fucked up my sentence structure.

There was another soft knock at the door, so soft it grated and caused my hairs to stand on end. And then I heard a tiny, muffled cartoon voice.

"Jeff. Hello, Jeff."

It was Jean trying to humor me with a knock-knock joke, but it felt like she was poking me with a stick.

"Jean, I'm writing!" I snapped.

Then suddenly, the door cracked open and the gray head of Booter the cat popped in. Jean held Booter and waved its paw at me.

"Boo wants to say hi," she said. "Hi, Jeff!"

I'm rather disgruntled when I'm writing under pressure . . . especially when I'm super horny and afraid to get laid.

"Fuck Boo!" I yelled. "I'm trying to wriiiiiiite!"

I snatched that cat out of Jean's arms and threw it out the window. Jean screamed with horror! So I grabbed her by the ears and threw her out the window, too, followed by a computer chaser.

Well, there was nothing like good old-fashioned violence to jump-start the imagination and loosen the blockage that had gummed up my creative gears.

"Jean, I'm trying to work," I yelled.

Jean pushed open the door. I hadn't thrown her out the window after all, and that damn bug-eyed cat was still in her arms. But boy, what a fantasy!

"Jeff, you've been holed up in this dark room all day and I just want to make sure you're okay."

"I'm okay, Jean."

A writer who can't write is never okay. Jean had never seen this side of me before and I felt bad for yelling at her.

"Do you need anything?" she asked.

"No," I said. "I just need to write. I'll be fine."

Jean and I were living in two different worlds now. She didn't understand the pressure of having to crank out page after page, even when I didn't feel up to it. Nor did she experience the same fear and frustration I had about sex. She didn't know what it was like to have a crush on a guy and in the middle of the date, have him deliver the heart-wrenching news, "Oh, by the way, I'm HIV-positive." From my perspective, her heterosexual life was fun and carefree, or so it seemed. What I didn't know is that Jean was experiencing a different kind of pressure. She was thirty-two years old. She wanted a husband and a home. She didn't want to spend her life hustling for auditions, waiting to get a part. She yearned for a more fulfilling role. But curiously, finding a nice guy to date in the City of Angels was just as hard for her as it was for me.

So that day, while Jean left to go play softball with a singles group and Holly worked at Wacko, I stayed inside my bedroom and banged out ten pages that sort of made sense.

Later that afternoon, I printed those pages and walked to Lizards to clear my head. I needed some fresh ideas and new inspiration. Maybe I'd run into my friend Keith and catch up on the latest gossip. Or better yet, maybe I'd see handsome Ron-Jon, the beautiful young bodybuilder whose piercing blue eyes were always focused on a book.

When I walked into Lizards, John and Clinton were sitting around a table with a few of the regulars, and everyone looked solemn. When I asked what was wrong, John told me Ron-Jon had died that morning of pneumocystis pneumonia, an AIDS-related infection also known as PCP.

"He went into the hospital a few days ago," John said. "He was twenty-one years old."

There was no escaping the AIDS nightmare. It lurked in the background like a macabre organ grinder who cranked an eerie, dreadful tune that was ubiquitous and unremitting. On this day that song was loud and jarring, other times it was soft and barely noticeable. But regardless of its tone, it was always there, a weirdly ominous melody, that played and taunted while the grim reaper's monkey danced and tipped his hat.

A few weeks later, Holly got the news that her good friend Peter Dallas was sick and had slipped into a coma. Within a week, he was dead from AIDS-related brain cancer. Holly was terribly upset. She had lost most of her friends in New York. Now the funerals began in Los Angeles. I accompanied her to Peter's wake, which was held at Forest Lawn Hollywood Hills, not far from the Warner Bros. lot where he worked. The casket was closed. It was dark gray with silver metal handles and looked like it was made of cardboard. I'd never seen such a strange-looking casket and I couldn't believe that Peter's body was lying inside. Just the thought made me feel sick and uncomfortable.

Holly and I sat toward the back of the chapel. We did not engage with the other people who were there. No memories were shared or condolences exchanged. Holly grieved in silence, dressed in her dark suit with her eyes hidden behind plain modest sunglasses and her hair pulled back. This was not a time for glamour or vanity. It was not a time to look fabulous wearing Christmas tree pearls and black velvet pumps. It was a time for reverence and respect, which Holly showed with great class.

This Silence=Death poster from 1987 was created by activists to spread the word about AIDS. The triangle in the center is pink. It's the same symbol used by the Nazis, when persecuting homosexuals in the '30s and '40s. All homosexuals in concentration camps wore a pink triangle emblem on their uniforms.

Courtesy of Avram Finkelstein, Brian Howard, Oliver Johnston, Charles Kreloff, Chris Lione, Jorge Socarrás, and The ACT UP Foundation.

A group portrait of Andy Warhol's "girlettes" (a.k.a. transgender superstars), whom Lou Reed sang about in "Walk on the Wild Side." Jackie Curtis (top), Candy Darling (right), and Holly Woodlawn (bottom).

Photo by Jarry Lang, courtesy of the Jarry Lang Estate.

Holly Woodlawn: The Ultimate Superstar... or so I wanted to believe.
This portrait thrills me every time I see it because it's haunting,
mysterious, and stunning.

Photo by Jarry Lang, courtesy of the Jarry Lang Estate.

One of my favorite portraits of Holly. She's rocking the K-Mart
Christmas tree pearls that I gave her, and her wig looks great.

Photo by Peter Palladino, courtesy of the Peter Palladino Archive.

Holly in later years. By now the illusion was starting to fray and the reality of her decline was just awful.

Photo by Greg Gorman, courtesy of the Greg Gorman Archive.

All dolled up like a 1940s movie queen, looking forward to the day she'd attend her own glorious Hollywood premiere.

Photo by Greg Gorman, courtesy of the Greg Gorman Archive.

Miss Woodlawn, tarted up in her new "Delta Burke" wig, which
looked great... until she made the mistake of washing it.

Photo by Greg Gorman, courtesy of the Greg Gorman Archive.

Holly in later years, flashing a wad of cash she should have given to Miss Teresa Conboy to help pay for some of the debt she incurred while managing her. With the divine Udo Kier, star of *Andy Warhol's Frankenstein*.

Photo by Greg Gorman, courtesy of the Greg Gorman Archive.

A rare and wonderful portrait of Holly that made me gasp the first time I saw it in 2023. The saturated color is so rich and so fa-ha-habulous!

Photo by Peter Palladino, courtesy of the Peter Palladino Archive.

Holly came from Miami, F-L-A and took New York City by storm as one of Andy Warhol's greatest superstars. Circa 1970.

Photo by Laura Rubin

HOWARD HUGHES
presents
REPUBLIC PICTURES Presents
PHIL REGAN
LEO CARRILLO
ANN DVORAK
TAMARA GEVA
JAMES GLEASON
featuring
TED LEWIS AND HIS ORCHESTRA
CAB CALLOWAY AND HIS COTTON CLUB ORCHESTRA
KAY THOMPSON AND HER ENSEMBLE
JOE DiMAGGIO
HENRY ARMETTA
LUIS ALBERNI
MAX TERHUNE
SMILEY BURNETTE
LOUIS PRIMA AND HIS BAND
and introducing that singing western star
GENE AUTRY
MANHATTAN MERRY-GO-ROUND
A REPUBLIC PICTURE
A REPUBLIC PICTURE
A THREE RING THRILLER OF THE AIR
THE AIR CIRCUS
COCK of the AIR
with
Chester Morris
DIRECTED BY TOM BUCKINGHAM
PRODUCED BY HOWARD HUGHES

CHAPTER 20

"**Y**OU LIKE BIG HAIR! VERY BEAUTIFUL," SAID A small Chinese saleswoman in the Wigs Galore shop on Hollywood Boulevard, who didn't seem to mind that Holly was an unusual-looking man shopping for a woman's bouffant.

"I love it!" Holly said. "I'm calling this my Delta Burke wig."

"Fifty dollar. Good deal," said the saleswoman. "You take!"

A gorgeous haystack hairdo that Holly could plop on her head at a moment's notice without any fuss seemed like a prudent investment.

When "Holly Woodlawn - Superstar" made a public appearance, the wig was a necessary part of the illusion. It was the pièce de résistance and so much more attractive than Holly's natural hair. The wig was fuller, it had more body, and it was styled. Without the wig, Holly had a beautiful movie star face and the hair of a scarecrow.

Holly bought the new wig for a photo shoot with a well-known photographer named Greg Gorman, who was famous for his celebrity portraiture. Somehow Greg learned that Holly was in Los Angeles working on her memoir and he reached out to her. This was a big deal for Holly. Greg Gorman didn't photograph just anybody, so this was quite an honor. The shoot took place in the evening on Santa Monica Boulevard outside the tawdry Pussycat Theatre where XXX-rated films were shown. I was very excited about Holly working with Gorman. He shot a well-known advertising campaign for a Los Angeles-based eyeglass company on Melrose called l.a.Eyeworks, and I hoped Holly's collaboration with him would lead to Holly being featured in a future ad. It was an exciting possibility because if that happened, the publicity would be fantastic.

One glorious Saturday morning, I knocked on the wall to see if Holly would like to grab coffee at Lizards and review some pages I'd been working on.

"Come on over, honey," she said. "The door's open."

When I entered her apartment, I found Holly sitting at her kitchen table, bent over with her head down while a nineteen-year-old gay queen feverishly stitched something to her scalp.

"Good morning, darling!" Holly sang. "Guess what I'm doing?"

"I have no idea," I said, almost afraid to ask.

"I'm getting hair extensions! They're going to be fabulous."

I spotted the tray of golden-brown tresses the kid was working with, and I wasn't so sure.

"I'll be able to wash them like my own hair. So much easier to manage than that polyester wig."

Really? The wig sat in the closet on a Styrofoam head form. How much easier could it get? But Holly had been convinced the extensions were a better idea.

"I'm getting a great deal, too, because Javier here is in beauty school, and he's giving me the beauty school discount. Only three hundred dollars!"

"You're kidding," was the only thing I could think to say, particularly after learning she'd met this beauty school enrollee at Wacko.

Good hair extensions and weaves weren't cheap; they easily cost over a thousand dollars. What did Holly think she was going to get woven into her head for only three hundred bucks?

Later that day, when Holly and I got together to work, Holly's new hair extensions didn't look any better than her own hair. In fact, it just looked like she had more of her own hair and ten cowlicks. As we reviewed pages, Holly scratched at her head. It soon became clear this bargain beauty binge yielded nothing more than an itchy mess of tangles and knots. Later that night, when Holly tried to sleep, the hair knots irritated her.

"I can't stand these things!" is how she put it the next day. As she picked, poked, and scratched at them, one by one they started to fall out, and I would find them, these knots of golden-brown hair, on the floor of her apartment, in the elevator, and in the lobby of our building. I even spotted a few in the liquor aisle at the supermarket. Within a week, Holly had ripped what was left out of her head and threw them into the trash.

My ball and chain: a 1986 Pontiac Fiero. Holly was so blinded by its flash, she once mistook it for a Ferrari. After its hubcaps were stolen, that car suffered one awful indignation after another. But despite the abuse, it just kept running.
Photo by Ed Evans.

"What a disaster!" Holly exclaimed. "I never want to see another extension for as long as I live."

Life with Miss Woodlawn was at times a comedy of errors . . . but not all of those errors were funny. Such was the case one afternoon when Holly and I were on our way to the grocery store to see our favorite checker, Miss Melons. We got into my Fiero and the edge of the passenger side door got caught in the parkway turf adjacent to the curb. Holly yanked at the door to close it, but it didn't budge.

"Honey, hold on. Let's get out—," I began to say as Holly yanked the fiberglass car door with all her might. Suddenly, there was a loud horrible CRACK! as the car door slammed shut.

"What was that?" I blurted, overcome with a sense of dread. Holly shot me a sheepish look. We stared at each other in stunned silence.

I got out of the Fiero and walked around to the passenger side. My jaw dropped. The car I was still struggling to pay for now had a huge chunk ripped out of the passenger side door.

"Oh, my God!" I cried out, staring at the gaping hole. Holly got out of the car. She was horrified.

"Oh, hon, I'm sorry."

Holly felt terrible. With a $500 deductible on my auto insurance, I felt even worse. But I wasn't going to spend $500 to have it fixed. What was the point? I certainly wasn't going to hit Holly up for the cash. She had enough expenses now that she was enrolled in fashion school.

"Honey, who cares," I said. "It's just a car."

"Jeffrey, when the book gets made into a movie, you'll get a new one," Holly said.

"I'm not going to worry about it."

Driving a less-than-perfect car didn't bother me like it did when I first moved to Los Angeles. I just didn't care what people thought anymore. I was writing a crazy story that I loved and I was enjoying my time with Holly. That's really all that mattered.

In March, I mailed finished chapters to our editor, Michael Denneny, to get his feedback. We were on pins and needles waiting for his response.

"Keep 'em coming," he said.

He seemed happy with our work, and I was so relieved because I didn't know what I was doing. I was just doing it, following my creative intuition, forging ahead. The greatest challenge was Holly's memory, which at times just sputtered and gave out entirely.

"But what happened in the back room of Max's Kansas City?" I pressed one night in Lizards coffeehouse. Max's Kansas City was the famous hangout where all the Warhol superstars partied, and I was writing an entire chapter about those uproarious times.

"Darling, I told you. We were all drunk and carrying on," she said.

"Yeah, and that's great. But I need to take that one line, 'drunk and carrying on,' and turn it into twenty pages with a beginning, middle and end. So who were you carrying on with? What was going on?"

"Well, darling..." she said, pondering her thoughts. She sipped her coffee, sat back in the chair, thought for a moment and laughed. "How the hell do I know? That was thirty years ago. I was bombed out of my mind!"

"Holly, I need more information or this chapter is going to read like a first-grade primer. 'See Holly go. Go, Holly, go.'"

"Honey, I was the fastest go-go girl anyone had ever seen!" Holly laughed. "Shoot me full of speed and I'd go all night."

Oh, that Miss Woodlawn was always up to something . . . but I just needed more richness, more color, more texture . . . and more juice. Suddenly, Holly perked up, and her eyes flashed with memory.

"Truman Capote came up to me one night and said I had the face of the seventies! And Jane Fonda, she was there! Her and Roger Vadim," she said.

"What were they doing?"

"Oh, you know Jane," Holly chuckled, and I could see her flash of memory dim. "Always causing a ruckus. Just carrying on, honey! Carrying on like the rest of us."

While Holly did remember a lot, there were some things she couldn't remember at all. And to connect those dots, we planned a trip to New York City in April 1990 so I could interview some of Holly's old friends and Warhol colleagues. It would also give us the opportunity to meet our editor, Michael Denneny, which we were both very excited about.

This trip would be an important milestone for me as I'd never been able to afford a trip to the Big Apple before. And while this trip was expensive, we got a huge discount on our hotel accommodations, thanks to my employer's travel division. Holly didn't have a suitcase big enough to hold everything she wanted to bring, so a day before we left town, our agent Robert lent her a nondescript black one that was large enough to hold all her clothes, makeup, wigs, high heels, and a few headdresses, just in case.

For whatever reason, on the day we boarded our United Airlines flight that was bound for Newark, Holly was in a foul mood. Perhaps it was the stress of getting packed and going to LAX at the crack of dawn. Regardless, with her man-do pulled back and hiding behind dark, Greta Garbo leave-me-the-fuck-alone sunglasses, I could tell she was irritable.

Since we were tight on cash, I smuggled aboard two mini bottles of vodka in my pants pocket. When the stewardess, who had just served me a cup of orange juice from the drink cart, noticed that I was going to spike it with my own liquor, she got angry.

"You can get arrested for that," she said.

I had no idea it was illegal for passengers to open their own liquor on board an aircraft. According to the stewardess, I had violated federal regulations. Only liquor provided by the crew could be opened during the flight. I was embarrassed and apologized. Holly reacted to the stewardess' tone of voice.

"Honey, he didn't know," Holly snapped. "We're sorry."

Holly's short angered tone was one that I came to know all too well. She was disgruntled and crabby, and this was not the way I wanted to start a six-hour flight to New Jersey, particularly since we still had five and a half hours to go. This situation would take some sly manipulation to improve, so I called the stewardess over moments later, and I apologized again.

"I'm really sorry about that," I said. "We're just so excited because, well,

The most fun I'd ever had on an airplane, drunk and carrying on, and posing for photos with the crew. The other passengers must have thought we were nuts! April 1990.

this is my friend Holly Woodlawn, and she's an Andy Warhol superstar, and we're on our way to New York because we just got a publishing deal to write Holly's life story."

With the spotlight now shining brightly on Holly, her mood changed for the better.

"You're writing your life story?" the stewardess asked Holly, genuinely impressed.

"Oh, yes, honey!" Holly squealed with excitement. "We got a book deal with St. Martin's Press and we're jetting off to meet our editor. Dieu!!"

The stewardess leaned in with interest.

"What's your name again?" she asked.

"Holly Woodlawn."

"Holly was the inspiration for the Lou Reed song 'Walk on the Wild Side,'" I said.

"You remember, honey," Holly chirped. "'Holly came from Miami, F-L-A,' and how I hitched my way across the U.S.A. Plucked my eyebrows and carried on with those colored girls do-do-doing. That was me, darling!"

"But her name actually came from the Holly Golightly character in the story, Breakfast at Tiffany's," I interjected.

"Oh, I love that movie," the stewardess said, covering her mouth in awe.

Truman Capote's inspiration for *Breakfast At Tiffany's*, Miss Holly Golightly (or so they thought!) poses with her fans. April 1990.

"Oh, wasn't Audrey Hepburn fabulous?" Holly said, and suddenly the two were chatting like old girlfriends, reminiscing about their favorite parts in the movie, culminating with Holly whistling for a cab.

"I've always wanted to whistle like that!" the stewardess said, then fondly reached for Holly's hand. "I have to run up front, but it was so nice to meet you."

Within a few minutes, the starstruck stewardess came back with several other members of the flight crew.

"This is Holly Golightly!" she said. "She inspired Truman Capote to write *Breakfast at Tiffany's!*"

The crew fawned over Holly and presented her with a free chilled bottle of chardonnay and two real wine glasses from first class. While they might have gotten their facts crossed, they got the wine right, and that's all that mattered. Once we finished that bottle, another one came, and then another. We laughed and carried on like drunken, bombastic lunatics, and the flight crew was so enamored with Holly that they invited us into their galley where we posed for photographs.

By the time our plane landed in Newark, New Jersey, Holly and I had laughed ourselves into a stupor like two pie-eyed hyenas. We bid the crew farewell, never to see them again. But I will always cherish the photos I took of them on that wacky, all-you-can-drink flight.

When Holly and I staggered into baggage claim, we were both bleary-eyed and exhausted. We grabbed our suitcases as soon as they appeared on the carousel, and then Holly taught me how to hail a cab, and she did it with a loud whistle, just like Holly Golightly. When the cab pulled up, Holly warned we had to watch out for shyster taxi drivers.

"You have to always look and make sure the cab has a number on the windshield, so you know it's an official taxi. Otherwise, we could be kidnapped, robbed, and held for ransom."

Holly pointed out the number so I could see where it was, then we got into the car.

"Where to?" the crusty old driver grumbled.

"The Hotel Dorset on West 54th Street," I said, prompting the driver to take off like a bat out of hell. The cab ride to New York City was more like a white-knuckle thrill ride that made me queasy. By the time we got to the hotel, I wanted to throw up, and nearly did when I saw the fare.

"Forty dollars?! Are you kidding me?" I was wrecked.

Forty dollars to go from the airport to our hotel was crazy. I couldn't believe we had spent that much money to avoid being screwed by a shyster.

"Jeffrey, don't worry about the money," Holly said. "Let's just check in."

I worried about money because I only had $300 cash on me, and I just blew $40 of it on Mr. Toad's Wild Ride. But that was the least of our worries. When we approached the front desk and the clerk asked me for a credit card, I was thrown for a loop.

"But my hotel room has been prepaid in advance by my employer," I explained.

"Yes, but we still need a credit card on file for incidentals."

"But I don't have a credit card," I said. Neither did Holly.

"But you need one in order to check in," the desk clerk replied.

"What do we do?" I asked. "We just got off a plane from Los Angeles. No one told me I needed a credit card to check in. This is horrible."

The desk clerk looked over his reading glasses and stared at me in a way that told me he was not in the mood for this stupidity.

"We have to check in," I insisted with a hint of panic in my voice. "We don't have anywhere else to go."

"Get back to the turnip patch, doofus!" That's what he could have said. But instead, he was more kind.

"One moment," he sighed. "I'll speak with the manager."

After a few minutes, the desk clerk came back and explained that in lieu of a credit card, we could make a $300 cash deposit. I only had $260 on me and Holly was broke! So we ran to a nearby bank, withdrew as much loot as we could from my savings, and ran back to the Hotel Dorset, where the desk clerk FINALLY let us check in. As my dear friend Jean would say, "Jesus! Mary! And Joseph!" Who knew our New York arrival would be so problematic? The only bright side to this fiasco was that it was all a tax write-off, which I reminded myself as Holly and I made our way to our tiny room with two beds that we agreed to share to cut back on expenses.

"All I want to do is take a hot shower and go to bed," Holly groaned as she hoisted her suitcase onto the bed and opened it. She stood there, dazed, staring at the contents.

"What's wrong?" I asked.

I walked around to the other side of the bed and looked inside the suitcase.

"Some asshole stole my shoes," Holly barked. Indeed, her black high-heel pumps were missing. In their place was a pair of black businessman's oxfords.

"I can't wear these with a dress," Holly frowned, picking up the stodgy oxfords and examining them closely. "I wouldn't even wear them with my suit. Darling . . . where is my suit?"

Holly rifled through the suitcase.

"Where's my wig?" she demanded.

A $40 chill ran up my spine.

"Oh, no," I said and wanted to cry. "Oh, no, Holly. Oh, shit! Holly, you got the wrong suitcase."

In our pie-eyed state, we didn't know one black suitcase from another, and we forgot to check the name tag. We were so stupid, in fact, that we spent $40 to take a cab back to New Jersey to exchange the suitcase and another $40 on a cab back to our hotel. Our first night in Manhattan was a debacle! We spent $120 on cab fare and didn't get anywhere.

CHAPTER 21

T HE NEXT MORNING I LOOKED OUT OUR HOTEL window and watched the bustling street scene below. I was already showered and dressed, waiting for Holly to come out of the bathroom. I lifted the window's sash to let in some fresh air, but it only went up six inches. After smelling the exhaust fumes wafting up from the street below, I decided six inches was all I could take and pushed it closed.

"Honey, I'll be ready in a minute," Holly said as she opened the door and smeared her face with moisturizer.

"Holly, do we have to ride the subway?" I asked.

I had a phobia of the New York subway system because I'd heard all sorts of horrifying tales about how people were beaten, robbed, stabbed, and even pushed onto the tracks. In my mind, the subway was nothing more than an invitation to hell, and I was afraid we'd get lost, wind up in some godforsaken neighborhood, and get mugged by hooligans with pantyhose pulled over their heads.

Mugged! Just the thought of it made my skin crawl. I'd heard all about New York muggings on TV when I was a little boy, and back then, I thought it was like getting beat over the head with a large coffee cup. In my small Missouri town, we didn't have that kind of crime. The worst thing I'd ever

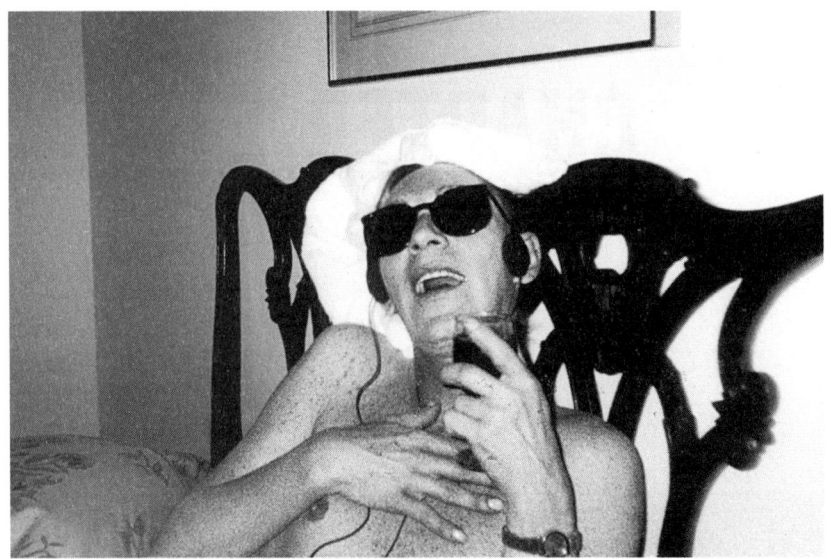
Holly, wearing headphones, relaxes in our hotel room at the Hotel Dorset in midtown Manhattan after we blew most of our money on cab fare. April 1990.

experienced was getting yanked off the monkey bars and having dirt rubbed in my face. Or getting jumped by masked punks who stole all my Halloween candy. Then there was the time a friend and I were ambushed by a mean, nasty ten-year-old thug named Rosie, who pushed us off our bikes, grabbed my friend by the hair, slashed his bicycle seat with a knife, and lit it on fire.

Well, holy shit! I'd been mugged more times than most New Yorkers by the time I was twelve . . . and I didn't even know it. Despite this revelation, I still refused to ride the New York subways because I was certain that experience would only end in disaster. Besides, we'd already been robbed by cab drivers. We couldn't afford to be robbed by derelicts.

"I don't want to take the subway, Hol," I said.

"That's fine with me, hon. I can't stand the subways."

Within minutes, Holly was dressed in a blue silk shirt, shorts, and sneakers. Her hair was combed back away from her face, and she looked more like an androgynous man than a glamorous Warhol superstar.

"I'm your Auntie Holly, darling. I'm going to show you things in New York you've never imagined!"

And she did. Visiting this city was a treat beyond my wildest dreams, and to experience it for the first time with Holly Woodlawn was nothing short of fascinating.

"Whatever you do, hon, don't look up," Holly said as we walked down the street and I looked up at the soaring height of the skyscrapers. "All the tourists look up and get distracted, and that's how they get mugged. New Yorkers don't look up. They stay focused. They've got places to go, people to see. Just like us, honey. We're going places."

The first place we went was a donut cart on W. 57th Street. We bought coffees and donuts, then we walked around the corner to Tiffany's on 5th Avenue so we could literally have breakfast there. Afterward, we wandered the city and journeyed into Holly's colorful past. We visited Bryant Park, where Holly used to sleep when she was a homeless teen, explored the West Village, visited the street corner where she met and befriended the legendary Candy Darling, saw Sheridan Square, and walked by the historic Stonewall bar where gay liberation was born. Holly also showed me the locations of Andy Warhol's Factory and Max's Kansas City.

That night, with flickering bulbs and glowing neon dancing in our eyes, we explored Times Square. The song "Good Life" by Inner City blasted on a boom box while street kids gyrated to its techno beat. Theatre marquees boasted live nudie revues and sleazy peep shows, and I was captivated by every sordid and vivid triple-X detail.

"Oh my God," I said, feeling a bit uncomfortable with the overt carnality that was thrust into the open for everyone to see. It was the most despicable display of lust and perversion I'd ever experienced, and I was visibly appalled and secretly titillated.

"Holly, this is outrageous!"

"Darling, outrageous is putting it mildly. But this is where my New York adventure began, hon. Right here in 1962. Holly hitchhiked her way across the U.S.A. and got dumped off in this shithole. The nerve of that truck driver!"

Holly laughed and I cringed as we walked by the questionable characters who lurked on the streets, wallowed in the gutters, and receded into the darkened doorways.

"Whatchyou want, whatchyou need," asked an old ruffian as we walked past him on the sidewalk. "Crack, cocaine, hey-rone," he offered.

"Darling, ignore the drug dealers," Holly said, grabbing my arm and pulling me close to her. "Just keep walking and stay focused."

"Hey, bro! Hey!" A disheveled vagrant called to me as we approached. He was dressed in rags and sat on the curb with his dirty hand extended. "Bro, can you help me out?"

I remained silent and felt ashamed for ignoring his plight.

"Let's grab a cab and get out of here," Holly said as she put two fingers in her mouth and blew an ear-piercing whistle that was so loud it startled the hooligans. I tried to whistle like that myself and only blew hot air.

"How do you do that?" I asked as a cab suddenly pulled in front of us and Holly opened the door.

"I just do," she said as we got into the taxi and sped off into the night.

In 1990, New York's Times Square looked hard and brutal, and I could only imagine what it was like for a runaway child. For Holly to wind up in that merciless and depraved jungle

Holly and her good friend, Lenny Dean, chat about their illustrious past. In the '70s at night, Lenny worked with Holly as an actor on stage and an MC in her cabaret act. During the day, he played Holly's guy Friday, screening and scheduling her appointments when she was an upscale Park Avenue call girl.

at the age of fifteen with no money . . . it would have been every kid's worst nightmare. But Holly made the best of it. I had already written a chapter about the struggles Holly endured as a kid living on the streets. I knew how she survived. But to be on that street and experience the grit, grime, and desperation for myself was a bit unnerving. No amount of flashing neon could make that dismal reality any better.

The next morning at 10 a.m., we arrived at the home of Paul Morrissey, the filmmaker who directed Holly in the movie *Trash*. It looked like Paul Morrissey had done quite well for himself because he had a grand living room with high ceilings and beautiful crown molding.

Paul told us how he first discovered Holly by reading an interview she did for an underground newspaper called *Gay Power*, wherein she falsely claimed she was an Andy Warhol superstar. Paul thought she was nervy and funny and had a hunch she would be good on film.

"Holly was always totally natural and spontaneous," he said, then explained how George Cukor petitioned the Academy of Motion Picture Arts and Sciences to nominate Holly for an Oscar. Paul also confirmed

Hanging out in a pub with Harry Koutoukas, Holly, and Lenny Dean. Harry (a.k.a. H.M. Koutoukas) was a fascinating New York-based playwright whose absurdist work helped create the Off-Off-Broadway theatre movement in the 1960s and '70s. April 1990.

interesting details about Warhol superstars Candy Darling, Jackie Curtis, and Andrea "Whips" Feldman.

"Andrea used to run around saying she was married to Andy," said Holly.

Paul agreed. "She said she was married to Andy, or she was Andy, or she was his sister. And then she thought she looked like Andy. She was genuinely comical."

We spent an hour chatting with Paul, then we hopped into a cab and ricocheted throughout Manhattan like two manic pinballs, meeting one cohort after another while I jotted notes and tape-recorded what I found to be interesting and useful.

One of the best interviews was with a man named Philip Locascio, who had managed Max's Kansas City. Holly and I took him to lunch in the West Village, and Philip shared many wonderful memories, like the time Holly was invited to have dinner with Federico Fellini. Fellini was one of the most famous and revered film directors in the world.

"What?!" I said, then turned to Holly and asked, "Do you remember Fellini?"

"No," Holly replied.

"He was very quiet," Philip continued. "He invited Holly over to the table. And he was with an actor named Hiram Keller. It was when he was taking

Taylor Mead, Warhol Superstar and poet, poses with Lenny Dean and Holly. I believe we're at a cocktail benefit event for the La MaMa Theatre. April 1990.

Hiram Keller out of *Hair* to cast him in *Satyricon*. I wasn't at the dinner table, you know, so I don't know what the conversation was. But I remember one thing. Andrea Whips came over and sat down at the table. And I'll never forget the look on your face. Andrea took her shoes off, put them on the table, and then opened up her purse, took out those liquid Crayolas, and she proceeded to color her entire face."

Philip's memories were rich and colorful. He told stories about Holly's adventures with Marty Balin (co-founder, Jefferson Airplane) and Jim Morrison (lead singer, The Doors), he remembered Jackie Curtis setting up a chemistry set to make her own methamphetamine, and he remembered details about Holly's act at Reno Sweeney, a popular Greenwich Village cabaret.

According to Philip, Holly's show at Reno's attracted some of the most fascinating entertainers in the world, including Ethel Merman, Leonard Bernstein, Liza Minnelli, Lauren Bacall, Lou Reed, David Bowie, and Mick Jagger.

"I'll never forget Mick Jagger and David Bowie," Philip said. "They sat at table A8, all the way in the back room. They sat and watched your whole show holding hands. They ordered a bottle of Dom Perignon and they sent a bottle of Dom Perignon to the waiter's station. And in those days, Dom Perignon at Reno's was $110 a bottle. Now think about that. That was a lot of money, so we were all just ecstatic."

Taylor Mead hams it up for the camera as he and Holly reminisce about their wild days in the NYC underground theatre scene. April 1990.

Later that night, Holly and I paid a visit to one of her best friends, a transgender prostitute named Tilda, who lived in an old Victorian apartment at the top of a winding, crooked staircase. Tilda's home was a modest, unkempt hovel, and as we settled in for an hour of tea before her next trick, the two laughed and reminisced about their colorful antics as women of the night.

"Darling, always get the money first," Holly advised, and Tilda concurred.

With all the money we were spending on carfare and restaurants, it didn't take a brilliant mathematician to know that our cash supply was dwindling fast. Although we weren't smart enough to figure out how to take a bus from Newark, New Jersey, to Manhattan to save $120, we both knew how to survive when our backs were against the wall and we were left with few options. Canned tuna and boxed macaroni & cheese were my fallbacks for saving money when I was close to being broke. But Holly had other ideas.

"Jeffrey, don't you worry about money," Holly said one morning as she put on her lipstick. "Your Auntie Holly has an appointment today with a stockbroker at noon. I'll only be a couple of hours."

Holly got all dolled up in her pinstripe suit and high heels and tied a red camisole around her neck like a scarf.

"Now doesn't that look fabulous?"

Holly on her way to make some moolah, wearing a red teddy as a scarf and her "Delta Burke" wig that had seen better days. April 1990.

I'd never seen anyone turn a camisole into a scarf before, but Holly proved that anything could be possible. Then she put on her Delta Burke wig, which looked like it had been through the spin dry cycle one too many times.

"Who is this stockbroker?" I asked.

"Oh, he's just one of my old clients from Park Avenue."

My best friend was back to being a prostitute, at least for a couple of hours, and it bothered me. While Holly day traded on Wall Street, I grabbed a coffee and prepared questions for our next interview. But what I really wanted to know is why Holly didn't have more self-respect. Her life was on the upswing now. There were other ways we could have gotten the money if we put some thought into it. She didn't have to prostitute herself. But she wanted to do it; she enjoyed it. That's what disappointed me most. Her choice challenged my own moral convictions. Holly could be a fun-loving whore on occasion because she wasn't saddled with the same cultural restraints that made me so conservative and uptight. She had freedom. I had obligations and responsibilities. She wallowed in sin, I wanted to save her, and that was just stupid. Holly didn't think being a hooker was degrading. If she didn't have a problem with it, why did I? Why was I so prudish about turning a trick for some easy cash? What was wrong with me?

I was a blue blood. Blue bloods don't turn tricks. We had too much integrity and class. And as I sipped my coffee and chewed on that thought, I realized that was the biggest bullshit ruse of all.

Love Holly for who she is, not for what you want her to be . . . that was my trick to turn. Prostitution might not have appealed to me, but if Holly liked it, bully for her . . . even if it was against the law. For me, it would have been degrading, but for Holly it was fun, lucrative, and humanitarian. She provided a service that fulfilled a need, and when she was a high-priced call girl living on Park Avenue, she told me she genuinely cared about her regular customers. Holly's compassion was one of her most endearing qualities. If someone was physically or mentally disabled, Holly's knee-jerk reaction was to take that person under her wing and make him feel better. One of her favorite clients was a man who was missing a leg.

"I love a man who isn't perfect," she said. "All it takes is one little flaw and my heart melts."

Later that afternoon when Holly sauntered into the hotel lobby with three hundred dollars cash, I had to laugh at the absurdity of it all.

"Three hundred dollars, darling," she said, flipping the cash before my eyes. "Isn't that fabulous? Now we can eat."

THE BROADWAY MELODY

ALL TALKING · ALL DANCING · ALL SINGING

ROBERT Z. LEONARD Presents

MAE MURRAY
in
BROADWAY ROSE

B. EDMUND GOULDING

METRO

A TIFFANY
Production

PICTURES CORPORATION
EXCLUSIVE DISTRIBUTORS

Alice
WHITE

Presented by · RICHARD A. ROWLAND
Directed by · MERVYN LE ROY

A FIRST
NATIONAL
PICTURE

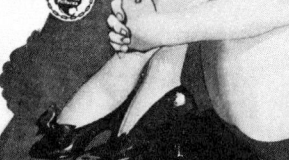

BROADWAY
BABIES

CHAPTER 22

QUENTIN CRISP WAS A BRITISH WRITER/RACONTEUR whose autobiography, *The Naked Civil Servant*, was made into an independent film that starred John Hurt. His book was published in 1968 and chronicled his life as an out and proud flamboyant homosexual, who refused to hide his identity, even when such behavior was criminalized. When he met us in our hotel lobby, he was elderly and well-coiffed, and looked more like a grand old lady than a man.

"Hello, Quentin, darling!" Holly called as she spotted him across the way.

Holly was similarly dressed: men's slacks, a blue silk shirt, and a black blazer, with her hair pulled back and tied into a man bun behind her head.

They were genuinely delighted to see each other and while they embraced and exchanged pleasantries, I couldn't help but notice other hotel patrons swirling around us who reacted to the reunion with frowns, smirks, and rude stares. Holly and Quentin were oblivious because they were engaged with one another, but as I observed the whole scene, it made me uncomfortable.

I'd experienced similar situations in Los Angeles when Holly and I were out and people shot her the stink eye. People didn't always take kindly to an effeminate-looking man who had unnaturally thin eyebrows and no facial hair because of the electrolysis he did in his youth. One time we were at the Yum Yum donut shop at five in the morning, and there was a small group of Mexican laborers standing at the counter. When they saw us enter, they stared at Holly and snickered. I heard one of them utter "puto." I knew the word meant "fag" in Spanish, so I stood in front of Holly and blocked their view. I was apprehensive because I knew this situation was potentially dangerous. The last thing I wanted was to be harassed or attacked.

Another troubling situation occurred in the French Quarter restaurant when Holly and I were standing at the host's station, waiting to be seated. We were minding our own business when a short bodybuilder pushed his way by Holly, gave her a look of disgust, and muttered the word "freak."

The book's title was inspired by Crisp's work as a nude model for art schools in the United Kingdom. Because he was paid by the U.K.'s Department of Education, he was technically a civil worker.

"What's your problem?" I said, which was a huge mistake because it caused the little muscle goon to explode into a steroid-fueled rage. He stomped around, called us names, and threatened to kick my ass!

"Don't say anything, darling. Just ignore him," Holly said. "He'll go away."

But he didn't go away. The little fucker just kept yelling at us, spewing all sorts of homophobic hatred. By now, everyone was staring, trying to determine what had caused such a violent outburst. We were mortified! We probably should have pushed him into the adjacent koi pond. That would have cooled him off. But then we would have been arrested for assault, and that was the last thing I needed.

Now we were in the lobby of the Hotel Dorset, and I was on high alert because even in Manhattan, there were intolerant people who made no effort to hide their disdain.

"Darling, I'm an authoress, can you believe it?" said Holly to Quentin, then she grabbed my arm and pulled me closer. "I even have my own co-author, Jeffrey Copeland. Isn't he divine?"

Hobnobbing over lunch with the delightful Quentin Crisp. April 1990.

Quentin Crisp was very warm and gracious, and soon we were in a cab, weaving through cars and flying through stoplights. When the cabbie finally came to a screeching halt, we found ourselves outside the Americano Cafe in the Tribeca neighborhood.

Over lunch, Quentin recalled meeting Holly at the London nightclub Country Cousins, where she was performing. It was the same place where she met Freddie Mercury.

"The act was lovely," Quentin explained. "It's the only drag act in the world where she's not malicious. No bitchiness in it at all. It was just great fun."

A woman came over to our table and told Quentin she was a huge fan. He thanked her and told her she was very kind. Then Quentin said, "America is the only place in the world where you don't have to do something well enough or even—as in England—long enough to become famous. You just do fame. That's a career in itself."

Holly's ride on the roller coaster of fame didn't yield the most lucrative opportunities, but it did land her an acting role in an independent film called *Night Owl*, which she was scheduled to shoot that weekend in New York's Greenwich Village. The filmmaker, Jeffrey Arsenault, had tracked Holly down at Wacko, after reading in Michael Musto's column in the *Village Voice* that Holly worked there. When Jeffrey learned she was coming to New York, he offered her the part, a role he wrote especially for her.

That Friday night, Holly went to Jeffrey's apartment to rehearse with another actor, John Leguizamo, while I explored Manhattan on my own. The next morning, Holly got all dolled up in her wig and high heels, and we took a cab to the film location in the West Village. It was a club called J's Hangout at 675 Hudson Street. I escorted Holly inside and made sure she was in good hands. Everyone was busy fixing lights, pulling cables, and bustling in all directions. I wanted so badly to be part of the independent filmmaking scene. This was exactly the type of movie that I wanted to make with Holly when we first met, and it was odd, being on that set, seeing someone else achieve the goal that was once my dream. I felt like an outsider, so I left the set, explored the Village, and came back a few hours later to find the crew giving Holly a standing ovation.

"That was magic," said one of the producers. Holly was thrilled. Not only was she a success, but she was also paid in cash.

Later that night, we had dinner with Richie Berlin. Of all Holly's friends, Richie Berlin was the most entertaining. She was uptown New York royalty, a genuine blue blood who was the daughter of Richard and Honey Berlin (her father ran the Hearst publishing empire and her mother was an esteemed socialite). More interestingly, she was one of Warhol's early Factory players and the sister of Brigid Berlin, one of Andy Warhol's most outrageous superstars. She was also a good friend and roommate of Edie Sedgwick.

Richie was charming, and I was fascinated to learn that she worked as a bicycle courier in Manhattan. It was an unlikely job for a woman of great wealth, but she genuinely liked it.

We went to dinner at a nice restaurant of her choice. The place was beautiful, with mood lighting, white linen tablecloths, and a well-polished clientele. Now this was the way to experience New York. Somehow our conversation shifted from the Factory and La MaMa to Broadway, and Richie, who was plowed on cocktails, started singing show tunes. The more she sang, the louder she got. That gal was having her own Broadway revue in the middle of the restaurant, and people around us were annoyed. I didn't know what to do. I looked at Holly and Holly looked at me. We were beside ourselves! Holly gently patted Richie's arm.

"Honey, you know I love you but you've got to keep it down—"

"Keep it down?" screeched Richie, then she looked around the room and saw all the people looking at her.

"Ahh, fuck 'em!" she howled, then burst into "Big Time" from the musical *Mack And Mabel*.

Richie got so loud, the maître d' came over and told her to shut up. And when she didn't, we were told to leave. I probably should have been mortified, but I loved the whole debacle. Somehow getting kicked out of a restaurant with Richie Berlin and Holly Woodlawn made the evening all the more special.

The pinnacle of our trip came that weekend on Sunday morning when we met with our editor, Michael Denneny, who hosted a brunch for us in his Victorian apartment. Michael Denneny was an established New York writer and editor, and an ardent champion of LGBTQ authors. He worked with straight authors as well, but he pushed to strengthen the voice of queer writers because when he was a young man coming of age, their stories were rare and hard to find. In the 1970s, as one of the few openly gay editors in major publishing, Michael Denneny became a trailblazing force, created the first gay imprint, Stonewall Inn Editions, and worked closely with many acclaimed, award-winning, and best-selling authors, including Ntozake Shange, Randy Shilts, and Edmund White. And to think he was throwing a brunch for us! That was mind-blowing.

"Oh, God!" I said as the cab pulled up to our destination. "I hope I make a good impression."

I was excited, but nervous.

"Darling, you're with Holly Woodlawn. You're going to be fine," Holly said as she freshened her lipstick, dropped the tube into her violin case, and snapped it closed. She looked like a million bucks, decked out in her two-piece pinstripe gangster suit, black high heels, and a gorgeous face painted to perfection.

We knocked on Michael's apartment door, and when he opened it, we were both thrilled. He was an attractive middle-aged man with strong, handsome features, dark brown hair and eyes, and a deep masculine voice that was so sexy, I wanted to push Holly out to the street and keep him all for myself.

"Hands off, scaintch! He's mine!" were the only words that came to mind as Michael gave Holly a friendly hug and then invited us into his home. I knew Michael Denneny was impressive, but I had no idea that he was Prince Charming, living in a grand nineteenth-century apartment with hardwood floors and nine-inch baseboards. The minute I saw those, I was ready to move in.

Once inside, Michael introduced us to some of his work colleagues. Holly was warm and charming, while I wrestled with social anxiety and tried my best to act like I belonged there. It was all going well, until I was introduced to a St. Martin's marketing executive. I got tongue-tied, and while struggling to spit out my words, I literally spit! A spitball hurled out of my mouth and nearly smacked this lovely woman in the face. Good God! Thankfully, it veered off to the side. Who knows where it landed . . . probably in the vegetable dip. But the stunned, wide-eyed look that we both shared made me cringe. There's no recovering from that kind of social blunder. It was worse than getting kicked out of a restaurant! While I smiled and acted polite, inside my anxiety swelled and I was miserable the entire time.

"Oh, who cares if you almost spit in her face," Holly said later. "At least you didn't belch, fart, and stink up the place. Honey, if you did that, even I would have been plucked."

Despite a handful of mishaps, our trip to New York was a success. We never did make it to the Statue of Liberty, though.

"Too many tourists, honey!" said Holly. "You can wave to her from the plane. She's just as green as ever."

I thought about that iconic statue on our ride back to the Newark airport. I'd work her into the book somehow. But for now, I was excited to have so much rich material to help flesh out Holly's story. I couldn't wait to get back to Lizards in Hollywood, where I'd sit for hours, fueling my wild imagination with tongue-curling java while embellishing our manuscript with fabulous new jewels.

20 Great Stars

EBONY PARADE

HARRY M. POPKIN PRESENTS

"GANG Smashers"

WITH

NINA MAE McKINNEY

ALL COLORED CAST

LAWRENCE CRINER · MONTE HAWLEY
REGINALD FENDERSON · MANTAN MORELAND
Directed by Leo C. Popkin · Original Story by Ralph Cooper

A MILLION DOLLAR PICTURE

OSCAR MICHEAUX'S
PRODUCTION

"GIRL from CHICAGO"

FROM THE STORY
"JEFF BALLINGER'S WOMAN"
WITH

Grace SMITH · Carl MAHON

AND AN ALL STAR
COLORED CAST

DISTRIBUTED BY MICHEAUX PICTURES CORPORATION, NEW YORK CITY

SIE
/THE
EL LEE
/ERETT
FLOWERS

BILAIRES

DOROTH
RAY DAWN and DUSK BILAIRES

RELEASED THRU ASTOR PICTURES CORP.

CHAPTER 23

OUR WEEK-LONG VISIT TO NEW YORK CITY GAVE ME enough material to write two hundred more pages, which is exactly what I needed to finish the book. While I listened to audiotapes and pecked notes into the computer, Holly was next door in her orange apartment, enjoying her own creative frenzy. She had also cut back on her drinking again . . . somewhat. These were happy times that were often punctuated by upbeat knocks on my wall, which usually came late on a Saturday after we'd spent all day working.

"Hey, Lola! Answer your wall!" yelled Holly.

I left my computer and stuck my head out the window to see Holly's face beaming with excitement.

"Darling, come over and see this fuss I'm making!"

"I'll be right over," I said, grateful for a much-welcomed break from the arduous task of listening to all those audiotapes.

Next door, Holly was very excited to show me her new creation.

"I'm calling this one 'Puerto Rican Madness'!" she said, running a mess of fuchsia polyester through the sewing machine.

"Isn't it going to be divooon?"

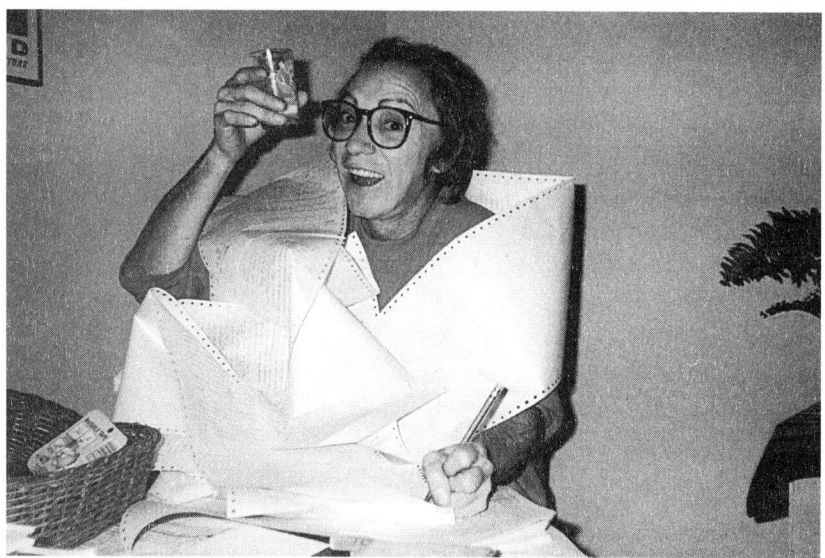
Holly, wrapped in a mess of continuous pages, makes notes on a chapter. 1990.

There's no such word as "divooon," but that didn't stop Holly from saying it, or me from writing it down.

"We're artistes," Holly reasoned. "We're creative! We can make up our own words if we want. In fact, I think I'll make a few right now out of hot pink taffeta."

Holly could sew just about anything she wanted. She enjoyed going to fashion school, made good grades, and loved working on her own designs. She had talent, and I knew if she worked hard, she'd be able to carve a niche for herself in the fashion world. The opportunities were endless, particularly because she was liked by so many famous and accomplished people. Her future looked brighter than ever now, and I was happy for her.

In the fall of 1990, we completed the manuscript and sent it to St. Martin's Press. Holly was happy, and I was relieved but still a bit apprehensive, because meeting our deadline didn't mean the manuscript was acceptable. What if Michael didn't like the book in its entirety? What would we do then? I was so tired of writing I didn't even want to think about the possibility of a rewrite.

Overall, writing Holly's story was a great experience. We had only one major disagreement, and it all came down to one word that started with "N" and rhymed with jigger. Holly insisted on using that word in the first chapter to describe a cellmate in jail who sexually harassed her.

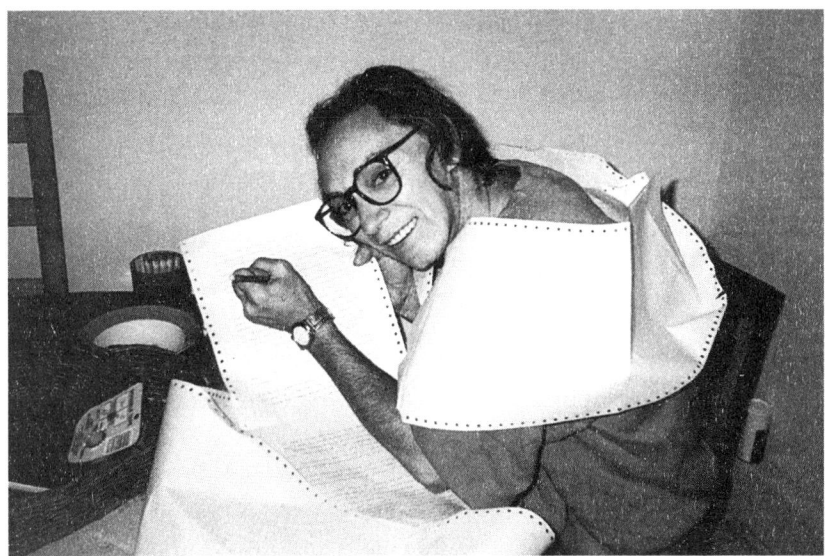
The best of times, working on a rewrite, and knowing we were on to something big. 1990.

"Holly, we can't use that word," I said.

"Honey, that's what he was! That's the word that best describes him."

I cut it out of the story and Holly demanded that I put it back. Even our agent, Robert, tried to get the word changed but Holly refused. It was like that scene out of the movie *Sunset Boulevard* when Joe Gillis makes a decision to cut a scene from the screenplay Norma Desmond has written, and when she finds out she curtly demands, "Put it back!"

Holly was impossible to deal with when it came to this one issue. I couldn't reason with her. So a few months later, I covertly cut that word out again. When Holly found out, she had a fit.

"He was a n*gger!" she screamed.

"That sounds horrible!" I yelled back.

"Well, he was horrible!"

"That word is offensive. What if Oprah reads this book, Holly? What's she going to think?"

"Why would Oprah care? She isn't a n*gger. Why would she be offended?" Holly was adamant and unreasonable.

"Holly! Using that word makes you look like a racist," I argued.

"I'm not racist!" Holly snapped. "Jeffrey, I'm not saying *all* Black people are n*ggers. I'm just saying that asshole in jail was a n*gger. And he was!"

This argument lasted for about nine months, until Michael Denneny insisted the offending reference be changed. Only then did Holly relent.

Shortly after we delivered the full manuscript, we got word from Michael that he condensed the final chapters to improve structure and flow. Holly didn't mind the cuts, as long as St. Martin's Press was cutting another check. We were due another $10,000 payment on our advance. The biggest change, however, concerned our title, *On the Wild Side*.

"What do you think about calling it *A Low Life in High Heels*?" Michael asked. It was inspired by a line in the book, that I took verbatim from Holly's mouth.

"That Jackie Curtis was a low life on a high heel," Holly said one night with a chuckle.

Robert, our agent, objected at first because it denigrated Holly's image, which we had all worked so hard to elevate. There was also concern it would be a blow to Holly's self-esteem. Yet we knew a self-deprecating title would work well with the book's over-the-top, self-aggrandizing tone. We discussed it for about five minutes and decided that Michael's suggestion was brilliant. "On the Wild Side" was lackluster. "A Low Life in High Heels" was outrageous and eye-catching.

"Darling, I think it's fabulous," Holly said. "Yay, honey! *A Low Life in High Heels*! I can already see it on the theatre marquee!"

We were galloping down the final stretch now, fast and furious, and time was running short. Legal clearances had to be obtained for photos we wanted to feature inside the book. We needed permission from Lou Reed to use lyrics from "Walk on the Wild Side," which he initially declined. We had to get a written introduction from Paul Morrissey. A strategic publicity campaign on both coasts had to be coordinated. Photographs for the front and back covers had to be taken. And if that weren't enough, we had copy editor notes that had to be addressed.

"This was a doozy!" the copy editor wrote in a letter. "The writing and typing are quite sloppy and often inconsistent." Then she rambled on about all of my overwritten, run-on sentences, parallel constructions, and inconsistent pronouns. Well, boo hoo, Mary! I would have been embarrassed, if I'd had the time. There were so many tasks to complete, we had no choice but to stay focused and push forward. Thankfully we had friends who helped us get it all done.

One of the first people to step up to the plate was Thomas Cunningham, a photographer we both knew from Lizards because his studio was right next door. Tom was a gruff old curmudgeon who had long gray hair that he refused to cut until a Democrat was elected to the White House. He was gay and creative, and when we first met and he learned I was working with Holly on her autobiography, he was so enthusiastic about the project he said, "I want to shoot the book cover!"

When the time came to shoot the photos, Clinton volunteered to work as Holly's stylist, and another friend, Tyr Jung-Hall, came along to assist. Holly brought a variety of outfits for different looks that would be shot in black-and-white and color. It was a fun night of inspiration and creativity. When Clinton found a few yards of gold lamé fabric in a corner, he spun it into a large turban and stuck it on Holly's head.

"Oh my!" exclaimed Clinton.

"Isn't it fabulous, darling?" Holly quipped. "All it takes is a little sissy magic."

Another photo shoot took place in Holly's apartment with Evie Bibo. Evie was one of Holly's co-workers at Wacko who was studying to be a movie makeup artist. She'd been part of the L.A. punk scene, and she had a mop of dark, thick shaggy hair, an infectious smile, and beautiful energy that was just wonderful. Evie wanted to practice what she'd been learning in school and Holly was happy to help, so they set up a photoshoot in Holly's apartment with one of Evie's friends, a photographer named Julia Sloan.

For a backdrop, they hung some heavy black cloth. Holly didn't get dressed for the shoot. She simply draped herself in a red ruffled shawl. Julia shot black-and-white film and the resulting images were astounding. Holly looked like a movie star from the golden era of Hollywood. Some people said her high cheekbones and ethereal gaze were reminiscent of Marlene Dietrich.

Teresa Conboy volunteered to help with Holly's publicity. St. Martin's had its own PR and marketing team in New York, but the idea of having a publicist in Los Angeles to help supplement the efforts seemed like a good idea to me. So Teresa came on board and began strategizing a nationwide campaign.

Lindsay Root, a videographer I'd met while working at Paramount, produced and edited a beautiful promotional video about the book that St. Martin's Press could use at the annual booksellers' convention. Lindsay got us a professional TV studio, lights, cameras, and a fancy editing suite, and he did all the work. If we had to pay for that service with a production company, it would have easily cost $10,000! Lindsay gave it to us for free.

The encouragement and generosity of our friends was the positive force that pushed us toward the finish line. As we got closer to our publication date, Robert coordinated an advance reading at a gay bookstore in Silver Lake called A Different Light. Holly and I were very excited about the event. Now that we had resolved our "N"-word issue, I printed Holly a revised chapter so she would have a fresh, correct copy from which to read. I gave it to her while she was putting on her face. About an hour later, she was dressed up in her pinstripe suit and high heels.

"Holly, do you have the pages I gave you?" I asked as we got into the Fiero.

"I have them right here," she said, patting her violin case, where they had been safely stored.

A Different Light bookstore was located in a quaint Tudor storefront in an area of Silver Lake called Sunset Junction. The building has since been torn down, but back then, this little bookstore was a community hub for the gays and lesbians who called Silver Lake home.

When we parked the car, we were excited to see such a large crowd had turned out for the event. The store was packed.

"Oh, look at them, darling! They're here for us!" Holly beamed.

"Well, they're here for you, my dear, but thank you for including me."

"How do I look? Is my wig on straight?"

By now, Holly had traded in her old Delta Burke haystack for a newer model, and she looked beautiful.

"You look great," I said.

Holly was a nervous wreck and so was I. The event coordinator introduced Holly to the crowd and there was resounding applause. Holly's face lit up with a smile as she took to the podium.

"A Low Life in High Heels. Chapter one, page one!" she announced with great theatrical flair. Everyone laughed and from that moment on, she had them in the palm of her hand. I stood in the back and reveled in the laughter. It was wonderful to hear the crowd's reaction. Holly Woodlawn was many things to me in the times I knew her. She was a friend, mentor, confidant, and at times a pain in the ass. But at that moment, she was a bright and radiant star, and I was more proud of her now than I'd ever been.

And then I heard the word "N*GGER"!

I was gripped with horror. Somehow Holly had grabbed the uncorrected draft.

Holly kept reading, words flying out of her mouth like a turbocharged chatterbox. I was so upset and embarrassed that I got dizzy and thought I was going to faint. I couldn't believe she said that word! I felt terrible. Holly finished the reading to much applause, but for me, the evening had been ruined. I couldn't wait to get out of there.

"How do you think I felt, honey?" Holly said as we drove home. "With

This book is dedicated to my parents who have loved me, cried for me and supported me when I was up, down and sideways! It is also dedicated to those who have known the struggle of being different, endured the fear of rejection and have mustered the courage to survive.

Dear Dorothy,
There's No place
Like Home!

This is the original dedication page before it was properly punctuated. I wrote it, Holly approved it, and before we sent our finished manuscript to Michael Denneny, Holly handwrote a personal note to my mom: "Dear Dorothy, there's no place like home!"

those two gorgeous Black men sitting in front. I was plucked!"

We drove home in silence. I fought for a year to get that word deleted from the manuscript. Had Holly been rational and listened to me in the beginning, this fiasco would never have happened. But Holly didn't listen. At times, she was hard-headed and irrational, and that led her to make bad decisions that, unfortunately, we would both pay for in the end.

MUSICAL REVUE in Technicolor!
HOLLYWOOD PARTY
CHARLIE CHASE
AHERN SISTERS
JOE MORRISO
Joan CRAWFORD
Gary COOPER
IN
TODAY WE LIVE
ROBERT YOUNG
FRANCHOT TONE
ROSCOE KARNS
A HOWARD HAWKS PRODUCTION
-Mayer PICTURE
HARRY RICHMAN JOAN BENNETT
PUTTIN' ON THE RITZ

CHAPTER 24

WHEN MICHAEL DENNENY SENT US THE PRINTED book jacket in the mail, the design was more subdued than Holly had originally imagined. Holly loved explosive colors. This jacket was predominantly an old black-and-white photo of Holly with a tan inset, where Tom Cunningham's gorgeous color photo had been reduced to a two-inch square.

"Oh, no!" was Holly's first reaction. "That's not how it's supposed to look."

But after a few glasses of wine, Holly grew to love it.

"It is rather tasteful," Holly said as we both admired the jacket in the light of her apartment.

"Well, it's not Day-Glo green and fuchsia," I concurred.

"Understated elegance," she smiled.

Holly was elated and proud.

The book was published in October 1991 to much fanfare, thanks to Teresa Conboy, the St. Martin's team, and a slew of ardent supporters. In New York, the St. Martin's publicity department organized a huge book launch party at the Limelight nightclub and a big signing at B. Dalton in Greenwich

Village. It was a momentous and triumphant occasion for Holly. I stayed back in Los Angeles because I couldn't take time away from work, but I didn't mind. Manhattan was Holly's city. For her to go back a winner with a memoir to tout was huge, and I wanted her to relish that time and savor the glory. This was her moment to shine and I didn't want to horn in on it.

"Darling, it was fabulous!" said Holly of the B. Dalton event when she called me the next day. "Honey, there were people lined up down the block to get in! I kissed so many books my lips were numb."

St.Martin's Press
INCORPORATED

Dear Jeff,
Well here's the fruit of your labor (not loins).
You two should sit and gloat over it.
Best
Michael

175 FIFTH AVENUE, NEW YORK, N. Y., 10010 • Telephone: (212) 674-5151
Cable Address: SAINTMART • TWX: 710-581-6459 • FAX: (212) 420-9314

Holly often signed the book "Love you madly, Holly Woodlawn," and then kissed the inscription to leave an imprint of lipstick. It was a beautiful and distinct insignia that epitomized her gratitude for the people who remembered and supported her.

The publicists lined up several print and television interviews to promote the book's release. One of the best interviews was a public access show with Stephen Holt, which was hilarious. All seemed to be going well, until one morning, as I was getting ready for work, I got a call from Keith Kahla, Michael Denneny's assistant at St. Martin's Press.

"Holly won't put on her wig," he said matter-of-factly.

"What?"

"She won't put on her wig for the press."

"I'll call her," I said and quickly hung up and dialed her hotel number.

"Hello!" she sang into the phone.

"Hi Hol, St. Martin's just called. Why aren't you wearing your wig?"

"St. Martin's Press called you about my wig?" she said. "I've gone *au naturel* and everyone is in an uproar. Darling, what's wrong with these people?"

"Holly, you need to wear the wig for the photographers. I'm begging you as a friend. Please put on your wig."

"Oh, puh-leeze! Why is everyone so worked up about that goddamn fucking wig?"

Because your natural hair looks like dry, unmanageable straw! That's what I wanted to say, but that was not the way to negotiate the situation.

"Because you look beautiful wearing that wig, Holly."

"I'm sick of that wig, Jeffrey! It stinks!"

"Holly, listen to me. You're in New York. These are your people. Do you think the ancient Egyptians wanted to see Cleopatra without her wig?"

A sly reference to ancient Egypt and Cleopatra always helped grease the wheels of positive thinking with Miss Woodlawn.

"Oh, all right!" she snapped.

But it was too late; the damage had already been done. The *New York Daily News* published a feature story about *Low Life* that included a large photograph of Holly with a beautiful face and hair that looked like the wiry fur of a terrier. The St. Martin's team faxed the article to my office, and I cringed when I saw the photo. I was so disheartened. It took so much work and so much time to get to this point. We were at the pinnacle of our success. Why would Holly pull this kind of stunt? What was she thinking?

Teresa was beside herself.

"Goddamn it, Holly!" she cried out later when she saw the photo.

There were so many photos of Holly taken at the Limelight party when she was looking spectacular. It was too bad none of those images made it into the *New York Daily News*.

In Los Angeles, there were so many people who reached out to laud and promote the book's launch. The DuPont Twins, celebrated social darlings of the Warhol set, paid to have the book cover printed on dozens of T-shirts as promotional giveaways. Art maven Joan Quinn, the former West Coast editor of *Interview* Magazine, touted that book every chance she got. Joan

It's the wacky paper doll gimmick that just won't go away! Teresa sent this out to magazine editors to stir up publicity. I drew the doll on the left and Holly drew the dress on the right. Then it was xeroxed on thick paper stock and Holly hand-colored it with markers. 1991.

promoted Holly and the book on her local TV show, then she and chef Michael Roberts hosted a posh book launch party at Trumps, his trendy restaurant in West Hollywood.

A few weeks later, restaurateur Mario Tamayo threw yet another book launch party at Atlas Restaurant on Wilshire Boulevard. Joan Quinn was there, too, lending her support with actress Sally Kirkland and actor Dennis Christopher. The event was highlighted by a mock protest staged by two drag queens named Marge and Eleanor, two very funny guys who were our neighbors on Las Palmas. They dressed up as conservative, uptight moralists and picketed the party with signs that read "Burn the Book!" My favorite moment was when Eleanor read aloud the book's most offensive lines and demanded they be changed.

"Chapter one, page 10," she yelled. "Don't fuck with me motherfucker, or I'll cut out yo' gizzard and shove it up yo' ass. Now we believe that should be changed to: 'Don't bother me, young man. You're making me cross.' Chapter one, page 11: 'I'll break your arm, faggot!' should be changed to 'I'll give you such a pinch!'"

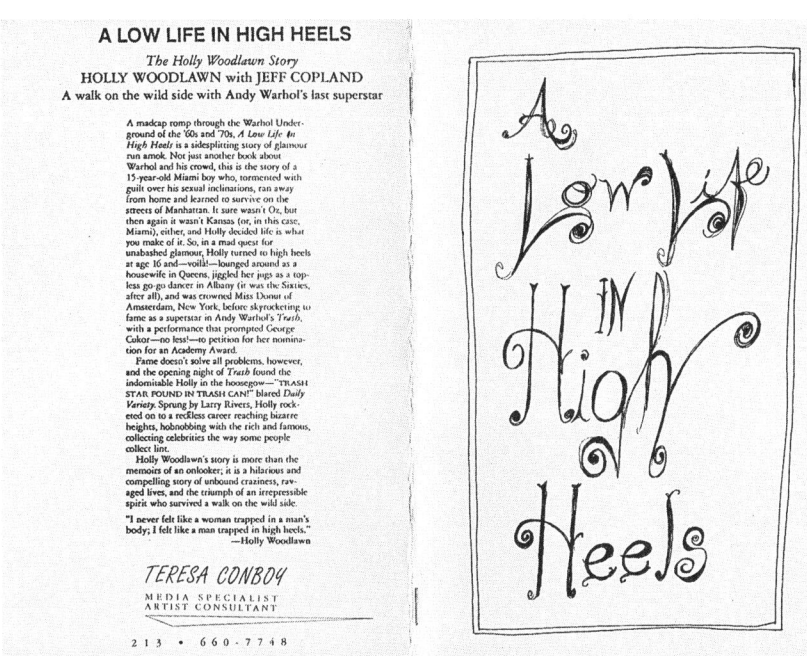

A LOW LIFE IN HIGH HEELS

The Holly Woodlawn Story
HOLLY WOODLAWN with JEFF COPLAND
A walk on the wild side with Andy Warhol's last superstar

A madcap romp through the Warhol Underground of the '60s and '70s, *A Low Life in High Heels* is a sidesplitting story of glamour run amok. Not just another book about Warhol and his crowd, this is the story of a 15-year-old Miami boy who, tormented with guilt over his sexual inclinations, ran away from home and learned to survive on the streets of Manhattan. It sure wasn't Oz, but then again it wasn't Kansas (or, in this case, Miami), either, and Holly decided life is what you make of it. So, in a mad quest for unabashed glamour, Holly turned to high heels at age 16 and—voilà!—lounged around as a housewife in Queens, jiggled her jugs as a topless go-go dancer in Albany (it was the Sixties, after all), and was crowned Miss Donut of Amsterdam, New York, before skyrocketing to fame as a superstar in Andy Warhol's *Trash*, with a performance that prompted George Cukor—no less!—to petition for her nomination for an Academy Award.

Fame doesn't solve all problems, however, and the opening night of *Trash* found the indomitable Holly in the hoosegow—"TRASH STAR FOUND IN TRASH CAN!" blared *Daily Variety*. Sprung by Larry Rivers, Holly rocketed on to a reckless career reaching bizarre heights, hobnobbing with the rich and famous, collecting celebrities the way some people collect lint.

Holly Woodlawn's story is more than the memoirs of an onlooker; it is a hilarious and compelling story of unbound craziness, ravaged lives, and the triumph of an irrepressible spirit who survived a walk on the wild side.

"I never felt like a woman trapped in a man's body; I felt like a man trapped in high heels."
—Holly Woodlawn

TERESA CONBOY
MEDIA SPECIALIST
ARTIST CONSULTANT

213 • 660-7748

Front side of the *Low Life* paper doll promo. God only knows what inspired that ridiculous title font. Probably too much of Lizards' coffee. 1991.

It was silly, fun lunacy. And of course, "free pussy" sent her off the deep end.

"Now I know for a fact that you're not talking about giving away kittens, Woodlawn!" Eleanor ranted. "Free pussy has got to go!"

Book readings and signings were staged at Book Soup on Sunset Boulevard, at Larry Edmunds Bookshop on Hollywood Boulevard, and at A Different Light in West Hollywood and in San Francisco. Billy Shire, who owned Wacko, threw a book launch party for Holly at his La Luz De Jesus gallery on Melrose. Even my parents threw a book party back in Missouri.

Meanwhile, Teresa Conboy was working with the St. Martin's team to get Holly as much media coverage as possible. One of the biggest achievements was when Holly was interviewed by Terry Gross for National Public Radio. That was like hitting the publicity jackpot!

I was relieved that the book got some pretty good reviews. There were a few critics who didn't care for the story's over-the-top, self-aggrandizing tone, and one attacked me personally, saying I was an embarrassment to all

Our book launch party on Melrose Avenue at the La Luz De Jesus Gallery with me, Holly, and Teresa Conboy. Teresa is wearing one of the T-shirts the DuPont twins had printed to help promote the book. 1991.

Photo by Sean Hahn. Courtesy of the Teresa Conboy PR Archives

A San Francisco book party with Stephen Parr. Parr was a San Francisco film archivist who specialized in odd, avant-garde film footage. Holly is wearing her favorite orange silk blazer and black button blouse. The book she's holding is the green preview galley that St. Martin's sent out to the press before it was published. 1991.
Photo by and courtesy of John A. Mozzer.

of humanity, and if I ever wrote again, it would be take-out orders at the Dairy Queen, because that's the most my talent would allow. Thankfully, there was only one bitter queen who raised a stink. The most meaningful responses, however, came in the form of cards and letters from gay men who were dying of AIDS. These men were fighting a losing battle, and they took the time to write Holly, tell her how much they loved her book, and thank her for making them laugh out loud. Those letters were poignant and touching and caught us by surprise. They far outweighed any of the biting, scathing rhetoric that some of the sarcastic naysayers spewed.

The book launch was like an exhilarating thrill ride. Dazzling lights! Cheering faces! Time was wondrous and blurred. It was all so precious, so beautiful, so rich . . . and so fleeting. Holly's celebrity status was now elevated in the Los Angeles social circles. Anyone who was hip and relevant knew the name Holly Woodlawn, and that was evident by the seemingly endless party invitations that she received weekly, which were always followed by an exuberant knock on the wall.

LE GRAND HOTEL
UN HOTEL INTER·CONTINENTAL

PLACE DE L'OPÉRA - 2, RUE SCRIBE - 75442 PARIS - CEDEX 09 - TÉL. : (1) 42.68.12.13 - TÉLEX : 220875 F - FAX : 42.66.12.51

Feb 5, 1991

Dear Holly,

Very often when I found myself laughing out loud I was tempted to write in the margin Very Good or V.G. then I realized that I would be filling up all the pages with V.G.'s Really Holly the whole thing is Very Good, meaning Very Funny! It is really enjoyable and a great read. It sounds so much like you and really captures your great personality. I congratulate you on doing such a good job and I know that Jeff must have really been a great help in getting it all down in such a consistently entertaining way. You were very lucky to have teamed up with him, as I was when I teamed up with you. Once again you've delivered another great performance.

L'HÔTEL N'EST PAS L'EXPÉDITEUR

Regards
Paul

A handwritten note from Paul Morrissey, raving over the book. Having him write that it made him laugh out loud and that "it is really enjoyable and a great read" made me feel like, WOW . . . finally, I'd hit a home run.

Please feel free to use the following comment in publicizing A LOW LIFE IN HIGH
HEELS by Holly Woodlawn

Thank you,
          dear Mr. Tennony,
                              for sending me the galley
of Holly Woodlawn's autobiography.
                              I greatly enjoyed
reading it; I liked the slangy, campy style that so
vividly reminds me of Holly, tinselled with immortal
one-liners such as 'I was a pretty good cook when it
came to heroin .'
                    I congratulate Holly on having crow-
ded so many bizarre adventures with such a wide variety
of famous people into half a life time and Mr. Copeland
for having shaken this cocktail of depravity into
some kind of order and you for your courage in publishing it.
          As always, quote me as saying anything that
will promote the sales of this tormented, terrifying
but in many ways touching story.

        "I congratualte Holly on having crowded so many bizarre
    adventures with usch a wide variety of famous people into half a life time
    and Mr. Copeland for having shaken this cocktail of depravity into
    some kind of order and you for your courage in publishing it."

(Signed) Quentin Crisp

(date) 3rd August '91

    (Quintin is a very famous writer. His autobiography was turned into a movie
    called "The Naked Civil Servant" twenty years ago. He's very old -- at least
    85!)

A wonderful blurb from Quentin Crisp. I was thrilled that he wrote "tinselled with immortal one-liners such as 'I was a pretty good cook when it came to heroin'" because that's the kind of fluff I had to put in the book to meet our page count. September 1991.

"*Detour* Magazine is having a party, darling!" she said excitedly. "We're going to have a hoot of a time."

And so did *Interview, Fame, Buzz,* and *L.A. Style.* The parties thrown by magazine publishers were a veritable Hollywood trough for all the gossipmongers, narcissists, and opportunists. I didn't care for this kind of pretentious slop, but Holly and I always made the best of it. I went to these parties hopeful and optimistic that maybe I'd meet someone interesting to date. I never did . . . probably because we arrived in a Fiero that was now missing its hubcaps, had a dent on one side, and a chunk missing from the other. The

Every time I see this image of fan letters that Holly received from people who loved *A Low Life in High Heels*, I think of a specific scene in *What Ever Happened to Baby Jane?* Do you remember it? Here's a clue: "Oh, how kind people are." 1991.
Courtesy of the Teresa Conboy PR Archives.

looks of dismay and confusion on so many faces as we valeted the car were just priceless. The only thing that could have made a worse impression was bird shit.

Then we'd enter the trendy restaurant where the event was being held and I could feel the eyes of haughty, opportunistic wolves sizing us up at every angle. These folks were all about Chanel handbags and Gucci shoes. They didn't know what to make of Miss Woodlawn's violin case or the strand of cheap Christmas tree pearls that she draped around her neck. They gawked and stared, but once we got our hands on the free hooch and fancy hors d'oeuvres, it didn't really matter. All we really cared about was a cheap good time.

My favorite parties were those that were held in private homes. The invitees were hand-picked, not computer-generated, so the crowd was more interesting and usually of a higher echelon.

"Yoo-hoo, darling!" Holly called, knocking on my wall. I stuck my head out the window to see what was up. "Steven Arnold is having a salon," she said. "It's going to be fabulous!"

Holly, wearing a dress of her own design, greets a fan at a fabulous book launch party at Atlas Restaurant in 1991.

Steven Arnold was a gentle force and an extraordinary human being who worked as a painter, sculptor, and photographer. He was a protégé of the great Salvador Dali, one of the most famous surrealists in the world. I loved Steven's work; he created some of the most interesting, surreal, and thought-provoking tableaux I'd ever seen.

Steven Arnold's visions were exquisite, absurd, and whimsical. I was most familiar with his ethereal depictions of nude male angels floating in black celestial space. These photographs were a tribute to the many friends he'd lost to AIDS.

"Darling, a salon is not just a party," Holly said. "Oh, mon Dieu! A salon is a gathering of interesting, fashionable, and creative people. You're going to love it."

I didn't quite know what to expect, but we were dressed up, so I assumed it was going to be special. Holly looked stunning in a vibrant ensemble that she whipped up especially for the occasion. Her face was beautifully painted—she looked like a movie star.

We crammed ourselves into the beat-up Fiero, which barely had room for our shoulder pads, and ripped down Melrose into the wilds of Silver Lake.

"Oh, there it is! That's Zanzibar!" announced Holly, and pointed to a run-down hovel as we drove past.

"Are you kidding me? That's it?" I was shocked.

"Isn't that a sight to behold, darling? It used to be a pretzel factory."

Zanzibar is what Steven Arnold called his home/studio on east Beverly Boulevard in the less than desirable Rampart division of Los Angeles. This was not the fabulous artist studio I had envisioned. On the outside, Steven's house looked like a dilapidated California bungalow that had been modified and expanded

12/21/91 – MOMENTS BEFORE APPEARING ON THE DAWN Freedman SHOW.

Me and Holly riding the wave of publicity, waiting to go on camera for a television interview. December 1991.

to accommodate an attached commercial structure. Painted dark green and perched on a small hill that was overgrown and unkempt, the compound was discreet and private and looked like the home of an elderly widow who spent her days and nights looking after cats. No one would ever suspect that so much fabulous creativity was bubbling in such a nondescript, seemingly forgotten area of town.

We parked the Fiero around the corner and down the block on a side street. The hubcaps had already been stolen, so there wasn't much to worry about, and the neighborhood didn't look nearly as bad as what I imagined from my judgment of the commercial corridor.

Within a few minutes, we had arrived and wandered through a thicket of brush and bougainvillea to find a plain, indistinct entrance. When the door opened, the real magic began as we entered an enchanted wonderland that had all the decadence of a carnival funhouse. I'd never seen such opulent and delightful jewel-toned elegance. Beautifully draped fabrics, a gold altar, a fantastic array of props and relics, a large antique papier-mâché head of a clown, decadent red sofas, and royal purple velvet chairs with tall whimsical backs that looked like something out of a Dr. Seuss story. I felt like I'd just walked into a fantasy.

"This is Jeffrey Copeland," said Holly, introducing me to Steven. "He wrote the book with me. It's all his fault."

Steven Arnold took my hand.

Holly, looking radiant at a book signing, wearing the dress she made called "Puerto Rico Madness." December 1991.

"Jeffrey, it's so nice to meet you," he said. "I loved your book."

I wasn't used to anyone giving me sole ownership like that and it made me feel uncomfortable.

"Thank you," I said.

Steven Arnold smiled. I felt his energy and was taken by his spirit. He was warm and soft-spoken and reminded me of Jesus Christ.

The small crowd milling about was eclectic and interesting. I mingled with a lovely European countess, an accomplished Latino film actor, writers, artists, and a bevy of handsome models whose youth and naked beauty had been preserved forever in silver gelatin prints. The power of Steven Arnold's unbridled creative expression was magnificent.

I treasured all the wondrous sights of this magical world. It was spectacular. I knew it was a privilege to be there. This was the inner sanctum reserved for a special few, and I loved relishing it with Holly. She was radiant and beautiful, and I was so fortunate to be included in her dazzling orbit, which only seemed to get more exciting with every knock on the wall.

"Yoo-hoo, darling!" she called out a few weeks later. "Allee Willis is having a huge hootenanny this Saturday so get out your tails, top hat, and ukulele. We're puttin' on the ritz, honey!"

Allee Willis was quirky, delightful, and beloved. Holly knew her from New York when Allee worked as the coat check girl at Reno Sweeney, where Holly performed regularly. Now Allee was a huge success as a songwriter whose string of hits included "Boogie Wonderland" by Earth, Wind & Fire and "Turn It Up" by Patti LaBelle. Allee was also known for throwing some of the best wingdings in Hollywood.

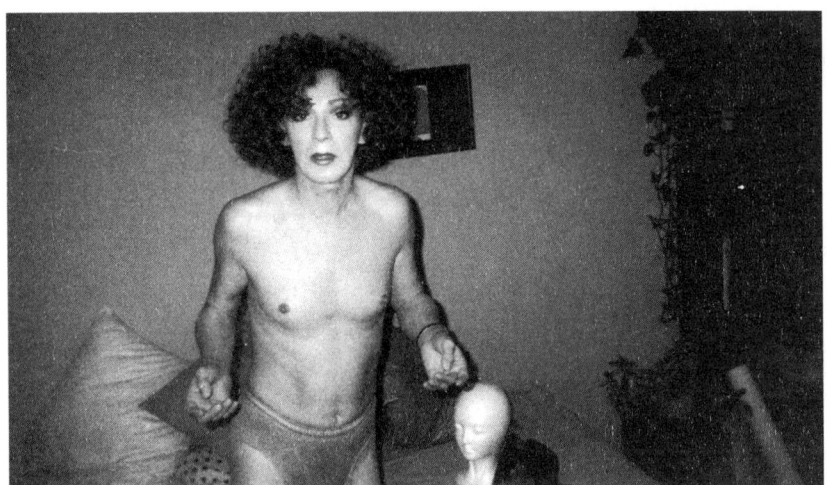

Holly getting ready for a night on the town. At this stage of her life, Holly didn't feel the need to do female hormones or get breast implants. She was happy with her natural body. 1992.

That Saturday night, while Holly got all dolled up in a red sequined gown, I went to see Miss Melons at the grocery store and bought a fruit tart for us to take to the party. Then we hopped into the Pontiac Fiero and tore over the Hollywood Hills to the San Fernando Valley, where Miss Willis lived on Otsego Street in a modest, Streamline Moderne Art Deco villa. That place was jam-packed with vintage tiki treasures and more stars than a Bob Hope Christmas special. Teri Garr, Shelley Duvall, Buck Henry, Cyndi Lauper, Laraine Newman from *Saturday Night Live*, Andrea Martin from *Second City TV*, David Cassidy from *The Partridge Family*, and Angelyne, in all her hot pink glory, who was famous for being on Hollywood billboards. Paul Reubens was probably there, too, as he and Allee were good friends, but we never crossed paths.

Allee's backyard was set up like an art festival, with a variety of stations where guests could make all kinds of fun, creative things. Holly and I arrived later than most, so we didn't get in on the art-making action. But we did enjoy being there with all these fabulous people. Holly and I wandered the compound, trying to take it all in. We wound up inside the house, chatting with the Del Rubio Triplets: three lovely and delightful old ladies decked out in white minidresses, white boots, and platinum bouffant hairdos, who would later perform a live rendition of the hit Devo song "Whip It."

Allee came up to us and gushed over how beautiful Holly looked. When Allee learned I was Holly's co-author, she raved over the book. Raved! Well, stick that in your pipe and smoke it, Skippy Perkins! Take that for some dictation, Mack! Even though Sol Finnegan said I couldn't write, I wrote myself a whole new reality. This was the best of Hollywood! There was no pomposity, no pretense. It was all good and it was genuine, intrinsic, and fun, and it was everything a fourteen-year-old gay kid with bad acne could have ever wanted. WOW! Insert the explosive Busby Berkeley musical number here, folks! This was it. Hollywood heaven! Thanks to Holly's magical coattails, I experienced it full throttle and relished every rich, ephemeral moment.

But this was a celebrity's world. It wasn't mine. In a short while, I'd go back to my own reality of responsibilities and obligations. I was a worker bee primed to serve its queen. Miss Francine's calls had to be answered. Advertising insertion orders had to be completed. The rent had to be paid. And the racehorse had to stay on track. We'd finished the book. Yay! But my race was far from over. Now there was a bigger prize to be won . . . that illusory golden carrot that kept me running all along. It shined in the distance, like a beautiful and sweet mirage. Who knew it would be so catastrophic?

CHAPTER 25

THE PONTIAC FIERO TORE AROUND THE CORNER AT Melrose and Fairfax as we drove north into West Hollywood, heading to the French Whorehouse (Holly's pet name for the French Quarter) to dine on our favorite eight-dollar plate of potato skins.

"The book is going to be made into a movie, I just know it," said Holly, and I agreed. We both envisioned the red-carpet movie premiere for *A Low Life in High Heels* as one of the most ridiculous spectacles in Hollywood history. Bigger than *The Birth of a Nation*! More historic than *Gone With the Wind*! And crazier than a bunch of drag queens on *The Price Is Right*.

"It's going to be a Technicolor extravaganza!" Holly said. "With bejeweled opening credits that twinkle like rhinestones!"

To see our names twinkling on the big screen was an exciting possibility. We imagined the night of our premiere to be a glittering, glamorous affair at Grauman's Egyptian Theatre on Hollywood Boulevard. Instead of a stodgy limousine, we planned to arrive in an old school bus.

"Ooooh, honey, we'll pack that bus with all of our friends. Allee, Joan, Jean, Clinton, the whole gang. Teresa knows how to work a stick, so she can drive. And we'll all be screaming, yelling, and carrying on as we jiggle

This postcard says it all. This is the kind of Hollywood premiere Holly and I dreamt about with a lot of fanfare, hoopla, and lights.
Courtesy of Theatre Talks Collection.

down Hollywood Boulevard. Everyone on the street will be appalled! And then we'll roll up to the theatre, where all the fabulous people are, looking all poised and piss-elegant," Holly said, lingering in thought. "And then the ol' bus will backfire and blow soot in all their faces!"

Holly howled with laughter.

"It's going to be fa-ha-habulous," she said as we drove up Fairfax. It was a fun moment . . . until Bette Midler horned her way into the scene. She sang "Wind Beneath My Wings" on the radio, which caused Holly to burst into tears. What a killjoy!

"Jeffrey, you're the wind beneath my wings," Holly cried. "If it wasn't for you, there wouldn't be a book."

"Oh, for God's sake, Holly!"

I was surprised by her sudden rush of emotion.

"I'd have to eat a shit-ton of beans to break enough wind to keep your wings afloat," I said, trying to lighten up her mood. But she continued to cry and I felt awkward and sad.

"Don't cry, Holly," I said, near tears myself. "Good grief."

"It's true," she blubbered.

"It's your life story," I said. "I just wrote it."

"You did more than that."

I sure as fuck did, and I appreciated her acknowledgment.

"It's okay," I said and patted her leg. "We have a lot to look forward to. There's no reason to cry."

And I honestly believed that.

The money we earned off the book didn't last long. When I received the final installment of our advance, I paid my taxes and then paid off my car. Finally, the Pontiac Fiero, my biggest financial mistake, was put to rest.

Meanwhile, Holly decided to take professional driving lessons.

"Darling, I'm finally doing it," she howled with glee. "I'm getting my learner's permit!"

May God help us all was my first thought. I'm ashamed to admit that terrible decision was my fault. Several months before, as we were driving back from the grocery store, I pulled into an empty parking lot and encouraged Holly to get behind the wheel. I thought it was important for Holly to learn to drive, particularly since she'd graduate from fashion school soon and would need a car to get to job interviews.

"You're living in Los Angeles, Holly. You have to learn to drive; otherwise, it's going to take forever for you to get anywhere."

"Are you out of your mind?" she said.

"It's easy," I said as I got out of the Fiero and headed to the passenger side. "Go on. Take it for a spin. You're going to love it."

That gal burned so much rubber the neighbors called the police.

Within a few months of that fiasco, Holly got her learner's permit. The way she handled a car and disobeyed the traffic laws, one would have thought she got her license through a correspondence course on the back of a matchbook in Tijuana. But somehow, some way, someone in California gave Holly Woodlawn a driver's license.

Now that Holly had cash from St. Martin's Press burning a hole in her handbag, she walked onto a used car lot and drove off in a faded, silver-blue Mazda sedan that sounded like an old lawnmower. Miss Woodlawn was not to be deterred by piddly details, like automotive mechanics. She figured that if the car started and it had tires, it was good to go. But there was always something wrong with that car. The brakes squealed like something out of a horror show, and the transmission jerked and shimmied like a coin-operated pony. Things only got worse after Holly drove over a curb and tore off the muffler.

It was a mistake to encourage Holly to drive a car. She didn't have the wherewithal to drive the writing of her own story. How could she possibly manage the responsibilities of owning and operating a motor vehicle? She couldn't! Holly could barely afford the gasoline to make it go, much less the repairs. When the car started to smoke, Holly smoked right along with it. If other drivers honked and hollered about the toxic cloud spewing out the back, Holly just waved back at them and screamed, "It kills the mosquitoes, darling!"

Luckily, that old clunker never broke down, and it propelled Holly forward in a way the Hollywood machine did not. We both wanted to see the book get a movie deal, but for some reason, our momentum in that direction was as sluggish as rush-hour traffic on the 405 freeway.

There was a lot of waiting in the Hollywood racket. Waiting on the set between takes, waiting for an agent's call, waiting for the right project to come along, waiting for a green light, and waiting for a union member to die so someone else could finally get a job. It took a lot of patience and fortitude to play the Hollywood movie-making game. It was bad enough having to wait for a publishing deal. Now we were counting on a movie deal to jump-start our careers and nothing was happening.

Our agent, Robert, who was now living on the East Coast, told me he pitched *Low Life* to John Waters while standing at a urinal, but I wasn't aware of any other packaging efforts. Our engine had stalled, so to speak, and we weren't getting anywhere.

Holly's car, on the other hand, took her anywhere she wanted to go. Not even a stoplight could hold her back.

"I'm from New York, honey, and the brakes are bad! Look out!"

Holly was on the go, usually downtown to the Fashion District. She looked forward to graduating from fashion school and thought about creating a clothing line marketed exclusively for transgender women.

"Those big-boned gals need all the help they can get," she said one day while cutting a pattern. "Lots of tulle and a shit-ton of feathers. That's what they need."

While Holly dreamt about a glorious future in fashion, I worked my day job and hung out at Lizards at night, jotting notes and writing scenes for the screenplay adaptation. Then one day, I read in *Daily Variety* that Madonna was forming a new production company called Maverick. The entity would have an independent film division that was dedicated to making unique independent movies. I called Robert and told him the good news.

"We've got to send the book to Madonna," I said. "Her company is looking to develop unique, independent films, and *Low Life* is perfect."

He didn't share my enthusiasm. In fact, his response was lackluster. So that night, I showed the article to Holly.

"We've got to get the book to Madonna," I said.

"Madonna?" Holly grimaced, clearly unimpressed.

"Holly, she'll be a great producer for the project."

Holly was indifferent to the idea, which made no sense to me. Madonna was the most famous pop star in the world. She had the Midas touch. Why wouldn't we want her company to produce our film? The soundtrack alone could have been amazing! But Holly couldn't have cared less about Madonna, and Robert didn't seem interested in pursuing her either. So I wrote Madonna a letter myself and sent the book to her company. A few days later, I called to follow up. In fact, I called several times. Finally, when I did get someone on the phone, I got a cold response.

"We don't accept unsolicited material," said a woman's voice, which meant if they didn't ask for it, they didn't want it.

Getting one's material read was the worst part of being a writer. I thought having a book published by St. Martin's Press would give me some leverage and clout. It did not. No one cared.

Not long after the book was published, Holly got bored with ringing up knick-knacks at Wacko. She had a published memoir now and was celebrated in the press. Working as a cashier just seemed so menial.

"Darling, I need glamour! I need excitement! I'm Holly Woodlawn. I can't work at Wacko," she said.

So Holly quit Wacko and got a job as a phone sex operator. I was floored when she told me the news.

"It's better than hookin', hon," she explained. "I don't have to get dressed up or put on a wig. I just show up at this office in Hollywood with the rest of the girls and talk cheap and dirty. But not too dirty. You don't want 'em to pop their cork too quick. You've got to string 'em along, keep 'em interested."

"What the hell do you talk about?"

"Oh, you know. I act interested. I ask them what they like to do. And then I make stuff up. I tell them what I'm wearing. Hot pink panties and black fishnet stockings. Meanwhile, I'm wearing a T-shirt and some Bermuda shorts."

Holly's foray into phone sex only lasted a few weeks because she was fired for drinking on the job.

"Darling, I was not plowed!" Holly emphatically declared. "It was just a teensy bit of wine in a glass or two. Maybe three. And those assholes acted like I drank the whole jug!"

One of the best decisions Holly made was to join Alcoholics Anonymous. She seemed to enjoy that experience. Upon achieving thirty days of sobriety and being awarded a token, she celebrated with a bottle of Glen Ellen chardonnay.

"Darling, thirty days is enough!" she angrily yelled. "I can't go to fabulous parties and not drink. I'll be bored out of my mind."

Well, she had a point. The party invitations were coming less frequently these days, though. And the celebrations fêting the book launch were over. All that remained in their aftermath were great memories, popped corks, and a deflated sense of NOW WHAT?

First National Pictures Inc. presents

The Lost World

Sir Arthur Conan Doyle's
stupendous stor...
By arrangement wit...
Watterson R. Rothacke...
Research and technical direct...
...H. O'Brie...

With
Bessie Love
Lewis Stone
...

"PRESTO CHANGO"
A MERRIE MELODIE
in Technicolor

A WARNER

THE LOST CITY

WILLIAM (STAGE) BOYD

EPISODE 6 "HUMAN BEASTS"

SUPER SERIAL PRODUCTIONS INC.
730 SEVENTH AVE. NEW YORK, N.Y.

THE BOGART SUSPENS...

PICTURE WITH THE

SURPRISE FINISH-

COLUMBIA PICTURES presents

HUMPHREY
BOGART
IN A
LONELY PLACE

with GLORIA GRAHAME

Frank LOVEJOY · Carl Benton REID · Art SMITH · Jeff DONNELL · Martha STEWART

A Santana Production
Produced by ROBERT LORD · Directed by Nicholas Ray

A First National Pict...

CHAPTER 26

"THE STREET IS CHANGING," WARNED GORILLA after a few of Melrose's trendy boutiques closed and relocated to other parts of town. I didn't pay him any mind. But according to Gorilla, it was an ominous sign that Melrose had hit its peak and was now on the decline. I thought he was crazy. How could a street as ultra-hip as Melrose lose its panache? But in Los Angeles, a city that was always evolving, change was inevitable, and it was coming to our lives in ways I never anticipated.

Robert said a movie deal was brewing and it promised to be big. So big, in fact, it would be life-changing. For me, that meant working as a screenwriter full-time. For Holly, it meant being a world-famous celebrity and fashion designer. And for Jean and the rest of our friends, it meant getting a break, finally! I would have written parts for Jean, Clinton . . . even Harriet! We'd figure out a way to squeeze them into the deal somehow. It was a great time, and we were all excited. All we had to do now was bide our time.

And so we waited again. Waited for another party invitation, waited for something good to happen, waited for yet another exhilarating ride on the Hollywood merry-go-round that would spin us in circles. While Holly and I hung on and eagerly hoped for the best, Jean got tired and jumped off. She'd

The corner of Melrose and Martel today, where the Soap Plant and Wacko used to be located. 2024.

gotten bored with the Hollywood hustle. The relentless struggle to get noticed just didn't mean anything to her anymore. She fell in love with a nice guy she'd met while playing softball and packed up Boo and left Las Palmas for good. I was happy for Jean. She chucked the pie-in-the-sky bullshit for a stable career as a school teacher and a charming house in the Valley with a comfortable bed, her own bathroom, health insurance, and a pension. It sounded like a good deal to me. I was still sleeping on an old Art Deco sofa, waiting for a movie deal to come my way.

But whether I liked it or not, the energy was shifting in my world. Changes were coming that were out of my control. One of the most upsetting was the day I walked into Lizards and saw John and Clinton dismantling shelves. I ordered a cup of hot coffee and asked, "What's going on?"

"We're closing down," John said in a matter-of-fact tone.

I was shocked. The news hit me like a sledgehammer. John explained that the building was sold and his new landlord slapped him and Clinton with an unreasonable rent hike.

"We can't make it," he said. "It's unfair. So we're closing shop."

I stood motionless, stunned into silence. Lizards was my sanctuary. What would I do without it?

"Here's your coffee," said John, handing me a mug. "It's on the house."

I felt so heartsick, I wanted to cry. Within a few hours, the neon lizard that was mounted outside was dismantled, and the tawdry district known as Theatre Row had lost the only place to hang after the show.

A few weeks later, Bob, the property manager of the Las Palmas Apartments, abruptly retired and drove his old Mercury off the front lawn. A younger manager was hired to take his place, a tall heavy-set immigrant from Guatemala. Her English was broken but good.

"Believe me when I say dis place no good. Look bery bad. I make beautiful," she said.

That gal tore through the Las Palmas Apartments like an Ajax white tornado. She scrubbed the front marble lobby, painted the dingy green walls a bright creamy white, raked the dirt yard and planted a beautiful lawn that she watered daily. In a short while, the shabby Las Palmas Apartments had transformed into a place that looked manicured and respectable.

But life at Las Palmas wasn't the same for Holly, not like it had been when we were writing the book. She was still in school, but she was out of work, running out of money, and desperate to recapture the limelight that was now starting to fade. Holly's knee-jerk reaction was to run away.

"Jeffrey, I'm moving in with Teresa," she told me one day. That week, she packed up everything—her clothes and wigs and high heels, her cosmetics, her colorful pillows, the bed, the vanity, and her gold Nefertiti. I was at work, shuffling papers, when Teresa came over in a pickup truck and hauled everything away. When I got home that night, I walked into Holly's empty, unlocked apartment and a sadness swelled inside me. The smell of fresh paint lingered in the air. The orange walls and chartreuse molding that were so outrageous, and so Holly, had been whitewashed earlier that day and lost forever. There would be no more knocks on the wall. No more chats outside our windows. The only thing that remained was that glorious, rent-controlled, million-dollar Hollywood view. I walked over to the window and savored it. It was so beautiful. I couldn't believe that Holly just dumped it, like it meant nothing more to her than an old postcard.

ERICH VON STROHEIM'S

From .... Novel

MAE WEST —
IN
SHE DONE HIM
WRONG"

With
CARY
GRANT

a
Paramount
Picture

VICTIM OF ATTACK!

OUTRAGE

IDA LUPINO Production
Introducing MALA POWERS and
TOD ANDREWS
Produced by COLLIER YOUNG Directed by IDA LUPINO
Written for the Screen by COLLIER YOUNG · MALVIN WALD · IDA LUPINO
THE FILMAKERS present a RKO RADIO PICTURES, INC.

"The Thief of Dreams"

EMIL JANNINGS RICARDO CORTEZ
BETTY BRONSON

GREED

Metro Goldwyn Mayer

POWIS

CHAPTER 27

We were both thrilled with the cover design on the Harper Perennial paperback. The cover photo is one of Holly's favorites.

IN 1992, HARPER PERENNIAL PUBLISHED THE TRADE paperback version of *Low Life*, which was exciting, but a far cry from the movie premiere we'd dreamt about. We were still waiting for a movie deal. To make money, Holly teamed up with an accomplished actor named Michael Greer, who co-created a live show for her. Michael was an older gentleman in his late fifties. He knew Holly because they had worked together Off Broadway in New York.

Michael Greer was tall and handsome, had an impressive career as an actor in TV, films, and theatre, and was also a popular performer. He was funny and talented and created a stage act for Holly that she could take on the road.

Teresa was now managing Holly and booked Holly's new act in cabarets and nightclubs around the country. It was a smashing success, not because Holly had sold-out performances, but because of the mere fact that Teresa actually got it booked. When Holly performed in West Hollywood, she drew a large crowd that included a handful of celebrities, including Lily Tomlin and Jane Wagner, and Dick Sargent (the second Darren on *Bewitched*).

Teresa and I were very proud of how well Holly was doing, so during one engagement, we invited a few good friends to see the show and share in our celebration. One of our friends, Eileen, now worked as a publicist at a major record label. Holly had worked so hard and looked absolutely incredible, so we were excited for Eileen to see her perform.

Holly with Gorilla at the opening of her cabaret act at the Rose Tattoo. 1992.

When Holly took to the stage, wearing a blue shimmering gown and blue satin gloves, Eileen's face lit up with fascination. But when the music started and Holly began to sing, Eileen's fascination turned to shock and disbelief. She nudged me, almost panic-stricken.

"What the hell is that?" she asked.

The same sentiment was shared by another friend, who turned to me and said, "Is this a joke?"

He thought Holly's voice was terrible and started to laugh until he realized he had to sit through an hour of Holly's caterwauling because I refused to walk out.

"We can't leave in the middle of her show," I whispered. "That's rude!"

"Not half as rude as her screeching," he retorted.

Holly's singing style wasn't for everyone . . . probably because Holly couldn't sing. But she could carry a tune, and she was funny and charming on stage, and that's why people came to see her. She was a personality, and despite her dubious talent, she packed the venues night after night.

Holy cow—it's Darren #2 from *Bewitched*! I was blown away when Dick Sargent showed up to see Holly's show. 1992.

The most memorable performance came one evening at a cabaret called the Rose Tattoo. Holly was in the middle of her opening monologue. I couldn't tell anything was wrong from where I sat, but suddenly Holly stopped her act and screamed, "Will you people shut up?!" *Jesus Christ*, I thought. *What the hell just happened?* Unbeknownst to me, three men sitting at a table in front of the stage were talking nonstop while Holly was trying to perform. Holly got distracted by their chatter and it threw off her comic timing. So . . . she exploded!

I'd never seen anything like it. The audience erupted in cheers and applause. The offending parties shut their mouths, paid their bill, and walked out. Holly laughed it off, got back on track, and continued her show as if nothing had happened. It was all about rolling with the punches when it came to live cabaret. Anything could happen!

While Holly was shimmying along the cabaret circuit, I was still looking forward to the movie deal that was headed our way, even though it was moving at a snail's pace. Then one morning Robert called. We had a deal, and the news was so big, it made Liz Smith's gossip column in the *New York Daily News*. Madonna was in cahoots with a big producer and a world-famous writer to make a movie based on Holly Woodlawn's autobiography. I couldn't believe it. No one gave two shits about Madonna when I pitched her. How did this happen?

"Darling, isn't it exciting?" Holly squealed over the phone. "Madonna wants to make our movie! Oh! I can't wait for the premiere."

Holly hitched herself to Madonna's gravy train and clung to the caboose like it was the last bottle of chardonnay on Earth. I was stunned.

Teresa, Holly, and a friend after Holly's performance at the Rose Tattoo. 1992.

The deal was being set up at Columbia Pictures through Dolly Parton's production company, Sandollar Films. The high-concept pitch was a retelling of the Marilyn Monroe classic *How to Marry a Millionaire*, only with drag queens. The famous writer was attached to write the script.

"What is going on?" I asked Robert. "I earned those screenplay rights. Those are mine."

I was furious. Robert was irritated. We got into a heated argument that he ended when he forced me to see the simple truth I'd refused to recognize.

"You're a with!" he shouted. "A with!"

He referenced my credit on the book jacket: "by Holly Woodlawn with Jeff Copeland." That "with" had been my choice. In hindsight, it was a terrible mistake. I could have had "by Holly Woodlawn and Jeff Copeland" on the cover. I had it on the copyright. But when it came to the book cover, I just didn't think it mattered.

Holly was not pleased that I stood up for what I believed was rightfully mine.

"I worked for this opportunity, Holly," I said. "This is the only reason I wrote the book, and now you want to take it away."

Opening night at the Rose Tattoo with Holly looking spectacular.
Photo by Teresa Conboy.

I was willing to compromise and collaborate with another writer, but that suggestion was out of the question.

"Then let me write the first draft," I offered. "That way I can at least get into the Writers Guild."

Becoming a member of the Writers Guild would have been a huge milestone for me. It would have given me a chance for a pension and health insurance. But in order to get that, I had to write at least one draft of the screenplay for a studio that was a signatory to the guild. The other writer could then rewrite it or toss it out completely. This happens all the time in Hollywood. But that suggestion wasn't acceptable, either.

I held out for a better deal to everyone's bitter frustration. Eventually, the famous writer sent Holly a postcard that said he was working on making the deal happen, but he didn't want to pursue it if it was going to hurt her co-author.

"Please tell me that he understands the workings of heartless Hollywood," he wrote. "'cause I don't want to be any part of breaking his sweet little heart. I'd rather walk away and do something else. Advise, please! Love, your servant..."

The workings of heartless Hollywood...

His sweet little heart...

Your servant? I read that and thought, *When was the last time he scrubbed Holly Woodlawn's kitchen floor?*

Where was this guy when Holly was a drunk mess? Did he take her under his wing and get her a job at Wacko? And curiously, Holly never mentioned him when we were writing the book. We never visited with him when we were in New York, interviewing her friends about her life. Now all of a sudden they were best chums and I was in the way.

Holly played Joan Crawford on stage in *Christmas with the Crawfords*. Miki Mootsey as Christina. 1997.
Photo by Peter Palladino. Courtesy of the Peter Palladino Archive.

I felt hurt and betrayed and refused to sign the contracts. Holly was livid. She called me on the phone and said in a firm, authoritative tone, "Jeffrey! I'm coming over!"

Oh, boy, I thought. *Mommie Dearest is on her way.* I could hardly wait for this admonishment.

Holly drove her gear-grinding, brake-squealing, smoke-spewing jalopy over to Las Palmas and met me outside. When she saw me she said, "Hon, we have to talk." She had a very serious, parental tone to her voice, which I found rather ironic and offensive, since I was the responsible one.

"Let's go for a walk," I said. As we began to wander up the street, I knew we wouldn't get anywhere.

"Jeffrey, this book is the only thing I've got."

"Where was this guy when you were broke and couldn't pay your rent?" I asked. "Where was he when you were sobbing into a pay phone outside the donut shop, drunk and lost and unable to get your shit together? I was the one who found you an apartment and got you a job. I was the one who carried the torch and wrote my ass off. And I'm the one who turned down jobs to write this fucking book, Holly."

Jesus Christ! I couldn't believe I turned down Paul Reubens for this horseshit.

I was furious. All the hard work and sacrifice I made were so meaningless now. No one remembered. No one cared.

"Columbia Pictures is offering $300,000," Holly said. "And you're getting forty percent of my pussy. That's a lot of money, Jeffrey."

Forty percent wasn't enough to make my heart feel any better. But it would buy me a nice three-story Victorian house overlooking a lake in St. Louis, which was certainly better than nothing. But that still didn't make it right.

"It's the principle, Holly," I said.

"Fuck the principle!" she screamed.

"NO!" I yelled back at her. "Why can't I work on this movie? I should at least be part of the screenwriting process. It doesn't make sense. I'm not asking for the world. I just want to help."

"Because you're not wanted!" she yelled. She lashed out now, delivering one painful, crushing blow after another. "No one wanted you. Not even Robert wanted you. You're not a writer. You're a typist. I talked and you typed. That's all you did, Jeffrey. Type, type, type! It's my life story. MY STORY! Now stop being such a pain in the ass!"

I was wrecked. This was worse than being pulled off the monkey bars when I was a little boy and having dirt rubbed in my face. And as Holly's true colors bled in ways that were spiteful and audacious, I stepped back and let everyone have their way.

I cared about Holly. I appreciated the opportunity she gave me. And despite my hurt feelings, I didn't want this fiasco to destroy our friendship. But in some ways it did. Our relationship could never be the same.

My friend Eileen, the major music publicist and one of the kindest people I'd ever met, couldn't believe the injustice of it all. Her Irish dander flared, and her blue eyes sparkled and flashed.

"Mark my words," she said. "Nothing good will ever come to that *thing!*"

It was a dire warning that rang familiar. I'd heard that tone before when people said Holly was a mess. But this time, I actually listened, and with much sadness, I believed it was true.

"She's troubled," my friend Derrick said one night after fixing me a drink. As we sat there in his beautiful 1920s apartment, I admired his collection of Art Deco furnishings that he had meticulously procured. "You did a wonderful thing for Holly, and you can be proud of that. But you have to move on now. You'll be fine. You'll write something else."

I smiled because I appreciated his confidence and tossed back the gin and tonic before releasing a heavy sigh.

"I'll write something better," I said.

So I let go of the *Low Life* screenplay rights. Holly was ecstatic. As we waited for the studio contracts to arrive, I had pangs of regret. Why didn't I fight harder? Why did I agree to take the short end of the stick? Why was I such a co-dependent mess? A screenwriting credit with a major studio could have launched my career. Now I was back to square one. Why did I do this to myself?

I loved Holly. I wanted things to get back to the way they were before the book was published. I wanted to hear her knock on the wall again. I longed for chats with her outside our windows. I wanted to relive those times when we would hang out at Lizards and review chapters, or take off in the Fiero when she was draped in Christmas tree pearls. I wanted so much to have that fun back in my life. And then one day, it came to me in the most unexpected way.

"Darling, I've got good news!" Holly sang over my 1940s telephone. "I'm starring in the gay pride parade! Michael Greer is producing this hilarious craziness, and the good news is he wants you, too! Isn't that fabulous?"

"Holly . . . what are you talking about?" I said.

"You're going to be a dancer, honey! In Michael Greer's Bette Davis Marching Drill Team!"

Who knew my work on *A Low Life in High Heels* would amount to such an honor?

"A dancer?!" I said. "Holly, no!"

There was a rustling on the line and Michael Greer got on the phone.

"Jeffrey," he said in a calm, soothing voice, which oddly sounded a bit like Ronald Reagan. "You're perfect. A big, corn-fed Midwestern farm boy is just what the drill team needs."

I wasn't from a farm and I couldn't dance. This didn't make any sense. But I agreed to do it because I wanted another adventure with Holly. Besides, I really had nothing else to look forward to, except a forty-hour-a-week day job that wasn't that exciting.

Five minutes into our first rehearsal in the West Hollywood Park auditorium, I realized this was a disaster. I didn't have any rhythm, I couldn't follow the dance steps, and I looked ridiculous.

"Michael, I'm sorry. I don't want to let you down," I said.

"Don't worry, you'll get it," said Michael. "You'll be fine."

The more rehearsals I attended, the more frustrated I got. In fact, I always quit after every rehearsal and Michael always cajoled me into coming back.

"You can do it, Jeffrey," Michael insisted as he slid up beside me and counted out the steps. "Step one, two three four, step two, two three four, turn, swivel…"

For some people, practice makes perfect. But in my case, when it came to swiveling, shuffling, and clapping my hands, I never improved. I was a mess when it came to doing the Hustle in 1978; how on Earth did I think I could pull this off?

"That's why you're perfect," said Michael.

"Jeffrey, you look big and fluffy," said Holly. "That's all that matters."

Fluffy was Holly's polite term for fat.

I knew I was a dancing calamity. I could just hear those snide West Hollywood queens pointing at me from the parade route sidelines because we all know they love to point and ridicule. I could just imagine the one with the sassy wedge haircut screaming out a sarcastic remark.

"Look at her! Look at her and her fat ass twirling around and tripping over her feet like a hot mess!"

I was not comfortable looking like a fool.

"Oh, honey, don't take it so seriously!" Holly said. "Who cares if you trip over your feet and fall on your ass. No one cares."

No one except for Miss Sassy Pants on the sidelines with the wedge haircut.

On the day of the parade, I was a nervous wreck. Holly and I met at the designated condominium where we joined the other drill team members and got into our costumes. Mine was a grass hula skirt, a weird feather-like headdress, and a coconut bra! Holly was made up to look like Joan Crawford in *What Ever Happened to Baby Jane?* She wore a black wig, a long dark robe, and black slippers.

After tossing back a few cocktails, we filled our plastic cups to the brim with more hooch and then staggered down to Santa Monica Boulevard where the parade entries were being assembled. It was quite an eclectic scene with glittering drag queens dressed in sequined evening gowns, oiled muscle boys wearing G-strings, potbellied leather bears wearing chaps that showed off their bare hairy asses, and the loud and uproarious Dykes on Bikes motorcycle club, who revved their engines and put every snippy queen on high alert.

Trying to maintain the order of all this craziness was a bossy little gal who zipped around in a golf cart, blowing a whistle and honking a horn.

Beep! Beep! Beep!

"Make way for Little Toot, honey!" chuckled Holly. "She'll snatch your cocktail and run you down."

Beep! Beep! Beep! Little Toot was laying on that golf cart's horn like she was blowing through town in a diesel locomotive.

Waiting in the hot morning sun for the parade to launch was almost as bad as waiting for a movie deal. When it was finally our time to go, the Bette Davis Marching Drill Team theme song blasted from giant speakers mounted on the back of a car, where Michael Greer and a famous Bette Davis impersonator named Randy Allen were riding and waving to fans. The theme was loud and bawdy and sounded like 1940s stripper music.

While I performed one misstep after another with the group of dancers, Baby Jane pushed the wheelchair in which Holly sat. As Holly rolled down Santa Monica Boulevard, waving to the crowds, her robe got caught in the spokes. The fabric got twisted into the wheel and it jammed. Holly was stuck! The front half of the parade continued to move along its course while the back half came to a screeching halt because Baby Jane and Blanche were at a standstill.

While Holly struggled with her wheelchair, I stumbled through the ridiculous dance moves and tried to keep up with the rest of the dancers. But within minutes, I had sweat in my eyes, a fallen headdress in my face, and a coconut bra around my belly. I literally had to stop everything just to get the headdress back on top of my head and the coconuts back on my chest. Once I got my costume situated, I started to "dance" again. Seriously, folks, an orangutan would have had more grace. Well . . . one twirl is all it took for that headdress to fall and the coconuts to drop. Thank goodness for the grass skirt, which stopped the coconut bra from dropping any further; otherwise, I would have tripped over those coconuts and fallen on my face! Now I understood the importance of a dress rehearsal, which we never had, so who knew our costumes would be so difficult to manage?

As I scrambled to get it together, I saw Holly frantically rocking back and forth in her wheelchair, trying to dislodge the caught fabric. Baby Jane was panic-stricken, running around the wheelchair, pushing, pulling, kicking, and screaming. No matter how hard those two pushed and pulled, that wheelchair wouldn't budge. Baby Jane abandoned Holly altogether to catch up with the rest of us, while Michael Greer jumped in and tried to get the stalled wheelchair to roll because it had now caused the parade to come to a standstill! In a fit of frustration, Holly got out of the chair, grabbed the caught fabric, and yanked it with all her might. She ripped it out of the wheel spokes just as Little Toot came zipping by in her golf cart, blowing her whistle and honking her horn, ready to take charge. But unfortunately, not even she, with all her butch bravado, could save the Bette Davis Marching Drill Team. It just got worse as the parade went along.

Adolph Zukor presents

Wallace Reid
Gloria Swanson
Elliott Dexter

in

"Don't
Tell
Everything!"

Three of the screen's biggest stars—in one of the screen's biggest pictures!

A Sam Wood Production
By Lorna Moon

A Paramount Picture

ADOLPH ZUKOR and JESSE L. LASKY PRESENT A

JAMES CRUZE
Production

THE ENEMY SEX

WITH

BETTY COMPSON

"THE SALAMANDER"
by OWEN JOHNSON

Paramount Picture

THE FAKER

Jacqueline Logan · Warner Oland
Charles Delaney · Gaston Glass

Directed by PHIL ROSEN

A **COLUMBIA**
PRODUCTION

CHAPTER 28

MONTHS LATER, OUR DEAL WITH COLUMBIA PICTURES was still in the works with no contracts in sight. Robert, our agent, sent me an Andy Warhol postcard, which read:

"I had the chance to read (again) lots of LOW LIFE this weekend and so felt compelled to send you this card reminding you of what a truly wonderful job you did; what a WOW! of a book it is."

I was touched and flattered, and it was nice of him to send. But big whoop. So I worked my ass off. What for? What did it matter? Who really cared? Well, according to the news media, Madonna. She was the best thing about that deal with Columbia. Her name alone created a publicity firestorm for the book that went around the world. Suddenly, *A Low Life in High Heels* had become a topic of international celebrity news, which resulted in more party invitations for Holly and a bit part in Madonna's music video "Deeper and Deeper."

"Don't even look at her, is what we were told," Holly explained of her experience working with Madonna. "So we all just, you know, chatted amongst ourselves and ignored her. And then between takes, she called out to me and said, 'Holly, the seam in your stocking is crooked.' And I said, 'Oh, thanks, hon.' And that was my day with Madonna."

Even though Holly's screen time amounted to less than five seconds, being part of that video was yet another sparkling jewel in her crown of celebrity. Not only was Holly an Andy Warhol superstar, but she was also now one of Madonna's royal subjects, or so people believed. I hoped it would bring more opportunities her way.

Around this time, Holly was getting ready to graduate from the Fashion Institute of Design & Merchandising. This was a huge accomplishment, and Holly's parents flew out for the occasion. Teresa had a small graduation party at home

Wow! What the heck is this? A rare snapshot of Holly and Udo Kier on the "Deeper and Deeper" music video shoot with Madonna. 1992.

Photo by Greg Gorman, courtesy of the Greg Gorman Archive.

to celebrate. While Holly's father seemed genuinely happy that his son had earned a diploma, he turned to Teresa and said, "He won't do anything with it." Later, when Teresa told me that, I thought it was terrible.

After graduation, Holly went on a couple of low-level job interviews in the Garment District. When she didn't get hired, she lost interest in finding a job altogether. Perhaps the idea of starting at the bottom of the fashion industry wasn't that appealing, but at least it was a foot in the door. Her friends, though, thought otherwise.

"You can't expect Holly to get a job," said one Andy Warhol Factory alum who was also an actor/writer/artist in her own right.

And Holly agreed. Now that she was basking in the glow of Madonna, she didn't want a job. She wanted fabulous parties, white wine, and enabling flatterers telling her she was great. And that's exactly what Holly got.

"Madonna is going to star in my movie, honey!" she said every chance she got. "We're in negotiations with Columbia Pictures as we speak."

Movie contracts took a while to type, or so it seemed. Even though Holly and I had agreed to all the terms, it took at least a year before our contracts were ready to sign. We agreed to an option fee of $10,000 for one year but had no idea it would take so long to get paid. By then, Holly had blown through all the cash that she earned on the cabaret circuit and was irritated that I was entitled to my fair share.

"He's got forty percent of my pussy, honey!" she complained to practically anyone who would listen.

Forty percent of a pussy that never really existed because it was all a ruse in the first place.

On the day our contracts were to arrive, we got word they weren't coming. There was a brouhaha amongst the producers that caused the entire deal to collapse. There wouldn't be a $10,000 option or a $300,000 payment for the film rights. After waiting with great anticipation for a year, we got nothing.

Holly and I felt battered and bruised by the experience. To make matters even more challenging, when we lost the Columbia deal, we lost our agent. Robert moved on. I certainly didn't blame him, but that left Holly and me to peddle the *Low Life* story rights ourselves, which was a hard row to hoe. We weren't agents, but we would do the best we could with our limited resources.

Shortly afterward, the company where I worked was restructured and I was laid off. I was twenty-nine years old, living on severance and unemployment, trying to find my way, but to what? So like every other starry-eyed dreamer in Hollywood, I wrote a screenplay. I was back on the Hollywood whirligig, low on cash but high on hope, living on strong black coffee and creative exhilaration. I was a full-time writer, and it was great. But by September 1993, my finances were dwindling fast. I had to get a job—one that would put me on the path that I should have been on all along. I pumped out résumés and got a few calls, but the money was so ridiculously bad, I'd wind up homeless if I took one of those jobs.

So I looked out my apartment window at that spectacular Hollywood view and wondered what to do, where to turn. For a moment, I felt lost. I knew where I wanted to go, I just didn't know how to get there. As I stood in that window, a calm settled over me. In that moment, I was like a mindless goldfish looking out of its bowl, not really thinking about anything in particular, as my eyes wandered over every iconic building and tourist attraction that now felt like a part of me: the Griffith Observatory, the Broadway department store sign, the Hollywood Roosevelt Hotel, and the Capitol Records building. I could even see Madonna's house in the hills because she painted it terra-cotta and it stuck out like a sore thumb.

In the foreground, I saw the top of a soundstage that was located two blocks up at the Hollywood Center movie studio. That studio was built

The guard gate at what was then known as Hollywood Center Studios. Built in 1919, it's one of the oldest studios in Hollywood. Harold Lloyd, Fred Astaire, Laurel & Hardy, Jean Harlow, and Mae West are just a few of the legendary stars who worked there.

in the Roaring Twenties, when pictures were silent, but the stars were loud, boozing, balling, and raising a ruckus in those fun, fast, carefree days. Imagined memories flickered and glowed, and the spirits called to me like ghosts who still wanted to play.

And I thought: *Wouldn't it be nice to walk to work?*

I remembered those flowers in a soda bottle that my mother fixed up for me so many years before. It was a brilliant strategy. Such a simple idea, but it was that kind of thinking that always saved me during the worst of times. Think out of the box. Cut to the chase. Get an inside tip. That's what I was thinking when I walked up Las Palmas to see the studio guard. Who the hell in their right mind asks a studio guard for a job?

No one . . . and that's exactly why I did it.

He was a young, husky Latino dressed in a blue uniform. He looked at me with a curious expression when I tapped on the glass door of his kiosk.

Hi there," I said. "I know this is going to sound odd, but I live right down the block, my rent is due, and I need a job."

He looked at me like I was crazy. But what did I care? I had no shame when it came to groveling for work.

"Do you know of any new productions on the lot that might be hiring?"

I explained that I'd been looking for a job for months and wasn't having any luck.

"I just need an inside tip," I said.

The guard gave it some thought and then scrawled two phone numbers onto a piece of scrap paper.

"These are two start-ups," he said. "They just moved onto the lot. They might need some help. Just don't tell them I told you."

I looked at those numbers like they were the secrets to a winning lotto ticket.

"Thank you," I said.

I went home and dialed the first number.

"No, we don't need your help," said the curt asshole who answered the phone and then hung up.

But when I dialed the second number, my fortune changed as I was greeted by a warm, friendly voice that belonged to a young woman named Jodi.

"We are looking for some help," she said. "When can you come in to meet?"

The following day, I had an interview with Kathleen French and Debby Reid. They were producing a PBS documentary series called *Future Quest*. Five days later, they hired me to work in their production office as a receptionist. The job paid $400 a week, "but you have so much experience, we'd like to start you at $450," Debby said. I got a raise before I'd even started! When does that ever happen?

Kathleen French and Debby Reid were generous with their experience and knowledge, and they opened the doors of opportunity that had been previously closed to me. Whenever I asked for help, no one smirked and snapped, "Don't you know who I am?" After eight long years of blowing around Hollywood like a wayward tumbleweed, I was finally in a place where my ideas were welcomed, my initiative was encouraged, and I could thrive.

While I worked in television during the day and wrote screenplays at night, Holly was back on the cabaret circuit, performing *A Low Life in High Heels* as a cabaret show in bars and clubs, and hustling for another movie deal to come her way. She gave up on her goal of being a fashion designer. As far as I knew, she stopped sewing altogether. Holly's sights were set solely on the big screen and she hustled her story to anyone who'd listen. In 1993, Teresa got her a spot on *The Joan Rivers Show* where Holly touted the book. She looked incredible, but an appearance on a national daytime talk show wasn't enough to sustain her. She was on TV for ten minutes. And while it was great exposure and fun to talk about, in the grand scheme of things . . . so what? It didn't amount to anything.

While Holly continued to hawk *Low Life*, my latest script got optioned by an up-and-coming producer named Michael Zoumas, who worked with an established, Academy Award-winning producer named Michael Phillips. Michael Phillips was huge. He produced *The Sting* and *Close Encounters of the Third Kind*, and got my script into the hands of a legendary director named Arthur Penn. It was an exciting time.

When the time was right, I sent Michael Zoumas a copy of *A Low Life in High Heels*.

"This could be a great movie," I said. "A fifteen-year-old misfit runs away from home, desperate to find his place in the world. He impersonates a woman, becomes Andy Warhol's greatest superstar in 1970, and lives a life of sex, drugs, rock and roll!"

Zoumas was intrigued.

"It's got all the elements of an award-winning film," I continued. "It's hilarious and poignant. You're going to love it."

At that time, Zoumas had no idea who Holly Woodlawn was, but after reading the book, he took *Low Life* under his wing and re-ignited its fire in a way that was fantastic and explosive. He sent the book to his friends Don Murphy and Jane Hamsher, two hotshot producers who'd just finished making Oliver Stone's *Natural Born Killers*. Michael, Don, and Jane put together a deal with a director named Rose Troche, who made a huge splash that year at the Sundance Film Festival with her first movie, *Go Fish*. Rose liked the *Low Life* book and was surprised by how much it resonated with her. She also had some exciting ideas on how to tell the story on film, which Holly loved.

Holly and I signed an option agreement, and on January 25, 1995, *Variety* came out with a huge article about the deal. The double headline was enormous:

"A NEW LIFE FOR 'HIGH HEELS'
Rights to Holly Woodlawn biopic wind up with Zoumas."

When we met Don, Jane, Michael, and Rose at the Abbey in West Hollywood to celebrate our new venture, Holly was so happy she swilled back one glass of chardonnay after another and got drunk. She got so plastered, in fact, that Zoumas took me aside and told me he didn't want her involved in any of the studio pitch meetings. It was an unfortunate situation, but I understood the reason. Holly didn't make the best impression when she was soused and out of control.

At the time, I was on hiatus from a TV series, so I was free to work with Rose on the script. We outlined the story structure during the day, and at night I wrote the scenes. Adapting a three-hundred-page book into a 120-page screenplay is a lot of work. Whittling that story down to its essence was a long and arduous chore, but within four weeks we had a strong working draft that everyone seemed to love.

"What kind of shit screenplay is this?!"

Everyone except Holly.

"Darling, this script starts with me overdosing on heroin!" Holly screamed over the phone. "You can't have me strung out in a bathtub on heroin!"

"Holly, it's one of the most poignant scenes in the book—"

"Darling, no! I'm Holly Woodlawn! I've got to be fabulous and glamorous. You can't open my movie with me shooting up and nearly dying."

"Well, fuck you, missy!" I hollered back.

I could have started that screenplay with Holly doing the can-can while bottle rockets shot out of her wig and it wouldn't have made any difference. Holly wasn't happy because she wasn't involved in the screenwriting process. She'd been tossed aside like she didn't matter. Thrown under the bus like she was a WITH! Now it was her turn to understand the workings of heartless Hollywood. The pain, the rage, and the betrayal I felt when I was thrown aside . . . it was all coming to an ugly head now. I'd never dealt with those feelings. I just buried them for the sake of keeping the peace, and now those raw emotions lashed out in a horrible, expletive-infused tirade that gave new meaning to the phrase "love you madly."

We tore into one another like two tigers tied by their tails, ripping and clawing until every festering wound had bled dry and there were no more tears left to shed. But no amount of screaming and cursing could turn things around for *A Low Life in High Heels*. While it was a fun book and a hilarious story, the films *Priscilla, Queen of the Desert* and *To Wong Fu, Thanks for Everything! Julie Newmar* pretty much stole its thunder. Did the American movie-going audience need another movie about drag queens? Not really. And to complicate matters, Holly was never a drag queen . . . she was gender-fluid. She wasn't a caricature or a clown, and no one seemed to get that, either. So the movie deal that got a huge headline and generated so much excitement went belly-up.

I was proud of my screenplay, though, and used it as a writing sample. In 1997, a respected film producer named Sandy Stern read it and liked it.

"This is a smart script," he said.

Stern produced the independent film *Pump Up the Volume* and was now partnered with singer Michael Stipe of R.E.M. and in development on a new movie called *Being John Malkovich*. When Stern casually asked about the motion picture rights to *Low Life*, I called Holly. I thought the possibility of optioning the film rights to a high-caliber independent film production company was exciting, but Holly balked at the idea.

"Fuck you, Jeffrey!" she yelled.

God bless Liz Smith! Her column always stoked the smoldering embers of Holly's fame, which died down over the years but never quite burned out. 2001.

For over ten years, there were many valiant attempts to make *A Low Life in High Heels* into a film. Holly even teamed up with some well-meaning friends and wrote her own screenplay. During that time, whenever an option to the *Low Life* film rights came up, Holly and I always fought over my attempts to protect our mutual interests.

"Holly, you can't just give your rights away to anybody who comes along," I said, trying to reason with her. "How many movies has this guy produced? What are his credentials?"

We had this argument over and over. Holly was usually drunk when we had these conversations. She didn't care about credentials or rights. Now she was the starry-eyed dreamer . . . and I was the pragmatic, nose-to-the-grindstone asshole who pushed for a better deal.

"Jeffrey, why are you so difficult?"

"Just option the screen rights," I said. "Don't let them have the stage rights, too, because you don't want to put all your eggs in one basket."

"Why are you such a pain in the ass?!"

"Because once you sell all your rights to that book, Holly, they're gone."

"What difference does that make?" she snapped.

"It makes a huge difference because I own forty percent And when you fuck yourself, you fuck me, too."

"You have ruined my life!" she screamed at the top of her lungs.

Madonna likes 'Long Hair' option, may star in pic, too

By CHARLES LYONS

Madonna's Mad Guy Films has optioned the script "The Long Hair Depression" from scribe Jeff Copeland.

Madonna, who is developing the project with Copeland, plans on producing the film and is considering starring in it as well.

In 1992, Dana Millikin inspired me to write a screenplay about my childhood, which I called *The Long Hair Depression*. It took eight long years to get it optioned! After years of development hell, it's now being turned into a hilarious book. 2001.

This kind of drunken hysteria usually came at me when she was pissed off because I played hardball, refused to sign a contract, and always held out for better terms. And it went on for years. Our arguments started when I was a production coordinator and continued until I was a supervising producer. I'd worked hard to build my career, but Holly never recognized it. At times, she treated me like an ignorant, backwater Missouri rube.

"Your name is not Holly Woodlawn," she once said in a recorded message. "Your name is Jeff Copeland. You have never done anything in your life. All you did was write a book about my life."

Then there was the time she yelled, "Honey! You should take what you can get!"

But much to her chagrin, I never did. I knew how to push for something better, but Holly wanted no part of that, even if it meant she'd benefit in the end. She'd get drunk, call me on the phone at the office or on location, and cuss me out so bad it was comical. It was the same old diatribe of rants and raves that always ended with, "You're getting forty percent of my pussy! You asshole!"

And then she'd hang up.

In 2001, when Madonna finally called, it had nothing to do with *A Low Life in High Heels* or Holly Woodlawn. She'd read one of my screenplays and liked it so much, she optioned the rights. Thanks to my agent, Lorianne Hall, the news was carried in the Hollywood trades and in newspapers and magazines around the world. That was the one thing I could count on with Madonna: a whirlwind of publicity. But even better was that she paid her bills! I didn't have to wait for the option money. When I told Lorianne I wanted the option fee doubled because I thought it was more reasonable, there was no argument from Madonna's camp. The check was delivered before the contracts were even signed.

The fact that I'd landed a movie deal with the most famous woman in the world never impressed Holly. It just irritated her. At the end of one angry phone message, before hanging up, Holly screamed, "And Madonna can go kiss my pussy for Israel!"

That pussy was nothing more than a sour lemon.

By now, Holly's alcoholism had gotten out of hand, fueling her irrational behavior and her poor business sense. The emotional toll was terrible and exhausting, but I wouldn't walk away. We were bound together by a copyright. That was the legal linchpin that kept us together. One could not move forward with a film option without the other. Every time someone expressed interest in the *Low Life* movie rights, I put them through the wringer because I wanted a fair and legitimate deal. When it came to business, I didn't have a "sweet little heart" and I didn't have patience for pie-in-the-sky bullshit.

In later years, Holly minimized my contribution to her story. "I talked and he typed," she said, conveniently forgetting that the typing wasn't the actual writing of the story. The structure, dialogue, jokes, and prose are where the real heavy lifting came into play. And the reason Holly and I had so many conflicts was because I stood up for what I rightfully deserved: respect.

CHAPTER 29

A S HOLLY'S ALCOHOLISM GOT WORSE, HER LIFE spiraled out of control. She needed help. But I couldn't be the one to give it to her now. I'd graduated from the Holly Woodlawn school of codependence with honors and moved on to bigger challenges. I was a workaholic now and had an all-consuming career. I didn't have time for her craziness. But I still cared about her, even though at times I chose not to show it. Sometimes the reality of her situation was just too painful for me to see. And so I kept myself distracted with burgeoning demands that made me feel important, accomplished, and safe.

Teresa looked after Holly for a few years, until Holly shit on her, too. One weekend, while Teresa was out of town, Holly packed up her belongings and left. For a while, she shacked up with a friend of hers in Beachwood Canyon who had a modest yet charming home that was built so close to the Hollywood sign, it was almost in the backyard. Coincidentally, Madonna's gated compound was right down the road, which added to the home's panache. Holly loved chatting about having Madonna as a neighbor and humorously complained that she never got invited over for coffee.

For a little while, Holly's life appeared stable. She loved living in Beachwood Canyon. But then her landlord sold the house, and Holly was

A candid shot of Holly and her friend Craig Vandenburgh (a.k.a. Tony LaVentura and Tony Zarr). Craig was a force of nature in his own right: a singer, actor, comedian, and model, who worked a lot on stage and in movies with top-notch talent. On the few occasions I got to meet him, his persona was that of an outrageous, over-the-top kook... and I thought he was crazy. 1994.
Photo by Peter Palladino. Courtesy of the Peter Palladino Archive.

forced to move. She hopped from one place to another until she moved in with an acquaintance who became a romance of sorts. They lived on Sweetzer Avenue, just north of Santa Monica Boulevard, in the corner unit of a low-rise mid-century apartment building. I thought they had a good relationship . . . until Holly told me he cracked her over the head with a wine bottle. She filed charges, he went to jail. Holly eventually assumed the lease on his apartment and stayed there for several years. Finally, America's guest had settled down.

Then one night, Holly left her apartment to go to the store. While walking along the boulevard, Holly tripped on a cracked sidewalk and fell. The injury caused nerve damage and impaired her ability to walk. For a time, she was in a nursing home. Doctors warned that if she didn't stop drinking, she would die.

Holly dried out for a while, but so much damage had already been done, her decline steadily continued. Her mobility issues, however, never stopped her from getting carried onstage to perform or attend film festival screenings in her honor. Every now and then, I'd catch a glimpse of her in West Hollywood

Park and I'd always go out of my way to say hello. By that time, Holly had a caregiver. Even though Holly was wheelchair-bound and her speech was impaired, she never once lost hope that the *Low Life* movie would be made.

"Euan Morton is going to play me and we're going to shoot in New York!" she proclaimed. "And the premiere! Oh, honey, wait until you see what I've got planned."

I always forced myself to smile and act excited, even though hearing Holly speak like that only made my heart ache. I knew that premiere, just like all the other premieres we had dreamt about before, would never come.

In December 2015, I got a call from Holly's good friend, Adriano, who told me Holly was dying. Holly had been diagnosed with terminal cancer that had spread to her brain. I was saddened by the news. Our conflicts had long been put to rest by now. I didn't harbor any resentments, and my hope was that she didn't either. It was terrible that things turned out the way they did. It didn't have to be this way. But there was nothing I could do about the situation now. Holly was on her way out, and I only wanted the best for her. In the end, she knew that.

Now the time had come to say goodbye. I went to see Holly with Teresa. When we arrived at the assisted living facility where Holly was to spend the last few months of her life, I was impressed at how beautiful the place looked.

Robert Starr, a close friend of Holly's, had arranged for Holly to stay there after her own apartment flooded during a rainstorm and became uninhabitable. Robert and Holly knew each other from the old days in New York, having met in 1969. Now he was her benevolent guardian, looking out for her needs. But sadly, some people turned against Robert and condemned his efforts.

Thanks to an online fundraising campaign, Holly's fans and friends made sure she was well taken care of in the end. When Teresa and I walked into Holly's private room, I was startled to see that Holly's face had ballooned in size because of her medication. But still, she looked happy, and her eyes lit up when she saw us.

"Darlings, I have cancer!" she announced with great vivacity to lighten the mood. Take the worst life has to offer and make it hilarious, that was her motto, whether she was face down in the gutter or standing at death's door.

Cancer . . . of all things.

I always thought Holly would live well into her nineties. I imagined she'd succumb to some ridiculous mishap, like falling face first into a swimming pool while wearing electric curlers. Or maybe her wig would accidentally catch fire and she'd explode, then rise from the ashes like a glittering phoenix, spectacular and awe-inspiring, leaving everyone flabbergasted and cheering for more.

We were all cheering for more, those of us who knew Holly on the upswing when times were good. Teresa and I visited her because of those good times, and we were just getting settled in our chairs to reminisce, when suddenly the door burst open.

"Knock, knock! Hello!" shouted a voice.

A loud brood of friends charged in, and the energy in the room changed completely. Our chance of having a nice, quiet chat amongst the three of us was gone. Now we were in the middle of a three-ring circus with everyone talking at once and Holly being distracted by a friend who dazzled her with gifts he had bought for her earlier in the day.

After the show-and-tell presentation, Holly said she wanted a cigarette. Smoking was not permitted in her room because oxygen tanks were present, so Teresa and I followed the entourage as they wheeled Holly onto the roof where a spectacular nighttime view of city lights played out in every direction.

All of Holly's friends lit up cigarettes. Teresa and I didn't smoke. As we'd gotten older, we'd both developed an allergic reaction to second-hand cigarette smoke that gave us terrible congestion and splitting sinus headaches. So, while the boisterous bunch gathered around Holly, chatting and laughing and blowing smoke, Teresa and I chose to stay several yards away so we could breathe. Once again, I was at a safe distance from all the chaos.

A few weeks later I went to see Holly again. This time she was alone. I brought her some gingerbread, which she ate and enjoyed. Despite the bloating, she looked good. Her eyes were bright. She seemed happy. She certainly didn't look to be on her last legs.

Then the phone rang. Holly answered it.

"Honey, you won't believe who's with me right now," she exclaimed into the receiver. "Jeffrey Copeland! He wrote the book with me."

Holly was on the phone with a French film director who was trying to spearhead a movie about her life.

"I want you two to meet," Holly said. "Jeffrey, this is the director making the movie. Oh, honey, the premiere is going to be fabulous."

Holly handed the phone to me to say hello. I had a brief chat with the film director. He seemed like a nice guy. I turned the phone back over to Holly.

She wrapped up the conversation, then asked me to take her to the roof so she could smoke.

Her feet were gnarled and crooked, and her entire body shook when I helped her stand and get into the wheelchair. It pained me to see Holly in such a state, and for a moment, I wanted to cry. I remembered how radiant she looked when we went to all those fabulous parties and salons. Now Holly was sick and dying, and we were alone on a rooftop with the diminishing sun. I felt awkward and was at a loss for words. She struggled with the cigarette pack and asked for my help.

"Sure," I said, gently taking the package out of her hands. I pulled out a cigarette and helped her light it. She puffed and I could tell the rush of nicotine made her feel better. I told her I liked the place where she was now living and praised her friends for getting her into such a nice facility. She spoke about the internet fundraising campaign that had been established for her care, and how she was genuinely touched by all the people who contributed.

"I can't believe it," she said. "They gave that much to help me."

It was very calm and peaceful on the rooftop that afternoon. We didn't say much. At that moment, I just wanted Holly to be happy and at peace.

"Oh, shit, Holly," I blurted, looking at my cell phone and realizing the time. "I have to put more money in the parking meter. I'll be right back."

I ran downstairs, down the block, and around the corner to feed the meter. It took about ten minutes. When I returned to the rooftop, Holly was struggling to wheel herself to the elevator. She thought I'd abandoned her. I felt terrible.

"I'm sorry it took so long," I said. "I had to park so far away."

I wheeled her into the elevator and back to her room. I helped her get back into bed and asked if she needed anything. Dinner was coming soon. She said she was fine. I looked around the nice room. It was a cluttered mess, and the unpleasant smell made me anxious.

"Honey, I've got to run," I said.

"You're leaving?" She looked surprised.

"I have a lot of work to do. But I'll come back soon. You take care, okay?"

I gave her an awkward hug, then walked out the door. I released a heavy sigh, trying to expel some of the sadness that swelled inside me. *This was horrible*, I thought. *Horrible*. And as I made my way to the elevator and down to the ground level, the memories of our lives together flashed through my mind. The first time we met. The success we shared and all the fun we had.

Holly and I visiting Robert at a beach house in Malibu, when times were good, and we had so much to look forward to... December 1990.
Photo by Robert Drake.

And the one explosive fight that ended with Holly screaming, "You have ruined my life!"

And then today, when she seemed genuinely delighted that I would bring her gingerbread. When she ate it with such voracity, I actually thought, *She's not dying. She's going to outlive us all.*

It was the last time I saw Holly alive.

Two weeks later, on a beautiful Sunday morning, I noticed my cell phone had a missed call from Teresa. She didn't leave a message, but I knew why she called.

"Did Holly die?" I texted her.

"Yes," she texted back.

My heart sank.

I'd spent over thirty years working in Hollywood. Of all the famous people I'd worked with over the years and of all the experiences I was fortunate to have, the one I treasured the most was the one that was the most challenged. But despite all the problems, the memories of my friendship with Holly Woodlawn were now priceless to me. The fun and the laughter we shared were all that really mattered in the end, and I was grateful those moments outshined the sadness.

Holly's invitation-only Los Angeles memorial would take place in a private bungalow at the Chateau Marmont in West Hollywood. I attended with Teresa and another friend, Dawn Moreno-Freedman. As I listened to people share their memories and fondness for Holly, I privately reveled in my own. I thought about the first time I saw Holly, the telephone operator who gave me her number, and the film script I wrote for her that wound up in a literary agent's trash. It was all so serendipitous and absurd . . . and proof that in some cases, stars do align, dreams come true, and goodness does prevail, even in the land of bullshit and glitter. And when that happens, it's important to be grateful. Good luck is a gift.

MAE WEST

IN

"I'm No Angel"

DIRECTED BY WESLEY RUGGLES

a *Paramount* Picture

EPILOGUE

N 2016, HOLLY WAS POSTHUMOUSLY HONORED AT the Academy Awards. I was sitting at a friend's house watching the telecast when I saw Holly's face fly up on the screen.

"WOW!" I yelled.

I was so happy and proud that she finally made it to the Oscars.

It was around that time when I began working on this manuscript. I didn't want to forget the fun times I shared with Holly or the ridiculous struggles I endured trying to make it as a writer. Within a few weeks, I had about two hundred pages of rough material and toyed with the possibility of organizing it into a book. But if I did that, what the hell would I call it? Sometimes thinking of a good title is the biggest challenge of all.

During that time, my friend Bill, who was living with me, went to a spirit circle hosted by a world-renowned psychic medium named Hollister Rand. When the spirit circle ended, Bill called me on my cell phone.

"Jeff, it was amazing!" he said. "Holly's spirit showed up!"

I was stunned.

"Oh my God!" I said. "What happened?"

"I taped it with my iPhone. I'll play it for you when I get home," he said.

Later that night, Bill and I sat in the living room and he played the recording. This is what I heard:

HOLLISTER: "I know this is going to sound so odd, but you don't know a drag queen who died, do you? Because there's a drag queen here with you. A big personality person. You know. She keeps pointing to me, so there's something about me that she either knows or we share something in common. So it could be a namesake. There's something we share in common."

(I was blown away because that commonality was the name Holly. Holly is Hollister's birth name.)

HOLLISTER: "God, she's bigger than life! I feel like she's passed somewhat recently. I don't feel as though she's been over there for very long. Do you know if her death was a bit of a surprise to people? Because she just yelled surprise to me, and she's talking about her death."

(Holly got cancer. That was the biggest surprise of all.)

HOLLISTER: "She's talking to me about a cemetery. She wants to be buried in a particular cemetery, a famous cemetery."

(Part of Holly's ashes were interred at the Hollywood Forever Cemetery, which is a famous cemetery in Hollywood and the final resting place for show business legends like Douglas Fairbanks, Rudolph Valentino, and Judy Garland.)

HOLLISTER: "I think she wanted a star on the Hollywood Walk of Fame."

(Holly did want a star and Teresa campaigned for her to get one, but they cost thousands of dollars to buy and Holly could never afford it.)

HOLLISTER: "She's delighted with herself, I have to tell you. She was a force to be reckoned with."

(You can say that again!)

HOLLISTER: "Strong-willed, and she would strong-arm people into her way of thinking, too. This is a tough customer. She's really kind of a tough lady. I mean, she was transgender maybe before it was popular. So she likes to think of herself as the first, honey. Although she says, 'Let's not forget about Marlene.' So she's bringing up Marlene Dietrich."

(On the backside of the *Low Life* book jacket is the Julia Sloan photo of Holly that's reminiscent of Marlene Dietrich. In fact, in the 1990s, many people compared Holly's look with that of Dietrich in the 1930s.)

HOLLISTER: "So, she's around you. She likes you for some reason. And I do think she likes to hang out around you and your friends. That's what she tells me. 'Pour me a drink, and I'll be there.' She didn't have trouble with alcohol, did she? Because that's the feeling she gives me."

Even in the afterlife, Miss Woodlawn was still whooping it up! After listening to that recording, I had to sit alone with my thoughts for a while. Bill knew who Holly was. In fact, he met her at one of the book signings at A Different Light when the book first came out. He's kind, gentle, and fun-loving. So of course Holly would enjoy being around him. As I thought about what had just transpired, I felt my arms tingle with a slight chill, followed by a warm feeling of comfort.

I lost the Holly Woodlawn I so fondly adored years before she died. She was like a pretty balloon that got blown away by a gust of harsh, bitter wind. Alcoholism had transformed the person I loved into someone I didn't want to know. At times, she seemed like a self-absorbed, self-destructive, disillusioned narcissist. Not once did she ask, "So how are you? What are you working on?" I just assumed she didn't care.

For years, I wished I could have the old Holly back. But she no longer existed, and even if she did, I could never recreate that wondrous time we had at Las Palmas. Everything was so different now. I was different. I wasn't a lost kid anymore, and Holly wasn't my beloved Auntie Mame.

My friend Ed Evans summed up our relationship best when he said it was a beautiful and darkly magical pas de deux and compared it to the movie *Harold and Maude*.

"Your presence in each other's lives is very much like two shamans. You each played Maude to the other's Harold," he wrote. "You both approached the union for selfish reasons and ended up helping the other immeasurably. It's similar to the way Mary Poppins arrived to help the kids through their difficult time and then left when her work was done."

I could not have said it better.

Holly and I were brought together when we needed each other the most. In later years, though we were friendly, we would never be close . . . not like we were when we both knocked on the wall, stuck our heads out our windows, and shared the same dream. There were just too many barriers in the way, mainly ego and pride. But on the night I heard Bill's recording, all that changed. There were no barriers anymore, just a rush of happiness. Finally, after all these years, the friend I lost had come back and her spiritual presence filled me with joy and gratitude.

As I worked on this manuscript, I could feel her energy, and at times, in my mind, I'd hear her voice encouraging me.

"Oh, honey, who cares if you screwed up the timeline! Just so long as it's funny and I look fabulous!"

Sometimes I poured a glass of white wine in her honor.

As I write this now, I feel she's with me, looking over my shoulder. She looks fantastic in a gown of her own design, face painted to perfection. I smile to myself and remember her signing books, kissing the autograph to leave a lipstick mark of affection, and making a smooch sound that sounds like "Mwah!" That same sound was how she ended her phone messages to me on my voicemail . . . when she was happy. "Mwah!"

"Darling," she says. "I've got the perfect title: *Love You Madly, Holly Woodlawn*. Honey, it'll be a great movie. Maybe even a Broadway show. With lots of singing, dancing, and carrying on! I can see the theatre marquee now. Oh! And wait until you see what I've got planned for the premiere. A gilded chariot! With me flying in, looking fabulous, decked out in feathers."

Then she shimmies in delight and lets out a hilarious, resounding "Dzieuuuuuuuuuu!"

And I laugh aloud because she's so funny, so radiant and so much fun . . . and I'm happier than I've been in years because in this moment, it feels like we're back at Las Palmas. I'm her racehorse. She's my jockey. And together we cross the finish line.

THE END

An aspiring screenwriter in Hollywood. *Photo by Ed Evans.*

ACKNOWLEDGMENTS

There are so many people who had a hand in the making of this book over the past six years, and to those listed below, I give my heartfelt thanks.

• Tam Warner, the first friend to read the manuscript in its entirety and say, "I think you've got something here." Thank you, Tam, for all your encouragement and support. And thank you for pushing me to take it to Andrew Lippa.

• Bridget Fiori, for her unwavering support, constructive criticism, and valuable insight. Your friendship means the world to me, Bridge.

• Ed Evans, for being such a great friend, photographer, and copy editor. Thank you for that striking film noir portrait you shot, and thank you for all the hard work you put into proofreading and correcting my manuscript. If it weren't for you, this story would be laden with grammatical errors, run-on sentences, and stoopid ~~mistpellings~~ mispellings. Your contribution was immeasurable, and I am so grateful.

• Teresa Conboy, for reading those early chapters, spotting errors, and helping me sort through memories and timelines. This story is as much yours as it is mine, and I'm thrilled that finally, after all these years, you'll get the recognition you so rightfully deserve.

• Lee Wilson, for reading early chapters, providing valuable writing advice, and encouraging me to write more.

• Angela Aiello, who screamed, "This is fabulous!" When the lit agents and managers all said "NO!" you said "Yes—Fuck 'em!" Thank you for all your encouragement and support.

• Rick Sparks, who took me under his wing, refined my pitch, and tried to help me find a publisher.

• Alan Bell, for his keen sense of story development and detail. Thank you for reading those early chapters and helping me find my direction.

• Cynthia "Cyd" Summers, for her unwavering support, encouragement, and inspiration.

• Jeanmarie Williams, for being a dear sweet friend who helped me get through some of the toughest times. There's more fun to come!

• Clinton Oie, my best friend, who read early chapters and helped me craft the early portions about Lizards. Get ready for the book launch, toots!

• John Gonzales, for taking the time to speak with me about those early days, even when he probably didn't feel like doing so. Thank you, John, for your support.

• Tom Cunningham, for being such a wonderful presence in our lives, and for taking those great portraits of Holly.

• Tyr Jung-Hall, Andy Krastins, and Beverly Bickle, for adding so much delightful color to Lizards coffeehouse.

• Ron Frederick, for giving me so much encouraging feedback and for lending me his wonderful music to use for my book promos. Thank you, Ron!

• Kelly Dennis, for always being such a doll and always making me laugh. Thank you for your support, Kelbo McHooter!

• Sandy Stern, for reading the first draft and giving me constructive story notes. Thank you, Stern! Your support and encouragement mean the world to me.

• Dawn Moreno-Freedman, for being a great cheerleader and friend. Thank you for reading early chapters, giving critical advice, and introducing my work to Felice Picano.

• Felice Picano, for taking an interest in my story and for trying to help me find a publisher. Your encouragement and support has meant so much.

• Don Weiss, one of the first editors to read my story. Thank you, Don, for your kind words of support and for helping me find my way.

• Beverly Cavaliere, for being the catalyst that got me to the party where I discovered Holly. Thank you for giving me notes and clarification about the early days of "The Lovely Carol."

• Tina Nelson and Marcia Copeland, my beautiful sisters, for their unwavering support and encouragement. Thank you for reading chapters and inspiring me to push forward.

• Peter Palladino, for his kind generosity in donating his incredible photographs for this book. Thank you so much, Peter!

• Doug Laughlin and Woolsey Ackerman, for reading the book in its entirety and giving me good, solid feedback.

• Natalie Venturi and Randy Lipnick, for being such fabulous and supportive friends.

• Robert Starr, for reading the final manuscript and giving me so much amazing insight, support, and encouragement.

• Brian Hamilton, for reading the final manuscript, clarifying important details, and encouraging this project.

• Aunt Carol Flinn and Aunt Fern Mreen, for reading early chapters and giving me valuable criticism and encouragement.

- Aunt Rhonda, for inspiring me to push forward.
- Suzanne Beauchamp, my high school English teacher, who said I could when everyone else seemed to say I couldn't. Your encouragement has meant the world to me, and to this day, I heed your advice: "Revise, revise, revise." Thank you!
- Rona Barrett, for being so thoughtful and kind.
- Steven Piorkowski and Eileen Thompson-Ray, for being there and making me laugh so much when the going got rough.
- David Jarbo, for always making me laugh.
- Christopher Schelling of Selectric Artists, for considering my proposal, offering valuable feedback, and being so kind.
- Nicholas Baker and Danny Poche, for their support, encouragement, and good times we had with Holly at Las Palmas.
- Kelley Dixon, for being a good friend and for winning that Emmy. So proud of you!
- Lindsay Root, for his kindness and support during the early days when Holly and I were working on *Low Life*.
- Geoff Story, Dallas Cupp, and Daumier Mageswki, for throwing my first book party years before the book was published. And to everyone who showed up: Mike Wyrock, Kirsten O'Loughlin, Tracy Collins, Paul Schankman, Shane Cherry, Barbara Lynn Clark, Natalie Zurfluh, and Chris Andoe.
- JenniferLynn Grega, my incredible attorney, who has always looked out for my best interests. I am so grateful. Thank you, Jennifer!
- Michael Musto, for taking an interest in this story, actually reading it, and helping identify the parts that dragged.
- Joan Quinn, for her unwavering support.
- Andrew Lippa, for encouraging the idea of a musical about Holly Woodlawn.
- Greg Gorman, for reading excerpts, giving his approval, and providing such beautiful photographs.
- Brianne DiMarco, for reading the manuscript and giving me such encouraging feedback.
- Tony Shibata, Mark Frazier, and Kevin Bershinski, for reading early chapters, giving feedback, and encouraging me to continue with this project.
- Jeffrey Arsenault, for clarifying details about Holly's work on his film *Night Owl*.
- Brent Pierson, for encouraging this project many years before it was a book, and for promoting it on his podcast.

Look, Ma! I finally made it! Nominated for an Emmy and livin' high on the hog!! With my wonderful mentor, Dana Millikin, at the 2014 Emmy Awards in Los Angeles.
Photo by Mike Sioss.

• Bill Gorin and Hollister Rand, for providing the happy ending to this story.

• Julia Stier, for reading an earlier, much longer draft, and saying it was fantastic!

• Michele Zeitlin, for making the time to read my manuscript and offer her honest opinion. Your constructive criticism helped me define my story's direction and cut the fat. Thank you so much!

• Kathleen French and Debby Reid Vigna, for launching my television career, and Tara Sandler and Jennifer Davidson, for giving me the opportunity to write.

• Dana Millikin, for taking me under her wing, giving me a chance, showing me how to write in an active voice, and making me a strong Emmy-nominated producer.

• Gary Benz and Michael Branton, for helping me survive those early years.

• Adriano Serafini, who took Holly under his wing and did the best he could to keep her on track.

• Harvey Fierstein and Howard Rosenman, for trying their best.

• Lorianne Hall, Steve Lapuk and Caresse Henry, for believing in my writing and introducing it to Madonna.

• Dorie Hannaway, for turning forty and throwing a party that would change my life in ways I never expected.

• Brett Kester, for his input on my passages about Steven Arnold.

• Tony Maietta, who co-authored *The Marble Faun of Grey Gardens*, which became a source of inspiration. Thank you for making time to give me valuable advice.

• Michael Zoumas, Don Murphy, Jane Hamsher, and Rose Troche for taking an interest.

• Lucy Moorman, for her friendship and encouragement.

• Carlos Vargas, for immortalizing Holly in a most fabulous way!

• Jay Jorgensen, for your kind words of encouragement.

• Robert Drake, who jump-started this journey in the first place.

• Madonna, for coming into my life on two separate occasions and giving me so much validation and hope.

• Jessica Parfrey and Christina Ward, who recognized this little book's potential, helped me refine its direction and tone, and gave it legs.

• LeeAnn Platner, for all the laughs and good times. I'm so sorry you didn't live to see this, but I know you pulled strings for me on the other side.

• C. Stephen Foster, for setting the bar for persistence and tenacity, and inspiring me to always push forward.

And finally, a huge thanks to everyone who reads this book. Your interest and support mean the world to me. Within these pages, I hope you find the inspiration to make your own dreams come true. Sometimes things don't always work out the way you want. But in the end, the most important thing to know is that you tried.

Fuck fear. Embrace risk. Live your dream. And always remember: Failure is temporary, but the regret of having not tried will last a lifetime.

GO FOR IT!